COMMONSPACE

Beyond Virtual Community

Seize the
Power of the
Collective

Mark Surman
Darren Wershler-Henry

FT.com
FINANCIAL TIMES

A Pearson Company

Canadian Cataloguing in Publication Data

Wershler-Henry, Darren S. (Darren Sean), 1966-
       Commonspace: beyond virtual community

ISBN 0-13-089361-7

1. Electronic commerce. I. Surman, Mark. II. Title. III. Title: Common space.

HF5548.32.W47 2000   658.8'00285'4678   C00-931451-2

ISBN 0-13-089361-7

Editorial Director, Trade Division: Andrea Crozier
Acquisitions Editor: Andrea Crozier
Copy Editor: Nancy Mucklow
Production Editor: Lori McLellan
Art Direction and Interior Design: Mary Opper
Cover design: Bill Douglas/The Bang
Production Manager: Kathrine Pummell
Page Layout: Monica Kompter

1 2 3 4 5 WC 06 05 04 03 02 01

Printed and bound in Canada.

This publication contains the opinions and ideas of its authors and is designed to provide useful advice in regard to the subject matter covered. The authors and publisher are not engaged in rendering legal, accounting, or other professional services in this publication. This publication is not intended to provide a basis for action in particular circumstances without consideration by a competent professional. The authors, their employees and the publisher expressly disclaim any responsibility for any liability, loss, or risk, personal or otherwise, which is incurred as a consequence, directly or indirectly, of the use and application of any of the contents of this book.

Visit the Prentice Hall Canada Web site! Send us your comments, browse our catalogues, and more. www.phcanada.com.

A Pearson Company

CONTENTS

PART 4: LONG LIVE COMMONSPACE: CONCLUSIONS

Acknowledgments

Commonspace is about the amusing/angering/inspiring/useful/banal world that is the Internet. Everyone who's been a part of its collective hum helped to write this book. We are grateful — not just for this book, but also for the fun we've had together.

We're also grateful to those who brought to this wonderful land in the first place.

Maureen James and Kirk Roberts (who never expected to see their names together in the front of a book) can take the blame for pulling Mark online. Before them, he was simply a fuddy-duddy young documentary filmmaker with an e-mail account. Maureen, Kirk and the rest of the people at Web Networks gave Mark the chance to immerse himself, experiment, make mistakes, learn and connect just as the Internet was exploding around us all. Mark also has his clients to thank for the fact that he gets a chance to play in the digi-lectual sandbox for a living. And, of course, he owes a deep debt to Tonya, his collaborator and life partner, with whom he hatched a good number of the ideas in this book.

It might seem strange now, but there was a time not all that long ago when institutions didn't necessarily *want* more people on the Internet. Despite the roadblocks created by various self-important administrative wonks, Darren did eventually get online, thanks to the the geeks at the University of Alberta in 1989 (especially crazy Bill Tucker), and those at the now-defunct Computer-Assisted Writing Centre at York University in 1990, who helped him figure out how to Telnet to the WELL. Ken Chasse's Sonic Interzone BBS (home of the only BBS/skate crew in Toronto at the time whose members were all old enough to shave) was the subsequent springboard for Darren's forays into USENET and the world of mailing lists. Darren would also like to thank Sour Skittles, Quake 3 and Lightnin' Hopkins for getting him through the last couple of weeks of the writing process.

There are many people who helped us gear up from Internet dreamers to authors who pushed this book out the door. The people at Pearson in Toronto convinced us to mutate Commonspace from a how-to manual about online community to a broad-based 'business book' (odd concept, really). Nancy Mucklow helped transform the manuscript from a pile of disconnected documents and e-mails into one long funky flowing blog. And the people at b2bScene.com provided us with an online home to collaborate and develop the book.

Of course, we have our families to thank most of all. We wrote this book through what was supposed to be a relaxing summer. Despite their better judgement, Tonya (again), Tristan, Liz and Georgia the big yellow dog, put up with the incessant glow of laptops at the cottage and in the mountains. Without the freedom and support they gave us, we'd probably still be on Chapter Three. We love you, and thank you.

PART 1

Geeks bearing gifts

Introducing commonspace

1

Seize the power of the collective

*The marketplace [of the Middle Ages] was the center of all
that is unofficial; it enjoyed a certain extraterritoriality in a
world of official order and official ideology, it always
remained 'with the people.'*
MIKHAIL BAKHTIN

The Internet isn't about dot coms, online malls or customizable coupons.
It's not about routers, servers, browsers, or any of those other fascinating
widgets and gadgets. It's not about the business hype or the eye candy. It's
not about the toys. Nope. In fact, the Internet isn't even about technology.

It's about us. The *collective* us.

The real power of the Internet lies in *the collective* — the vital, thrilling
interconnection of people and ideas that happens online. The juice that
makes the Internet hum is the direct result of people talking, sharing, collaborating, aggregating, and playing. It's the electric flow between five programmers on five different continents working together to track down
the same elusive idea and hack it into an elegant and useful algorithm. It's
the snapshot of what we're all thinking at any given instant: *This Sucks.
This Rules.* It's the sparks that fly when a million great ideas collide in one
place. People. Connected. *Commonspace.*

Think for a second about some of the things that are happening right now:

- **Open source software**, invented, constructed and maintained by loosely connected communities of programmers, is changing our whole notion of authorship and value. New companies are sprouting up out of nowhere, creating successful businesses by giving their software away — for free.

- **Business-to-business marketplaces** are bringing together entire industries to help speed up the supply chain and make transactions more efficient — through collaboration. Companies that were formerly bitter rivals are banding together to create marketplaces that they hope will make their industry better for everyone involved.

- **Grassroots activist**s are organizing themselves in ways that were previously impossible — over the Internet. From Seattle to Prague, they're creating a global equality movement that goes beyond tired ideas of right and left.

What do open source, B2B markets and grassroots online activism have in common? They certainly don't have the same goals, and they don't even use the same types of technology. The open source world uses its own powerful hand-built tools. B2B marketplaces use complex custom software packages written by the giants of the software industry. Activists use tiny, unsophisticated Web sites and e-mail lists to take on big companies and big governments. But the scale of the technology and the price tags attached to it aren't what drive the success or failure of any of these ventures. The common thread — the compelling, exciting factor that ties these phenomena together — is that people, connected online, produce interesting and unprecedented results.

Maybe this is obvious. But if it is, we as a society have developed a real knack for ignoring the obvious. Most discussion about the Internet lives in the past: it's tied up with old-fashioned business ideas and breathless gushing over 'way cool' technology. It entirely misses the real story: communities

The juice that makes the Internet hum is the direct result of people talking, sharing, collaborating, aggregating, and playing.

and other types of human connections. If these are mentioned at all, they are merely sprinkled on top of such discussions as pretty afterthoughts.

A consultant friend of ours was recently called in to assess an 'amazing offer' that one of his clients was considering. The company in question was a global market leader in its niche, well-organized and well-known. It had recently had a conversation with a big software company that went something like this:

Big Software Company: Why don't we help you build a huge B2B marketplace so you can dominate your niche?

Global Market Leader: Sure, why not? Sounds great!

Big Software Company: Okay, we'll be over with the software and the routers next week. Make sure you have a cheque for $10 million ready when we get there.

What's wrong with this picture? It should be obvious. There are no people in the equation, just wires. What are the people going to do once the wires are in place? Where's the community? For that matter, what are the products? What are the services? Unfortunately, such thinking is very common in the brave new economy. It's like thinking you can build a $10 million aquarium and then throw in a $1.95 packet of Sea Monkeys to make it come to life. Wrong. Wrong, wrong, wrong.

Put down your copy of *Wired*, stop spouting meaningless phrases like 'e-commerce solutions', and lose the Sea Monkeys. It's time to start thinking about the collective.

Commonspace is everywhere

This book is about one thing: commonspace. The power of the digital collective.

Why? Because commonspace is what makes the Internet different than other type of media . It's driving massive changes in work, home and play in our culture. The collective power of the Internet is morphing our tired assumptions about business and markets into something new and compelling. Fresh methods of interconnecting people online are transforming our notions of what constitutes a community.

In short, we are creating a digital gestalt — a new, more complex version of ourselves. We are growing a collective mind between the bits. And that is changing everything.

So far, the people who have understood this process of change the best are those who have built or participated in online communities. They should know, because they've been benefiting for years from the many to-many people connections of the Internet world. Unlike television or print, anyone can talk on the Internet: anyone can be on stage. This not only makes the Internet an incredibly powerful tool, but it also makes it a *fun* tool.

We learn new things: 'Don't buy Product X from ACME Accessories, Inc. I have one and it has this annoying habit of giving you a mild electrical shock every time someone in the neighbourhood uses a garage door opener.'

We make new friends: 'Wow, I had no idea there were any other people out their who posted photos of their handcuff collections online!'

We collaborate: 'The latest draft of the story line for the new video game really smokes, but it's still lacking something. It's time to implement the Secret Cow Level.'

And it's a blast.

But commonspace is a broader concept than 'online community.' Traditionally, online communities bring people together in the form of discussions. Pick up any classic book about the Internet — say, *The Virtual Community*, Howard Rheingold's ground breaking study of the WELL, or an *über*-capitalist tome like John Hagel III and Arthur G. Armstrong's *net gain* or the Faith Popcorn-style futurist punditry of Esther Dyson's *Release 2.1*. You'll find that most people's definitions of online community focus on three factors: membership, niche and conversation. While there are

Unlike television or print, anyone can talk on the Internet: anyone can be on stage.

Commonspace is
the collective,
many-to-many
world that we live
in online.

some disagreements about the precise details, these core components sum up what most people mean by the phrase 'virtual community.'

Today's world of many-to-many interaction is much, much broader than this narrow definition. Epinions and eBay, Napster, the Hotline and Gnutella, Ultima Online, QuakeWorld and Battle.Net — none of these are communities in the narrow sense, but all of them are built on the same principles as virtual community and are key examples of the evolving digital collective. To really understand the glorious mess called the Internet, we need to think in broader terms.

We are doing more with our online many-to-many relationships than talking. We are playing games, sharing data, doing research, fighting, falling in love (or at least in lust), booking tickets, buying and selling — in other words, we are conducting our lives online. And what's more, we don't always hang with people that think or act in exactly the same ways that we do. (How boring would *that* be?) It is this wider spectrum of collective activity that makes up commonspace: commonspace is the collective, many-to-many world that we live in online.

The metaphor that we've been using for years (along with many others) to get closer to the idea of commonspace is the town commons. As the public square at the centre of the action, the commons brings together the market stalls and the offices, the public lectern and the village green, the games in the park, the punks on the skateboards and the buskers on the sidewalks. At its very core, the commons blends commercial life, civic life and leisure. It is the epitome of the connected diversity that defines community. It reminds us that the social and commercial space that makes up our world is something that we all share. It is common space.

And so it is the Internet. We are drawn by the social collectivity, and the connections to many, many, many others. We are drawn by common space.

An armchair tour of commonspace

a. conversation

Online communities are where many of us first caught the commonspace bug in the 1980s. Glowing green text appeared slowly (sloooooowwwwwly) at 2400 baud, crawling across the black surface of the monitor:

>Hi.

[Pause]

>It's me :-)

[Pause]

>And me 8-P

[Long pause]

>And me ;-)

Speed wasn't the issue (a good thing, too). The glowing green letters on the screen weren't just empty pixels: they were other people.

Reaching out across the planet with tentacles of text, we have built entirely new social worlds. What's astounding is that we've been able to build these worlds so quickly. Almost overnight and in a completely organic manner, we've figured out the subtleties of community-building such as how to maintain membership, how to create niches, and how to fuel and manage collective online conversations. (Okay, we admit that there were decades of community organizing theory that could have helped us. But most of us didn't know about any of it when we first started building online communities.)

None of this is to say that online communities are one endless virtual picnic. Some online communities are certainly more redeeming than others. People go online to talk about everything from cleaning up the local river to improving their investment strategies to pretending that they're furry anthropomorphic cartoon mammals who like to shag each other. And as in

Reaching out across the planet with tentacles of text, we have built entirely new social worlds.

the real world, there are annoying neighbours and fights between friends. In fact, flame wars — vitriolic online word battles — became an online hot-button pretty early on. It's no wonder, really. Flame wars smart like a paper cut full of salt. The current practitioners of the flame-as-art-form still hang out on the alt.flame newsgroup and its various offshoots, but you don't really want to go there unless you thrive on abuse. The first entry from the alt.flame FAQ (Frequently Asked Questions) reads as follows.

```
1. Fuck off for starters.

Go away, newbie. Nobody wants you here.[1]
```

Like the newsgroup itself, the alt.flame FAQ becomes more hostile and offensive from there. But for a certain kind of personality — one of the kinds that thrives online — the alt.flame FAQ is like a dropped gauntlet, an invitation to jump in and get dirty.

Online communities aren't really about people being nice to each other: they're about experimenting, creating new worlds with new social mores and new standards of behaviour. What matters is the fact that the worlds we're creating are *ours*.

b. business

Despite the fact that most online communities started as forms of recreation, business has been quick to pick up on the power of the collective. Just think for a moment about what eBay has done for small business. Or, for that matter, think about what USENET has done to big business, or what day-trading has done to the stock market. As the authors of *The Cluetrain Manifesto* state so aptly, markets have once again become conversations.[2]

For the most part, the business world has been living outside the commons for the last hundred years. Businesses had moved physically and psychologically to the suburbs, disconnecting themselves from anything remotely resembling communities of impassioned, invested individuals. Corporations were content to be vast, mysterious entities that towered over the faceless consumers that bought their wares. But as online communities started taking off, some businesses started realizing that it was time to voluntarily reconnect with their customers — because the Internet was going to make it happen whether they liked it or not.

Ten years ago, the word 'business' and 'community' would rarely have been uttered in the same sentence (unless the speaker was droning on about the 'business community' at a Rotary Club rubber-chicken dinner). Now no one even blinks when titles like *Communities of Commerce*[3] appear on the shelves at the airport bookstore. People are starting to remember that businesses are us, and that they should be, a part of our communities — online and off.

c. open source

Community and business aren't the whole story. Commonspace has produced wild emergent behaviour and incredible outputs that we couldn't have predicted even a decade ago.

Think about open source for a moment: free software that's better than most of the stuff you can buy, a thriving community that appreciates anything you contribute back to it, and a strategy that allows you to make a comfortable living from giving things away. Open source is the digital collective on mental steroids, commonspace refined to its purest, most powerful form. Sure, the software always begins in the hands of one person or a small group. But from there, it grows strong on the fertile ground of the Internet collective mind.

The idea of open source has spread farther and faster than anyone could have imagined. With a little nudging from the likes of Eric Raymond and mouthy Linux start-up CEOs, even the most conservative business types have sat up and paid attention. There is a genuine acknowledgement that there is a business case — both social and economic — for open source. When IBM executives say things like 'I am increasingly coming to the conclusion that the Internet and open-source initiatives are the free marketplace way of dealing with the extremely complex software issues we are facing,'[4] something interesting is going on. Why are business bigwigs paying attention to open source? Well, some of them have probably asked the geeks down in their Internet service divisions about what software their servers were running, and have been more than a little surprised by the answer.

Maybe the success of open source in the business world is just a sign of co-optation, of 'selling out'. But it doesn't look that way when you examine the situation closely. Some people with real clout behind have seen the open source light, such as CEOs, public intellectuals and venture capitalists. At least in the world of bits, we are no longer in an economy based on scarcity. And there is no way to go back. You can't control prices by locking software (or films, or music, or books) in the warehouse, because someone already has a copy. Zap: now there are a million copies. The economy of abundance is here. This changes the rules for economics and business dramatically, and entire industries are running scared. Like the pirate captain said when the Spanish armada came over the horizon, bring me my brown pants.

Commonspace changes everything. Communities. Markets. Work. Intranets, Web forums, peer-to-peer networks and e-mail smash hierarchies flat, rendering entire layers of management obsolete. The collective has also ingrained itself in the world of play. From networked games to *The Blair Witch Project*, entertainment is becoming more about connection than about one-way spectacle. Even the world of government and politics has not been spared. As grassroots organizers clue in to the power of the Internet, politicians are forced to dip their toes into the pool of commonspace and to once again show their faces in the public square. Commonspace is everywhere, and it's getting more everywhere all the time.

But what is it? Can you touch commonspace? Can you buy a kit to create it, or at least control it? Sorry. No go. But you can begin to understand it and to see how you and your organization can be a part of it.

What makes commonspace?

The Internet is a gooey, bubbly swamp of an ecosystem. It's beautiful, and it's tranquil on the surface, but there's a persistent background stench, and it's a very difficult place to domesticate. The difficulty isn't due to any technological bugbears, though; it's a direct result of the fact that *the Internet is us.*

As each of us constantly contributes our latest two cents, commonspace continuously shifts and evolves. And while we might act with good intentions, our plans don't always work out as we might hope, because someone else has different ideas. This unpredictability is actually a bonus for the Internet, just as it is for any ecosystem. Diversity, the swirling together of millions of ideas, often leads to the creation of weird and wonderful paths.

While no one of us — or even a small band of us — can dictate the laws that control commonspace, we've come up with a few core principles that describe it. Sure, they're rough approximations of convoluted behaviour patterns, but it's always hard to suss out exactly what makes a complex system work. Over the last 10 or 20 years, we've learned enough about how we connect online as a collective to survey a little corner of the terrain.

Principle #1
The collective is the Internet's killer app.

The real difference between the Internet and all preceding media forms is the role it gives to people. More specifically, millions of people connected in many-to-many relationships make up communities, clans, and information gestalts.

In a many-to-many network, it is easy to form groups quickly and work collectively. The power of online collective work, creativity and thought was originally promoted by the people who homesteaded the first virtual communities. But others have seen it and named it since: connected intelligence, the hive mind, open source. Whatever you call it, the core principle is clear: the Internet lends itself to working and playing collectively. Under the right circumstances, online groups can produce astounding results in record time and make life more pleasant for everyone involved.

Principle #2
Online, we're always bigger than the sum of our parts.

Commonspace is a direct result of synergy. Whether they're aware of it or not, people create something bigger than themselves when they connect with each other. The results can be new ideas, new products, or innovative approaches to old problems: a piece of software, a collectively written book, a pool of aggregated data providing new insights. In other words, by leveraging the 'collective mind' and using collective resources, we can create something that is bigger than the sum of its parts.

Principle #3
In the economy of commonspace, you need to share power to thrive.

Traditional business logic says 'Consolidate power. Keep competitors and customers weak.' Commonspace business logic says 'Share power with your customers, your partners and sometimes even your competitors, if you want to succeed.' More simply, you need to share power to thrive.

Why share power? Because connectedness makes it easier for you to benefit from and build on the success of your users and partners.

Principle #4
Mutual self-interest builds community ... and beats the corporate drones.

The best kind of motivation is immediate personal need. But what happens when every time someone does something for themselves, they also happen to help out a hundred, or a thousand, or a million other people? Traditional ideas about value, leadership and money begin to shatter. In a many-to-many network that stresses sharing, everything that you do for yourself can benefit everyone else. Likewise, anything anyone else does can benefit you.

People and businesses that shift into this 'open source' mind-set will grow better, stronger, and faster, just like the six million dollar man. On the flip side, companies that keep their ideas proprietary don't benefit from the ideas and work of others. Everything they do becomes slow and costly.

Principle #5
In commonspace, 15 minutes of fame is better reward than money.

In many cases, the currency of commonspace is respect, small-time fame and ego-boosting.[5] Especially in technical endeavours, doing something smart and earning the respect of one's peers is of the highest order. As Eric Raymond and others have pointed out, in a digital economy that's based on abundance, ego-boosting — "egoboo" — is often the best reward.

From games to software development to traditional online communities, ego and pride are major driving factors behind the success of an online endeavour.

Principle #6
Distributed technology thrives. Siloed technology dies.

While the real power of commonspace comes from people, it can't happen without the right tools. This means having the right tools for the job (For example, you can't run eBay in a newsgroup.) More importantly, it means having tools that help people connect and tools that connect to each other. Successful implementations of commonspace have to enable many-to-many relationships between people. They also need to talk to other tools using open, commonly available standards.

In commonspace, distributed technology thrives, and siloed technology dies. Proprietary technology can survive for a while in isolation. But as soon as people want to connect to the outside world — and they will — these disconnected tools wither.

In commonspace, distributed technology thrives, and siloed technology dies.

Principle #7
Revolution comes from the strangest places.

It is almost impossible to predict where the next revolution is coming from in commonspace. Often, major breakthroughs come from the use of technologies in unintended ways. Or they result from organic, grassroots, non-commercial efforts that were never meant to be The Next Big Thing.

To see where commonspace is heading, look to the margins and the underground (if you can). But don't be surprised if you're sideswiped. Great new ideas in commonspace rarely come from a lab. (And when they do, it's often a 'mistake': Gnutella lumbered out of the Nullsoft/AOL lab like Frankenstein's monster on a killing spree.)

These principles are the essence of what we've learned about the collective, boiled down into little bouillion cubes of information. They're not immutable, and some of them aren't even very original (originality is overrated). But they are helpful if you want to get a sense of what the Internet is doing to our culture.

Don't be afraid. Just change everything about the way you work, think and play

If you'd just arrived from outer space, you might just think that the only reason that humans invented the Internet was to fuel new ways of making money and providing ourselves with amusing toys. But commonspace is about changes in the way we think and live, not new gadgets.

As customers connect to each other and markets become conversations, businesses have to change the basic premises by which they operate. Honest discussion is replacing hucksterism. P.R. weaselspeak is replaced by honest engagement *in* the conversation. Instead of standing back in a zero-sum *us* vs. *them* position, businesses are becoming a part of the sum-sum communities they serve. Certainly, not all businesses have made these changes. In fact, those that have already made the switch are by far in the minority. But these are the businesses that are thriving online and gaining the trust of their customers.

Many of these same businesses also know that the walls that separate the inside of the organization from the outside of the organization are becoming thinner. In fact, informal interactions between customers and employees and cooperation between companies working on the same project are constantly punching holes through these walls. Commonspace is behind it all and is making the lines that demarcate 'the organization' much fuzzier. Partnership becomes more possible, allowing businesses to focus on their core strengths. Of course, many businesses don't see the opportunities. They see disaster and stick their heads back into the swamp.

The same forces that are connecting customers to customers are connecting voters to voters, shifting politics (sloowwwwly — politicians *still* live in a 2400 baud world) back to the grassroots. And holes are penetrating the walls of government and non-profits just as they are the walls of corporations. Jurisdictions and service delivery are increasingly becoming fuzzy, and relationships with the outside world are becoming harder to control. For that matter, it's not even clear that the boundaries between nations mean anything anymore. Like business, politics and citizenship are going global.

These changes aren't coming from some weird, cynical techno-god. They are coming from us. We're involved and have a say through our day-to-day actions. If we can learn where the potential and the pitfalls are, we can navigate around them. The changes that commonspace brings aren't scary. They're exhilarating.

Buckle up.

2 | Fast Company or Fucked Company

The Industry Standard noted on Thursday that layoffs at Petstore.com presaged 'a long-awaited consolidation, and even the unraveling, of the beleaguered online pet-supplies retailing sector.' The very fact that there is a beleaguered online pet-supplies retailing sector at all makes me question whether we are actually living in a real world, and not some virtual reality satire dreamed up by a cynical novelist.

ANDREW LEONARD, SALON

Two decades of critical thinking and breathless utopian rhetoric about the potential of online communities says volumes about commonspace. What's real and what's vaporware?

Most of the existing books on the subject of online community, such as Howard Rheingold's *The Virtual Community*, Hagel and Armstrong's *net gain*, and Esther Dyson's *Release 2.1*. provide perfectly adequate explanations of the chat-based online culture of the early to mid 1990s. The problem is, there have been major changes in the habits and goals of Internet users since those books were written, and the original conceptual models haven't managed to keep pace with the phenomena they purport to describe.

While it's true that threaded online discussion really hasn't changed all that much over the last 15 years, people do a lot more online these days than chat with each other. They exchange huge music and video files, they use sophisticated workflow groupware, they shop, bank, trade stocks, and even frag headcrabbed zombies (or evil halberd-wielding cows, or whatever other digital foes their video games throw in their paths).

We can forgive Rheingold and company: they could hardly have anticipated the need to discuss the intricacies of zombie fragging. However, even recent writers on the subject of virtual community ignore online activity that doesn't meet these traditional definitions of virtual community — activities that are widespread and impossible to ignore. It's time to start thinking and talking about these broader models of interaction — the ones that make up the world of commonspace.

Homesteading the noosphere: Theories of online community

Howard Rheingold was the first widely read writer to inform the world that you don't have to 'become one with the Borg' or worry about the creeping peril of communism to realize that there are advantages to collectivity, especially online. And Rheingold, the Ascended Master of online punditry, should know. He is the former editor of the *Whole Earth Review*, a long-time member of the WELL (Whole Earth 'Lectronic Link), the author of many books, and a consultant to everybody under the sun.

In his groundbreaking book *The Virtual Community* (1993), Rheingold provides a definition of virtual community that is still the benchmark for contemporary discussions:

Virtual Community (defn) A social aggregation that emerges from the Net when enough people carry on public discussions, with sufficient human feeling, to form webs of personal relationships in cyberspace.[1]

Rheingold cites Marc Smith's notion of 'collective goods', the valuable things that people can only create by banding together online, to describe the power of the collective. On the WELL, such collective goods are:

The archive of
any discussion
group is a valuable
resource.

- **social network capital** - real-world relationships that benefit from online community;

- **knowledge capital** - collective knowledge pools and aggregated data;

- **communion** - empathy; what Rheingold calls the 'human feeling.'[2]

Of course, there are many other possible 'collective goods,' depending on the nature of the community — or commonspace — that creates them. The key point is that these 'collective goods' are now central to the culture of the Internet. Business managers, politicians, old people, young people — all kinds of people — are starting to understand this feature of the digital collective at a gut level. They know that accessing the collective goods of commonspace is essential to the success of everything they do online.

Conversation as content

You'd think that the relationship between communication and content would be self-evident. But it took John Hagel III and Arthur G. Armstrong's *net gain: Expanding Markets Through Virtual Communities* (1997) to identify it in print. Hagel and Armstrong, a principal and a manager in the influential consulting firm McKinsey & Company, pointed out that when members of a virtual community chat with each other, the conversation itself becomes new content.[3]

The archive of any discussion group is a valuable resource for both the community members and its organizers, especially if that discussion group has an extremely focused constituency — say, Labrador Retriever fanciers, PowerBook G3 users, or Quake Rocket Arena 3 players. People with specific questions can search the archive for solutions to their problems or locate experienced users to help them with digital or real-world problems (How much kibble can you feed a Labrador Retriever without making it really, really fat?). Additionally, the archive can be sold to advertisers or marketing companies, providing the agreement with the users allows for such a sale.

Esther Dyson goes one step past the theory. As a consultant and free-lance intellectual, Dyson makes a living by applying it to her own life. Her 1998 book *Release 2.1: A Design for Living in the Digital Age*,[4] which discusses the communication-as-content principle, is only one example. Her stock-in-trade is aggregating the opinions of others and selling them, and creating environments such as online forums and face-to-face (f2f) conferences that generate content. In turn, Dyson churns the principles she derives from these short-lived but highly focused communities into new material for her newsletters and printed books. Frequently, she even includes the actual postings and conversations from the archives of these events — it's a great way to boost your page count.

All aboard

After Hagel and Armstrong and Dyson had their say, everything to do with the Internet and the New Economy suddenly became Very Serious and Very Important. Fortunately, it wasn't long before someone (actually, several someones) with a sense of humour climbed up on the Internet soapbox when the Serious and Important people weren't looking.

Imagine *In Search of Excellence* crossed with *Fear and Loathing in Las Vegas*. That's how Thomas Petzinger of *The Wall Street Journal* described *The Cluetrain Manifesto* when it appeared in early 2000.[5] The *Manifesto* is the brainchild of Rick Levine, Christopher Locke, Doc Searls and David Weinberger, four IT professionals with a penchant for ranting and a healthy skepticism about the excesses of their own profession. You can (and should) read all 95 theses of the Manifesto yourself at <www.cluetrain.com>, but the important points are as follows:

- Markets are conversations between people, and these conversations should be conducted in a humane way, i.e. stripped of all forms of corporate rhetoric.

- The Internet and other forms of networking connect customers to each other as well as to businesses, and these inter-connected communities immediately render invalid almost all of the forms of 'communication' that the corporate world has developed for interacting with its customers.

Cluetrain presents an older-but-wiser version of the anarchistic ethos of the early Net community. Just because we geeks have grown up and had to get jobs, it argues, doesn't mean that we can't change the way that work happens *and* have fun in the process.

Polemical rants have always comprised a huge part of the overall discourse of the Internet, and the authors of *Cluetrain* have obviously had a lot of practice at them over the years. Christopher Locke's RageBoy® site <www.rageboy.com> provides some high-octane examples, including this fragment of a dialogue between a Really Concerned Thoughtful Journalist and RageBoy® about *The Cluetrain Manifesto* itself:

```
1. RCTJ : Let's turn to Cluetrain's focus on dis-
course. What point is the manifesto actually trying
to make about the 'human voice'?

2. RB : The fuck would I know? I mean 95 Theses? How
many people do you know who think that's even normal,
much less human? And 'discourse'? Give me a break!
Nobody talks that way. Except maybe academics, and
they can hardly be classed among the standard ho-
minids... Which reminds me, I have a paper coming out
soon on Barbie Doll dentition. Fascinating study ac-
tually.

3. RCTJ : Yes, that's all very interesting, I'm sure.
But getting back to your main point, you're saying
you don't agree with the idea that we should all num-
ber our sentences?

4. RB : I think you need to look at the issue on a
case-by-case basis. Sometimes numbering is useful.
Like say you're ticking off the various medications
you're currently taking. In my case:
5. Marijuana
6. Tylenol
7. Heroin
```

8. Psilocybin
9. NyQuil
10. Viagra
11. LSD-25
12. Prozac
13. Jack Daniels
14. Vick's Vap-o-Rub
15. Vicodin
16. Dimethyltryptamine
17. Tums
...and so on.

18. RCTJ: That's quite a list, and I can see how you'd need the numbers to keep straight, so to speak. But in other cases not?

19. RB: Of course not! If you were Julia Child, would you say:
20. Carrots are vegetables.
21. Vegetables grow in the ground.
22. The ground is basically dirt.
23. People get dirty when they pull up carrots.
24. What has a carrot ever done to you?
25. Leave those carrots alone you dirty fucker!

26. RCTJ : Good example.

Understandably, then, there is more than a little hyperbole at work in *Cluetrain*'s pages, but it's hyperbole with a mission. While items like thesis 74 ('We are immune to advertising. Just forget it') is probably more wishful thinking than truth, making the statement serves a purpose. Theorist Fredric Jameson claims that the function of utopian visions is to mark the limits of what's currently possible[6]. Our attempts to reach those utopias inevitably fail, but the process of reaching expands the borders of what's possible. In other words, hot air is what makes our balloons fly.

Geeks bearing gifts

At one or two points in his free-wheeling, hippie narrative about the wonders of the online world, Rheingold mentions something called the 'gift economy', but doesn't really go into much detail about it. Yet an understanding of gift economies is essential in any discussion of online culture.

Briefly, gift economies (sometimes called 'general economies' or 'potlatch economies') are based on the excess and free circulation of goods, with a general, intangible expectation of return from the broader community. They are an alternative to restricted economies (including capitalist economies), which derive their value from scarcity: in a restricted economies, one make profits by controlling access to the goods created. Yet the two types of economy aren't really opposites: the gift economy quietly percolates along underneath a restricted economy, occasionally erupting in wild and unpredictable moments of largesse.

In the early days of the Internet (say, pre-1994), something very much like an online gift economy was occurring. BBSes, FreeNets and USENET didn't cost a thing as long as you had a modem. How was this possible? Because people with a little computer savvy were willing to install a couple of extra modems in their basement and let other users into their spare computer. By giving people a place to congregate, they gained friends, conversation, shareware, software cracks and a constant source of amusement - in short, community. With the introduction of Netscape Navigator in 1994 — a FREE piece of software that provided access to a world of electronic wonder — *everyone* began to get a glimpse of what a gift economy was all about. And of course, this is where the problems began.

With the release of Netscape and the sudden availability of graphical user interfaces (GUIs) such as Web browsers and cheap, fast modems, regular people — not just geeks, scientists and students — began to flood the Internet. This online rush of people unfamiliar with the existing etiquette resulted in an erosion of the gift economy's ethos. In order for a gift economy to continue to function, *all* members have to be excessive in their generosity. Instead, nations of consumers simply rushed online, saw a lot of free stuff, and gobbled it all up without leaving much in return.

Of course, the gift economy hasn't entirely disappeared. Someone will always come along with the Next Big Free Thing, and all of a sudden, the rules for normal business will be turned on their heads again. In addition, gift economies have tended to be the source of the biggest changes and newest ideas online. Consider some of the recent 'gift' phenomena on the Internet today. File-sharing networks like Napster and Gnutella and open source software continue to demonstrate principles of gift economies.

The two sides of the coin

Open source guru Eric Raymond calls himself an 'accidental revolutionary.' This flute-playing, gun-toting, martial-arts-practicing, live-action gamer also happens to be one of the most convincing champions of the gift economy. In his 1999 already-classic *The Cathedral and the Bazaar,* he pushes open source as the way of the future. '[T]he open-source culture will triumph,' he writes, 'not because cooperation is morally right or software "hoarding" is morally wrong (assuming you believe the latter, which neither Linus [Torvalds] nor I do), but simply because the closed-source world cannot win an evolutionary arms race with open-source communities that can put orders of magnitude more skilled time into a problem.'[7]

But for many people, the gift economy still represents the long-haired intellectual version of the story. On the opposing side are John Hagel III and Arthur G. Armstrong, the golf-shirt-sporting authors of *net gain,* the book that helped fuel the dot-com goldrush.

In Hagel and Armstrong's biz-speak, the gift economy is a 'reverse market' — the opposite of the traditional economy of scarcity where businesses have the upper hand.[8] In a reverse market, the customer has unlimited access to information, which in effect gives *them* the advantage. Businesses that want to succeed in such an environment have to adapt, such as by supplying their customers with more and better information than what's already available.

The gift economy is a 'reverse market' — the opposite of the traditional economy of scarcity where businesses have the upper hand.

In a reverse
market, businesses
have to share
information —
and power — with
their customers

In a reverse market, businesses have to behave in unfamiliar ways. Moreover, they have to share information — and power — with their customers, for the site with the most information about quality and price will attract the most members. Sometimes power-sharing even necessitates a further (and seemingly heretical) reversion of common business principles: allowing users to have access to information from competitors. In some instances, it may even be necessary to cooperate with your competitors (something called 'coopetition') in order to maintain your user base.

The power of the reverse economy in online culture carries both a warning and a challenge for businesses: though the potential rewards are great, the world of online business is no place for stodgy thinking.

The cycle of community

In the summer of 2000, Blizzard released the 1.03 patch for their best-selling game Diablo II — and immediately infuriated many of their players. Some of the key skills of the favourite character classes — specifically, the Necromancer's 'Corpse Explosion' spell and the Barbarian's 'Whirlwind' attack — had been 'nerfed' or softened because the game creators had felt that they'd been too powerful and had disrupted the balance of gameplay. Many players promptly left in search of greener (or bloodier) pastures.

Mechanical changes, such as alterations to the overall site/service structure or user interfaces, can cause tremendous change to an online community. Such changes are common in the early years of a site's existence. They can be useful for attracting new users or new investors. But as the community grows, large-scale change can alienate long-time users. And this can do a lot of damage.

Changes in ownership — another frequent occurrence — can also send users fleeing. But this is not always the case. In 1999, the WELL, one of the first big online communities, was sold to Salon. There were probably a few scrupulous members who left at that time because they perceived that the service had 'sold out.' But the changes to the WELL's overall atmosphere were surprisingly minor. Moreover, the sale ensured its survival. Likewise, when AOL bought the ICQ service, some users were afraid it would be buried or nerfed in favour of AOL's competing product, Instant Messenger. But ICQ continues to post new releases and service upgrades and is still the most popular messaging community online.

Sometimes reorganizations and changes in mandate sound the death-knell for a community. In the late 1990s, Deja.com, the first people to bring USENET discussion onto a Web site, transformed their service from a product-rating system into something completely new: a consumer opinion site. Deja's more-or-less altruistic nature died, and it became a business. Once again, user resentment was high, and many of the long-term USENET readers abandoned Deja and returned to their newsreading software.

While the constituents of online communities tend to be very committed, the communities themselves do have a finite life span. As Amy Jo Kim points out in her 2000 book *Community Building on the Web,* these life spans tend to be cyclical in nature.[9] A community begins to gather around a topic or technology, grows, undergoes changes in ownership or mechanics, and loses and gains members. When it has outlived its usefulness to the members — for short-term projects and workgroups whose goals have been completed, or for games whose technological features haven't kept up with the pack — the community will fold up or simply fade away.

Kim rightly points out the difficulty of setting out to construct a particular type of community. Communities grow naturally and cannot be forced. Hotline Communications <www.bigredh.com> rebuilt their client software package enabling real-time chat, conferencing, messaging, data ware-housing and file transfer and viewing, with an eye toward the business community that Lotus Notes and Open Text's Livelink had already tapped. What they got instead was about three million script kiddies and crackers who download 150,000 files per month, many of them containing cracked and pirated software, porn and MP3s. But hey, it's a living.

In addition to the general cycles of commonspace, Amy Jo Kim also points out that there are rituals specific to particular sites. For example, gaming sites hold tournaments, mark changes in user status with specific icons, and hold f2f (face-to-face) events such as conventions. Other companies hold gatherings of product users (i.e. Saturn owners) on ICQ or IRC. These ritualized events mark specific phases of a community's life cycle.

They also help to create the community's sense of itself — in other words, its culture. Communities with a sense of culture are more attractive to users than those that lack culture, because they offer possibilities for participation and sometimes even a hand in the site's evolution. When users have a sense of personal investment in a site, they're more likely to to make a long-term commitment to it.

Like all life-cycles, the cycle of community includes a reproductive phase. Since reproduction is essential for long-term online survival, online enterprises are wise to capitalize on it. Communities that include features allowing members to assume control of sections of the community's functions over time or split off into sub-communities tend to be more successful than static sites.

There are many examples of successful second-generation sites. Gaming modifications ('mods') like Quake 3 Fortress and Quake Rocket Arena 3 use the game engine from Quake 3 to create new types of game play. These mods are so successful that between them, on an average day, they constitute more than half of the Quake death-matches in progress. For the eGroups site, reproductivity is its very lifeblood — the single purpose of the site is to spawn smaller subgroups, which then serve as highly specific target markets for various advertisers. In addition, the fledgling community of file-sharing sites is already experiencing cyclical growth. If ground-breakers like Napster cease to exist in their original form, there will be a number of new services (including Scour Exchange and Gnutella) to leap in to replace them.

Cyclical growth patterns suggest that we need to change the way we think about online communities. Given the unsteady ground of the Internet environment, a strategic, contingency-based model for maintaining communities of all types might be more realistic — and ultimately more productive — than one that expects them to remain unchanged forever.

Digital relics

From the (slightly) more sane perspective that the far side of the millennium affords us, it's obvious that things got a little silly in the late nineties in the world of online startups. The so-called 'dot-com revolution' spawned a lot of poorly designed 'instacommunities', most of which lived short, miserable and highly expensive lives. Simply 'being digital' (to steal a phrase from MIT high-tech cheerleader Nicholas Negroponte) isn't enough anymore, if it ever was. These days, an online community has to either have a bulletproof business plan or an unprecedented 'killer app' to stand any chance of attracting venture capital.

Despite its loss of momentum, the dot-com revolution still staggers on. However, both the general Internet community and the digerati have become considerably more cynical than they were in the early days of breathless enthusiasm.

In former times, we used to use *memento mori* — relics such as skulls — to remind us that our days were numbered, and that unless we got our act together sooner rather than later, there would be precious little to mark our passing. But for today's online businesses, we needn't bother with anything as grim and messy as a real skull. There are plenty of digital relics scattered across the Net that will serve just as well, perhaps better.

In fact, watching dot-coms go belly-up has become something of a spectator sport. Case in point: Fucked Company <www.fuckedcompany.com> is a death pool site, where users place wagers on which shiny new Internet companies are actually on the brink of going under. Sardonic humour is the order of the day:

```
Public Service Announcement

Stop fucking your own companies just to get points on
this stupid site. You know who you are (all of you).
On second thought, that's pretty cool — keep it up.

Posted: 6/10/2000
```

Watching dot-coms
go belly-up has
become something
of a spectator sport.

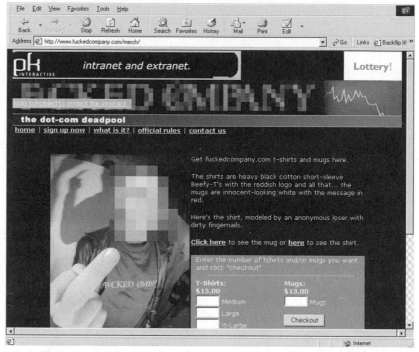

Rumours fly on the front page of Fucked Company. These people can smell impending dot-com disasters in the way that vultures can smell blood.

The turning point for dot-coms was arguably the failure of boo.com <www.boo.com> in early 2000, a trendy Eurpoean fashion site that soaked up millions in venture capital, only to fold within months of its launch. What was left of the company was broken up and sold off to various parties. The pickings were slim, though. The boo computers were leased, and the software already partly licensed. Bright Station ended up buying boo.com's highly advanced software for $374,900, a price that Bright Station's Andy Dancer estimates as being worth "about 0.6% of the cost of developing it!"[10] Though Fashionmall.com, a New York-based company that bought the company's domain and brand names, plans to relaunch the site, all that remains on the boo.com homepage is an e-mail notification form and a picture of an Ananova-style computer-rendered woman. Here's Fucked Company's take on the matter:

That cartoon Boo.com chick is cute though

fashionmall.com

I actually received a $50 gift certificate from
Boo.com a few days before they folded, so I never had
a chance to cash it in. While we're on the subject,
Fashionmall.com, which bought the stinking, maggot-
infested corpse of Boo.com, is now planning to re-
launch it. Boo.com's newly installed president Kate
Buggeln immediately demonstrated her ineptitude by
proceeding to insult and patronise its potential customers on cnet.com. 'While analysts and techno-geeks
know of Boo.com's troubles,' she said, 'most of its
everyday customers are not concerned with such
things. Susie Shopper doesn't care about that stuff.'
I think Susie Shopper should open a can of whoop-ass
on her.

When: 8/5/2000
Company: fashionmall.com
Points: 101

Since Fucked Company first appeared, there has been a positively ghoul-
ish surge in interest in dot-com failure. In fact, with the appearance of
Startupfailures.com <www.startupfailures.com>, failure is now officially
a growth industry. Apart from the news and discussion groups where con-
trite businesspeople are invited to 'Submit Lessons Learned' or receive
'Failure Feedback,' the site also offers entrepreneur coaching, jobs and resource listings, and general news. Even The Industry Standard has gotten
on the failure bandwagon, instituting a 'Dot-Com Layoff Tracker' and a
'Dot-Com Flop Tracker' after surveys revealed that as of September 21,
165 dot-coms had laid off at least 16,714 employees in 2000.[11] In addition, as of September 21, The Industry Standard counted 35 dot-coms
dead in the water[12] (a conservative estimate to be sure).

Aside from a general index of the Internet's current level of dark cynicism, dot-com death sites are useful sources of both rumours and examples of how not to run an Internet enterprise. Sometimes, learning the
hard way is the only way.

There is no one
information
highway. Rather,
there is a vast
web of roads and
communities.

Even more pathetic than sites that are currently in the throes of dying are those which have lapsed into 'bitrot' (net jargon for the condition of an abandoned and decaying Web site) but continue to exist in some marginal form as the digital equivalent of a ghost town. There are plenty of well-documented digital necropoli in Ghostsites, a webzine that's been around since 1996 <www.disobey.com/ghostsites>. In their short descriptions of failed sites, Ghostsites attempts to provide some analysis of the reasons that particular sites fail. Here again are negative examples that may be useful to online community builders.

Make a mental note to yourself: if your online enterprise fails, have the dignity to at least take the site down: it beats becoming part of the digital fossil record of evolutionary dead-ends.

Hazards on the Infobahn

Popular culture has become quite comfortable thinking about the online world as the 'Information Highway.' While the image is apt in some ways, it creates the impression of speeding along past poky little towns and side-roads to the heart of the matter: the information. Yet information only exists where there are people and communities to create it and post it and link it all up.

There is no one information highway. Rather, there is a vast web of roads and communities. Unfortunately we are trying to navigate our travels with out-dated maps — ones that don't show cities where villages used to be, or don't indicate new bridges over old barriers. Overall, the fastest way to change the Internet from a pair of gravel ruts in a farmer's field into an eight-lane superhighway is to use the right map.

Enough said: time to draft that map. What follows is a list of the major hazards of the Internet. A notion of the nature of commonspace will help you to avoid them, while guiding you safely to achieve your goals.

Naïve optimism

When it comes to Web sites, the attitude 'If we build it, they will come' is bullshit, pure and simple. Nevertheless, a surprisingly large number of businesspeople have paid for truckloads of it, only to discover that nothing will grow in it.

Successful complex systems don't appear out of nowhere: they evolve over time because of the demands of their users. Spending millions to create an online Taj Mahal before there's a recognizable need for all the bells and whistles your consultant told you were necessary will leave you with just that: a big, empty, expensive tomb.

What's more, it's difficult to determine the needs of your potential users through traditional market research. Often, a small response to a small need will grow into something unique and significant. When planning the first version of an online service, it's better to start small with your core functions and pay close attention to what features your users really want than to blow your entire wad on slick but impractical features.

Practical features are the ones that the users want — and determining users' wants takes time. ePinions <www.epinions.com>, a personal advice site, trades on the reputations of its community members for its success: more trustworthy users posting useful advice means a greater number of Net users will come to regard the site as a useful resource. For this reason, ePinions developed a 'Mistrust this User' function. The button has been very successful and makes this Web site stand out from its competitors. It not only provides some measure of control over the quality of postings, but also cleverly places the responsibility for policing on the membership rather than on the site's operators. This simultaneously gives users a sense of power and reduces the likelihood that mistrusted users will bear any sense of ill-will toward the site itself — all of which contributes to the site's longevity.

Spending millions to create an online Taj Mahal before there's a recognizable need will leave you with just a big, empty, expensive tomb.

Missing the forest *and* the trees

Despite all this techno-hippie rhetoric about the significance of the individual in the online world, beware of over-generalizing. The unique individuality of users isn't important to all online enterprises. For file-sharing networks, it's even a liability. Concentrating too closely on the individual users or focussing on the community itself at the expense of links to the outside may cause you problems if that's not what the users want or need. Worse, it might prevent you from noticing that someone has built a better networking technology that routes right around you and your service. The bottom line is that you have to think carefully about the individual, communal and technical needs of your site.

Beware also of trying to do too much at once. While elaborate user profiles can generate a lot of marketable data, consider the cost of collecting and maintaining this data. Are your users going to bother wading through huge, complex Web forms simply for the privilege of membership in your site? Can you justify collecting such data for the services you offer? Will your users be happy with the way you want to use their data, or just royally pissed off?

Every situation is different. If you're building a personal advice site, where users will want background information on each other, complex user profiles are justified. On the other hand, a file-sharing network requires almost no user information, and a 'minimal self' may even be preferable to a complex user profile. Napster, the most popular file-sharing site on the Web <www.napster.com> is facing a huge court battle over its right to allow users to share copyrighted material. Because of Napster's legally questionable position, the pseudonymity of its users is absolutely necessary. Gnutella < gnutella.wego.com>, the most popular alternative to Napster, has only a spartan interface that doesn't even have room for user names. Still it is at least as effective as Napster for the purpose of sharing files (if not more so) — and that's all the users care about.

Will your users be happy with the way you want to use their data, or just royally pissed off?

It's not just talk

Since Howard Rheingold's heyday, there has been not one, but two younger generations of Net users raised on William Gibson novels and gangsta rap MP3s rather than *The Whole Earth Catalog* and Grateful Dead bootlegs. Whether they're Gen-X e-commerce barons or Generation Next script kiddies and software pirates, odds are these new users take a more cold-blooded and pragmatic approach to online interaction than their long-haired predecessors.

So Rheingold's emphasis on the necessity of 'discussion' with 'sufficient human feeling' doesn't take into account the upswing in non-conversational online interactions, such as buying things, swapping files, and action gaming. Life is short, and time on the Internet is precious. Sometimes, like at the end of a Quake deathmatch, all there is to say is 'gg' (good game). This isn't inarticulacy or the decline of conversation; it's the register of a set of priorities for which Rheingold's definition fails to account.

The general conditions under which people participate in Internet culture have also changed greatly over the last five years. Rheingold mentions Jeremy Bentham (and Michel Foucault's) notion of the 'panopticon' — a prison in which all inmates are perpetually visible to the guards — to warn of the Internet's negative capacity to monitor people's actions and transactions.[13] From Rheingold's 1994 perspective and the influence of the WELL on his thinking, a panoptic Internet may have seemed avoidable. Today online privacy continues to decline as user-logging technology increases in sophistication. But the decline in user anonymity is more a result of data aggregation by online businesses than oppressive government interference   at least, so far.

Hello, my name is *][I_ I_ E G][I3 I_ E *

Esther Dyson's *Release 2.1* baldly states that 'lurkers' — people who only read or listen to online discussions — are not really part of the community. They may fancy themselves to be, but no one would miss them if they left.[14]

Odds are the new users take a more cold-blooded and pragmatic approach to online interaction than their long-haired predecessors.

Not true. This may have been the case before the invention of cookies and the widespread practice of user tracking and data aggregation. But in these panoptic days, even lurkers and casual visitors to a site leave a digital trace of their comings and goings that translates into valuable market research data for the site hosts, and even into potentially useful information for other users.

Consider Amazon.com <www.amazon.com> for a moment. The simple act of shopping for books online creates a large amount of information capital. Under every title, there is a 'Customers who bought titles by [this author] also bought titles by these authors' link, which represents the aggregated results of other shoppers' forays through Amazon. There are also editorial reviews, customer reviews and ratings of the title, as well as links to other books by the same author, and a search option that allows you to look for similar books by subject. As a content-creation strategy, Amazon has thrown every conceivable widget at its users. And it's worked.

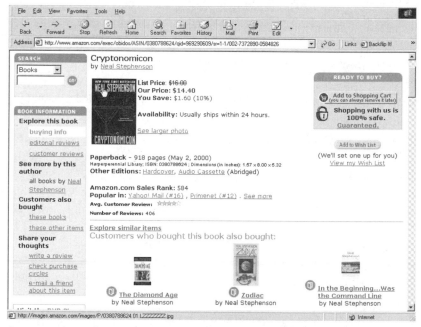

Anonymous data trails at amazon.com generate customer rankings and lists of items that are similar to the book a viewer is interested in purchasing.

And then there's also the question use of pseudonyms (also called userids, tags, handles and nicknames). Pseudonyms allow users to fabricate alternate identities for themselves, with varying degrees of detail. While Dyson recognizes that there are some positive aspects to the use of pseudonyms ('pseudonymity can also be a mask that allows a person to reveal a true identity rather than to hide one'[15]) she insists that pseudonyms have to be consistent for online community to work. For this reason, she excludes anonymous self-help sites from her notion of community, because 'A monologue explaining who you are does not bring you into a community, however good it feels and however cathartic or liberating it may be.'[16] Similarly, Elizabeth Reid, an Australian student whose research on IRC (Internet Relay Chat) users is cited by Howard Rheingold, suggests that one of the forces crucial to the development of online communities is the minimum certainty about identity that consistent nicknames provide.[17]

Once again, there is a wide gap between the theory and actual practice. Users adopt new online pseudonyms all the time. There are many reasons for changing pseudonyms, some good, others not so noble. In gaming circles, a user's pseudonym as a 'newbie' may be abandoned for another after they have gained enough expertise in a game to build a more impressive win/loss ratio. Some users maintain different identities for different purposes, such as to differentiate between the machines they use for logging in, to try on different avatars in a chat service or character types in a game, or simply to behave in a different manner (such as MorFing, a kind of digital transvestitism where a person pretends to be the opposite sex). In addition, on a service where a user has been banned for flaming or other annoying behavior, they may adopt another identity, maybe even several, to continue their activities, whether their continued participation is desired or not.

In fact, identity has become sufficiently alienated from actual users that it has become a form of capital. In her book on building virtual community, Amy Jo Kim provides the following tidbit on 'character as currency':

[Ultima and EverQuest] Players who have spent months, and even years, developing their characters and amassing wealth and property are now selling their

Adding a chat
group to a
sluggish Web
site probably
won't accomplish
anything if you
haven't already
captured the
imagination of
your present
and potential
members.

well-tended accounts to the highest bidder [on eBay]. Although many of these accounts are being purchased for their real estate (houses and castles are hard to come by these days in Britannia [the digital realm in which Ultima Online play occurs]), some people are obtaining fully developed characters, and then playing those characters within the game.[18]

When digital identity can be bought and sold, perhaps it's not so important who you are as who people *think* you are.

All talk = no action

Talk is cheap — so cheap that you can get reams of it anywhere in the on-line world.

But it's still only one element of commonspace. Adding a chat group to a sluggish Web site probably won't accomplish anything if you haven't already captured the imagination of your present and potential members by providing them with something extra, something they can't get anywhere else. In order to be attractive, an online service needs to offer its users a tangible reward for their participation. Information may have wanted to be free, once, but now it wants to get paid, baby.

There are plenty of options for what might constitute that reward. Money is the most mundane, though it's not necessarily the most attractive. Discounts on merchandise, club point systems, files, and even ego rewards (called 'egoboo') will suffice, under the right circumstances. Assessing the desires of your users is key to establishing what the proper incentive will be.

Almost all existing definitions of community place it exclusively in the civic sphere, separate from the workaday world. In other words, they contend that community is a purely recreational or educational pursuit. However, for many online people, work and recreation are inextricable. Either you play at work, or you work while you're playing, or both. The phrase 'I have no life' is a common refrain from anyone who has anything to do with the Internet.

Expanding the map of commonspace to include corporate intranets, business-to-business networking, and even the obligatory after-work Quake matches, then, make it much more useful than a purely recreational model.

What do you want, anyway?

The expectations of online community members aren't always clear, nor are their contributions always the same. Logging onto an online service is often about contingencies, short-term relationships and trial offers rather than long-term commitments. Commonspace has a shelf life, and perhaps we need to shift expectations for online experiences to reflect this.

Moreover, some people go online just to shop or to sell things, others to talk, still others to share files, flirt, or seek information. Then there are the people who are there to maintain the site, people with special posting or moderating privileges. In the old definitions of online communities, user roles are considered to be fairly symmetrical within any given community. But that is no longer the case, if it ever was. Accounting for different simultaneous modes of participation by making each as rewarding as possible will help to ensure the ongoing hardiness of commonspace.

Nobody likes a cop

Every culture has rules, and online cultures are no exception. But how strong do the sanctions that govern commonspace need to be, really?

Esther Dyson's notion of the necessity for punishment (or the fear of it) seems, well, a little draconian:

Community members should feel that they have invested in the community, and that therefore it is tough for them to leave. The ultimate punishment in a strong community is banishment, expulsion, excommunication, exile ... All those words signify the terror of being cast out of a community.

The community's rules should be clear, and there should be recourse if they are broken.[19]

Commonspace has a shelf life, and perhaps we need to shift expectations for online experiences to reflect this.

The Internet is not the Island of Doctor Moreau (with or without fat Marlon Brando). Paranoia and the urge to control are far too common in the business community's approach to online community. Corporations are anxious about the actions of their users because they are ignorant about the slightly irreverent and iconoclastic nature of online interaction. The failure to allow some room for unruly online behaviour is one of the quickest ways to kill a nascent online society. Clearly, there need to be some disincentives to causing mischief online; but just making it difficult and inconvenient should suffice in most cases.

Strictly business?

One of the biggest stock market crashes of the past decade suggests pretty strongly that the 'commercial orientation' that Hagel and Armstrong tout in *net gain* as the destiny of online communities is woefully inadequate. In spring 2000 the NASDAQ plummeted, taking the bloom off the high-tech stock market and venture capitalist money with it. It had a sobering effect on investors, who learned the hard way that adding '.com' to the end of your business name just doesn't cut the mustard.

That ended the first attempt of would-be net barons to take over the Net. But the techno-hippies, anarchists and idealists weren't out of the picture yet. In fact, many of them are still running the show. And the reason is that they know that the 'show' is.

While the dot.com empires are still rubbing the bruises on their greviously kicked asses and trying to figure out exactly what went wrong, the original spirit of the Internet continues to reassert itself. As the NASDAQ tumbled, Napster and other peer to peer networking tools were rolling into bedrooms, dorm rooms and courtrooms across the planet. At the same time, open source, which Microsoft CEO Steve Ballmer compared to communism, [20] was continuing to gain widespread credibility. The values of the older, anarchistic Internet are returning with a vengeance and are being taken seriously. The pendulum may swing back farther than the suits would like.

The upshot

What's necessary for a useful discussion of online phenomena is not the polemics of the various online factions, but a model that will take all perspectives into account, and be able to explain how opposites like the gift economy and the restricted economy can co-exist and interact.

The Internet is a much more complex beast than it was even a couple of years ago. Its increasing intricacy demands more sophisticated models than the received ideas about virtual community. Without some new theories, we're like the proverbial blind men trying to describe the elephant to each other while violently disagreeing about what each is experiencing. What follows is our attempt to take a step backwards and get a look at the larger picture (without stepping in a big heap of elephant shit.)

PART 2

The magnificent seven

Principles of commonspace

3

'It's people! The Internet is made of people!'

Everything$_2$ is made of people!
Geeks in Space is made of people!
Linux is made of people!
The Internet is people!
Soylent green is people!

FROM THE "EVERYTHING IS MADE OF PEOPLE" NODE ON EVERYTHING$_2$

The real difference between the Internet and all preceding media forms lies in its relationship to the public. Online, people aren't just the audience — they are also the content. The Internet is made of people.

Most forms of media from the last five hundred years (and there have been many of them; just check out the stack of corpses over at the Dead Media Project <www.well.com/user/jonl/deadmedia/>) weren't really made of people. They were made of producers and audiences, publishers and readers, talkers and listeners: binary opposites that establish rigid roles, with ideas flowing downstream, from the one with the knowledge to the many who thirsted for it. Before the Internet, the culmination of the top-down media model was big newspaper chains, broadcast TV, and Hollywood. Solid, predictable spectacle.

But the number of car chases, explosions, celebrity divorces, Backstreet Boys and episodes of Survivor any culture can absorb is finite. Spectacle has become boring, mind-numbing and repressive, and, thanks to the Internet, we actually have an opportunity at hand to institute a different way of doing things.

The Internet is the nail in the coffin of the disenfranchised spectator. Everyone can potentially see everyone else, whether in name or in action. More importantly, we all become a part of the show. People don't go online for the passive spectacle of a Disneyland parade, but for the collective carnival that we produce by being online together.

Think about how the Internet has changed the process of storytelling:

Then ...	Now ...
For our grandparents, the central narrative arrived in town every Saturday at the Bijou. After weeks or months trundling through the typewriters of paid hacks and the corners of big studio back lots, the Lone Ranger would ride off the screen in all of his predictability. He'd pick up where he had left off last week and end up where he was headed next week. And then all the kids would head home, don their masks and reenact the thin cultural gruel that flowed from the founts of Hollywood.	The central narrative for our children begins and ends within the game itself. In places like Battle.net or Ultima Online, hundreds of thousands of people weave tales of knights and sorcerers, noble alien races and bloodthirsty humans. The narrative unfolds in real time and is constantly changing. What's more, it no longer comes from the pens of paid hacks. It comes from the collective dreams of the players. As a product of 'the collective mind' it is engaging, compelling, magical.

'Now' is the time of commonspace, the many-to-many online world where audiences are simultaneously the performers in the main attraction.

The electric carnival

When describing the novels of Dostoyevsky, the philosopher Mikhail Bakhtin used the metaphor of carnival, 'a pageant without footlights and without a division into performers and spectators. In carnival everyone is an active participant, everyone communes in the carnival act.'[1] Yet Bakhtin could just as easily have been talking about the Web.

Of course, the many-to-many power of the Internet is changing more than just the process of storytelling. Business, Ideas, Politics, Music, Government, Games and Community — all of our institutions are morphing into strange new forms as the Internet enables us to work, play and act collectively. In such an environment, we are able to choose new methods of interacting with the people, projects and products that interest us. We feel more wanted and more engaged. We get and give more resources than we had access to in the one-to-many world. As a result, it becomes possible to make money, spend time, write books, build friendships, and start communities more quickly, effectively and enjoyably than has ever been possible before.

If this trend continues, the staid one-to-many ways of doing things are not long for this world.

One-to-many

So how did we end up here?

Gutenberg's print revolution in the 1500s symbolizes the erosion of the biggest one-to-many medium in recorded history — the Catholic Church. By making print cheap and easy, Gutenberg broke the Church's iron grip on the flow of information. Pamphlets were printed in the rough-and-tumble workaday language of the people (i.e. not Latin) and circulated as the printed word had never been circulated before. New ideas about God, religion, and power moved swiftly across Germany and the rest of Europe. As the Church's stranglehold on information disappeared, its monopoly on truth quickly followed suit.

Fast-forward to Thomas Paine and the American Revolution. According to legend, Paine used his printing press to spread the idealistic dream of a free society run by the people (well, actually by the men who owned land, but even revolution happens one step at a time), a society that balanced commerce and government, opportunity and the public good. His pamphlets found their way to all corners of the town commons — the tavern, the office, the church, the park. And as they moved, they helped build the fires of revolution. Just like Gutenburg, Paine and his printing press helped the 'little guy' pull down tired old ideas and replace them with new ones.

Fast-forward to the last half of the twentieth century. What happened to the little guy and all the new ideas?

When we think of the printing press now, we picture the faceless, industrial *ker-chunk, ker-chunk* of the factory floor. We see black-and-white *Citizen Kane* images of newspapers plopping off the press and onto the back of a truck, then distributed to a crew of plucky orphans in old shoes and floppy hats who deliver them to Norman Rockwell-style suburban white dads reading said papers in their slippers while smoking a pipe. At the dawn of a new millennium, print technology represents the orthodox, the inaccessible, the conservative and the boring.

At the dawn of a new millennium, print technology represents the orthodox, the inaccessible, the conservative and the boring.

If myth says print started like this ...

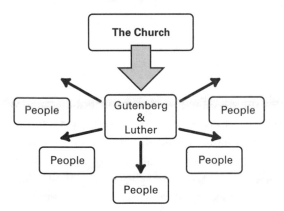

... how did we end up with this?

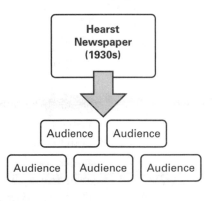

Figure 1: The evolution of print — from world-changing medium of the people to corporate pap.

How is it that we
started with hot-
blooded revolution
and got stuck with
slippers and pipes?

How is it that we started with hot-blooded revolution and got stuck with slippers and pipes? How did we end up with monolithic one-to-many media models, corporations, workplaces and schools? Blame it on the nature of the technology, and on a society that was content to use that technology in the most obvious way.

Certainly, the printing press has always lent itself to one-to-many communication. Even if you want to run a small newspaper or distribute political pamphlets, you need a press, paper and a distribution network. Print doesn't lend itself to massive dialogues between groups of people, or even two-way conversations. It is driven by small groups with a passionate message to communicate, or by publishers who see a mass-market of information consumers. The fact that print technology is cheaper and faster than groups of scribbling monks or the fussy and bureaucratic British colonial army made it an excellent tool for early revolutionaries. But it's never been a 'many-to-many' medium, not by a long shot.

As Marshall McLuhan observed in *Understanding Media*, the way that print culture organizes people as isolated individuals is antithetical to the ideals of an online culture:

Perhaps the most significant of the gifts of typography to man was that of detachment and noninvolvement — the power to act without reacting. Science since the Renaissance has exalted this gift which has become an embarrassment in the electric age, in which all people are involved in all others at all times.[2]

Because of this detachment, print was natural tool for the top-town, people-unfriendly world of the industrial era. At the level of social control, print helped to reinforce the command-and-control models of the military and big business. As a result, print eventually came to mean what it does today: words are written by professionals owned and paid for by 'the company.' There is no longer room for heretics like Luther or Paine, who might offend the audience or, worse, the advertisers. As society gradually sucked all of the fun and revolutionary potential out of print technology, the medium grudgingly came to fit with — and eventually reinforce — the rigid, de-skilled, industrial world that emerged around it.

Radio killed the radio star

Radio had a lot of potential in the early days. Much like the Internet, it started out as method for many-to-many military communication. Every radio set had both a transmitter and a receiver. Communication was cheap and provided limitless multi-directional connections within a certain radius. You could hold a conversation between two parties (ship-to-shore) or many parties (the whole fleet). It was a promising example of a many-to-many technology.

By the 1920s, radio had fallen into the hands of 'amateurs,' and the uses of radio had exploded well beyond the two-way transmission of logistical information.[3] Friends played records to each other over the airwaves (smells like teen Napster). Churches organized remote services complete with two-way hymn singing. Unions organized workers over the airwaves. Classes complete with question-and-answer sessions were held between the bedrooms and dens of amateur radio operators. Community and collective media were emerging — from the bedrooms, basements and garages of the 'little guy.' And this time, you didn't have to be a landowner to play.

And then it happened: society nerfed radio. RCA did the previously unthinkable and started pushing radio sets without transmitters (Imagine if, all of a sudden, you could only *receive* e-mail). Sponsored soap operas began to glob up the airwaves. The final nail in the coffin came when the U.S. government made it illegal to be a radio 'amateur.' By 1934, only people with commercial aims and big bucks could get radio licenses. Call it the landowners' revenge, if you like.

Despite the fact that radio began as a many-to-many technology, it ended up stuck in the same old one-to-many rut as print. The one-to-many mode of thinking had been so ingrained in people's minds — especially in the minds of the people who made money from media by restricting access to it — that there was no way radio stood a chance of remaining a many-to-many medium. Society trumped technology, and the 'broadcast model' was born. Taking its cues from existing print empires, radio stations (and television stations after them) became one-way pimps for the spec-

RCA did the previously unthinkable and started pushing radio sets without transmitters (Imagine if, all of a sudden, you could only receive e-mail.)

The game is
changing, and the
new rules are all
about diversity and
opportunity.

tacle. With the exception of a few stars, 'people' became more entrenched as the faceless, atomized audience.

Disconnected from each other.

Disconnected from the people telling the stories.

Disconnected even from the people selling them soap.

Drones.

And so it was, not only in media, but also in business, school and family: orders and info from the top, no room for the little guy or new ideas. Just a steady, predictable monochrome world — of drones.

And so it went, for a long, long, time.

Many-to-many

In contrast to the forms of media that were already grumpy and sclerotic by the Eisenhower era, it's easy to see how the Internet still holds the potential to be different. In top-down media, the audience simply sees the media product and 'the stars.' Through the Internet, we are beginning to see each other.

As a result, we're behaving differently. Certainly in the top-down, assembly-line parts of the world (and there are still many of them, because many different eras of technological development still exist cheek-by-jowl), corporate generals lead armies of workers to produce goods in the slow, traditional way. But here and there, workers are starting to operate without bosses. New products are flying out of basements and garages on a just-in-time basis. In a top-down world, conformity and follow-the-leader were the order of the day. But the game is changing, and the new rules are all about diversity and opportunity.

The transformations that the Internet has brought about require both the right technological conditions and the right cultural context. The world we live in is a mix of the technology we're using and the modes of thought that drive the use of the technology:

Print   One-to-many + Industrial thinking = Drones.

Radio + TV   Many-to-many + Industrial thinking = Drones.

Internet   Many-to-many + Commonspace thinking = People.

The Internet isn't creating these changes on its own. Rather, it is the fertile field for the kind of thinking that creates commonspace, thinking that has seeped out of the hacker margins to transform the mainstream.

At the core is the idea that given the option, we would rather be people than drones. Of course, no one wants to be a drone (except maybe Gary Numan, Kraftwerk, and other proponents of new wave music … but history dealt with them swiftly and harshly). And it's unlikely that we ever really were. If we had been, we would never have seen rock, hippies, punk or hiphop. We'd still be listening to Glenn Miller. Or Gary Numan.

Escape from the cubicle farm

Old habits die hard. Despite our cherished notions about the deep-seated human drive to be creative individuals, we persist in acting like drones. We still give ourselves role that are rigid, limited and tied to heirarchical organizations. We cut ourselves off from each other, creating a Dilbert world of tiny cubicles where even the average prisoner in a federal penitentiary has more room to move. (It could be worse: you could be stuck in a port-a-potty. After all, you have a laptop, right?)

But with the many-to-many culture of the Internet, the Dilbert world has the potential to change. Anyone has the potential to take on many roles at once. We can be producer, shopper, audience, friend or foe in the wink of an eye. While flitting between these roles and inventing new ones, we shed the rigidity that's required of drones and gain the opportunity to become people, creators, equals. When we start to climb over the cubicle walls, we see others all around us, shifting their roles and creating their dreams.

We create a Dilbert world of tiny cubicles where even the average prisoner in a federal penitentiary has more room to move.

Eggheads in fishnets

A group of cross-discipline knowledge, media and design academics at the University of Toronto describe their work style as a 'fishnet'. Connected by the Internet and intranets, they work together on collaborative projects. At any moment in time, any one 'knot' — or person — in the net can be pulled up. This person is the leader for the project for the moment. At another time, other knots can be pulled up in the same manner. Everyone is a leader and everyone is a collaborator.

U of T's fishnet is an example of a new type of online organization — one with fluid leadership. As Bakhtin points out in his description of the carnivalesque modern world, the inversion of traditional structures of authority is inevitable.[4] In the carnival of the Internet, everyone takes turns being leader and follower. And as ideas flow from online communities out into our culture, traditional hierarchies will weaken.

There is a strong connection between our shifting roles, the weakening of hierarchies, and the prevalence of collective, cooperative work online. If we take a close look at traditional roles, we can see how they are changing:

Bosses + Workers		Teams
Producers + Audience		Participants
Teachers + Students		Learners
Experts + The Masses	*become*	Collective Minds
Professionals + Clients		Hackers
Marketers + Markets		Transparent Data Trails
Sellers + Buyers		Traders

The fluidity of these new roles lend themselves to a flat, collective way of working.

It's important to stress that the roles people need to assume in common-space are neither rigid nor immediately obvious. Bosses and workers don't become teams simply because someone says so. The shift is subtler and (sometimes) scarier than that. You have to experience it and play with it to understand it. But it's a hell of a lot more fun than carrying pollen back to the hive.

The un-chain of command

Back in 1997, one of us (Darren) was employed on a project to write a video-game strategy manual with a team consisting of a project manager, a designer, and a play tester. The project manager and designer were at one end of the city of Toronto, connected to each other by an intranet and to Darren by the net and the telephone. The play tester was in the Phillipines. There was no face-to-face communication for the entire team — ever. The entire project took place in commonspace. Aside from e-mail, we communicated almost constantly via ICQ, which is an ideal device for sending quick query notices and organizing impromptu online conferences.

We began the project each in our respective roles. But as our communication developed, our roles shifted. Darren wound up doing a lot of organizing as well as writing, the project manager became an editor, the play-tester took on the design of charts and tables, and the designer offered arcane bits of technical advice. In a more structured situation, these skills might have gone unnoticed, and the finished product would have been much less competent as a result.

People like working on the Internet because of this blurring of role divisions. They perceive that the playing field is more level. Exactly how 'level' it really is corresponds to a number of factors, including the physical distance between workers and the amount of context ported over from the physical world. The further apart workers are physically, the fewer organizational imperatives from the regular work environment they have to deal with, and the greater their ability to define (and change) their own roles in commonspace.

If it also sounds messy and chaotic, that's because it is. But people are enjoying it. Typing messages, zipping back and forth through commonspace, reading e-mail, chatting — it all still possesses that 'gee-whiz' Tom Swift quality that makes it fun to use. And it makes us feel good, reminding us — rightly or wrongly — of the intimacy of village life, where people interact with familiarity, human-ness and little smiley faces :-).

Reciprocity and the fluidity of roles also has a leveling effect on narratives. Collective narratives change the teller and ultimately the world. In commonspace, everyone takes turns weaving new patterns into a collective story or beginning entirely new 'threads', like storytellers around a fire. The opportunity to participate is compelling because storytelling is an empowering and transformative act. The philosopher Walter Benjamin points out that retelling stories not only allows the teller to assimilate the tale into their own life experience, which makes it relevant for them (and changes them in the process); but it also allows them to embed a trace of themselves into the tale, a trace that will persist through all future tellers of that story.[5]

Collective storytelling is the entire purpose of Impromanga <www.im-promanga.org>, a site where participants construct sophisticated collective visual narratives in the style of Japanese comics ('manga'). The narrative evolves as new contributions appear. Even though it's possible simply to read the story, the assumption is that readers will write. Each new reader is automatically told which chapter will be theirs if they choose to contribute. The result is an exciting, organic story-line that reflects the personalities and imaginations of all the contributors.

People replace drones

Fluidity, commonality and reciprocity are the three factors that determine how many-to-many collaboration works in commonspace. Online communities help people feel like citizens again, reinjecting optimism and civic pride into even the most Grinch-like hearts. Where society makes us feel limited to pointless roles, commonspace offers opportunities to engage as free citizens. Online, we define the rules of the communities. We set the standards and act on them. We laud those that contribute or banish those who cause harm.

Hence the popularity of community. The WELL alone has over 260 active conferences. AOL, the largest private online service, has over 15,000 chat rooms in operation. And then there's good old USENET: a full daily feed is dozens of gigs of data from over 35,000 newsgroups. Given the number of people online, finding or building communities of interest is not difficult, no matter how 'specialized' an interest might seem. (After you've spent a little while exploring some of the dodgier corners of the Internet, you'll see what we mean. As Elvis Costello sang, we used to be disgusted, but now we're just amused.)

My employer can blow me

AOL's infamous purchase of Netscape in 1998 is a good example of exactly how wrong things can go when a top-down approach is imposed over a commonspace network. Seumas Froemke <www.seumas.com>, employed by Netscape as part of the Sun Alliance, explains the culture of Netscape before the merger:

Netscape is not supposed to be IBM. Netscape used to be the dyed-hair, pierced-whatever, jeans and tee-shirt, nerf-dart-infested, pool-playing, laughter-filled Internet company. We invented the web-browser. We were the first true Internet company.

...and the management structure afterwards:

When Netscape sold out to AOL, many employees left with their stock options which just happened to have vested during the same time period. Those who remained were mostly split up into two groups — AOL (client) employees and Sun/iPlanet (server) employees. Through an odd and yet not completely explained circumstance, there are Sun employees working on the browser and in management on the AOL side and AOL employees working on the server side with Sun....

While corporate executives were dreaming up dot-com empires to preside over, teams were replacing workers.

[E]ach of us end up having two sets of badges (a Sun badge and an AOL badge). We also end up having two managers (if you're a Sun employee). I'm a Sun employee and iPlanet is a Sun company, but it has AOL employees too. And AOL managers. So my division manager is an AOL employee, even though he's the manager of a division in a Sun company. I also have a Sun manager who is not the manager of the same Sun division, but is required to sign-off on any paperwork or technicalities that my AOL manager needs for those of us who are Sun employees.

The results of this kind of nightmarish bureaucracy on employee morale are neatly summed up by ex-Netscape/Mozilla employee Jamie Zawinski <www.jwz.org>: 'My employer can blow me.'

The conflict stems from the fact that while corporate executives were dreaming up dot-com empires to preside over, teams were replacing workers. The new worker expected more than top-down communication:

Figure 2: Online, the hierachies of information flow disappear.

E-mail was a key player in this shift. Workers became able to 'carbon copy' e-mail messages to each other, create document loops to guide workflow, and establish mailing lists to target specific slices of an enterprise. Because no single person controlled the communication now, workers began to regard each other as equals, regardless of their pay-cheque. Furthermore, e-mail made communications transparent and replicable, so that workers began to expect to be kept appraised of what's going on.

By the time intranets arrived on the scene, the technological stage was set for teamwork. Intranets introduced a whole new set of sophisticated tools for fine-tuning workflow and collaboration, such as document checkout and version control, digital bulletin boards and messaging, and charting and polling software. More importantly, people within companies who had

COMMONSPACE

never talked to each other before started forming relationships. Information flowed where there had previously been secrets. As a result, some businesses — the ones that 'got it' — started creating new kinds of roles within new kinds of companies. Of course, there were and still are many businesses that didn't get it. But some day soon, their desiccated corpses will line the shoulders of the information highway like so much roadkill.

And some industries really are 'getting it.' For instance, the New York City-based e-STEEL Corporation <www.e-steel.com>, the leading negotiation-based, neutral e-Commerce marketplace for steel products, counts nearly 3,000 companies from 90 countries among its membership. e-STEEL uses the b2bScene document management system to coordinate huge projects that span the globe. When a bastion of the industrial revolution like the steel industry decides to use commonspace to improve its operations, it's obvious that even the oldest dog can profit from some new tricks.

e-Steel demonstates that B2B can teach even the oldest dogs a few new tricks.

Everyone's a producer

'But what I really want to do is direct.' Really? You're in luck.

Like most of the societal structures that formed during the Industrial Revolution, the mega-print/broadcast model is hierarchical. It assumes that content flows downward from select pens, keyboards, microphones and cameras. Not surprisingly, most of these pens are located in the world's cultural Meccas: if you want to create a great magazine, you move to New York; if you want to make a movie, you move to Hollywood or India.

In some ways, this system makes sense, because concentration feeds creative synergy. On the other hand, concentrated hierarchies assume that unless you've bothered to scramble up the greasy corporate media ladder in the big town of your choice, you have nothing useful to say.

Wrong.

Commonspace is causing huge changes in the relationships between 'media producers' and 'media consumers.' The first five years of the Internet explosion have shown that amazing media products can appear out of the boondocks, courtesy of small guy with the computer. You don't have to look hard or long to find powerful examples, many of which began outside the big centres of media production:

ICQ

The first and still the best chat software in the world was invented in 1996 by four Israelis, all under the age of 27. Their servers were the first to handle 100,000 concurrent users online, and at their peak hours now handle hundreds of thousands of users at once.

Doom/Quake

On February 1, 1991, somewhere in the environs of Mesquite, Texas, John Carmack and his buddies began the most powerful videogame dynasty in the world, producing the insanely popular Doom and Quake titles. Quake is the nearest thing to an official sport that the Internet has. At one point, there were millions more copies of its predecessor Doom in circulation than there were legal copies of Microsoft Windows to run it on.

Mosaic/Netscape

The first of the big Internet startups was founded in 1994 by Jim Clark (the founder of Silicon Graphics) and Marc Andreessen (creator of NCSA Mosaic, the first graphic-interface Web browser, while he was still an undergraduate student at the University of Illinois at Urbana-Champaign). At one point, Netscape was the fastest-growing software company in history, and it's still the blueprint that most Internet startups aspire to match.

Hotmail

Indian-born Sabeer Bhatia, the inventor of Hotmail, made $400 million from the sale of his Webmail service to Microsoft.

The Blair Witch Project

Equipped only with a couple of cameras and $22,000 of borrowed money, three film students from Maryland created a horror mockumentary. Relying mainly on the viral power of the Internet to spread their word, they grossed $1.5 million in the first week of independent release and $29 million in the first week of wide release.

Many-to-many communication allows anyone anywhere to demonstrate that they have something useful to say. Of course, commonspace also provides a forum for a lot of fools spouting an astonishing variety of garbage. We don't have to provide any examples: you'll run across plenty of crap all on your own. But then again, Hollywood, network TV and good-old fashioned newsprint continue to produce endless streams of useless and offensive information by the minute. Online as anywhere else, we all need to keep our bullshit detectors and other heuristic tools in peak working order.

Relying mainly on the viral power of the Internet to spread their word, they grossed $1.5 million in the first week of independent release.

Death of the author

Anybody can be a writer too. Consider this exerpt from an Ultima Online role-playing game site <www.uo.com> titled 'Adventures on Dagger Island':

```
The cool fog caressed Jean-Luc's face as the ship
moved closer to the island shore. This was not a trip
he had wanted to make; but the guild had a new home
on the island, and the guildstone was needed there.
Mist, his faithful steed for so many years now, shuf-
fled and neighed behind him. Perhaps it was the cold,
or perhaps the mare felt the same sense of foreboding
that he himself felt.
```

It's not Shakespeare. But it's at least as good as the prose in the average heroic fantasy potboiler. And as writers such as this one become more experienced with collective authorship, the average quality of writing will improve. The important lesson here is that an audience is often as good as — or better — at 'writing the story' than real writers and producers.

That's because online collective authorship goes beyond the design team and down to the level of the players. In network games, everyone who plays is helping to author the unfolding story.

Actual play is dramatic enough, but it's also of sufficient interest to other players of the game that particular matches are often reported after the fact as either a sporting event or story. On Starcraft.org <www.starcraft.org>, one of the larger sites for players of Blizzard's hit real-time strategy game Starcraft, tournament games, complete with stills and captured action sequences, are reported in painstaking detail. Likewise, on numerous sites for Ultima Online, such as <www.uo.com>, players retell significant encounters, battles and community events, sometimes even in streaming audio.

Yet collective authorship isn't just about creating stories in the traditional sense. Online audiences are also authoring huge knowledge bases and research projects. Take the Open Directory Project <www.dmoz.org> as a stellar example. This huge weblogging initiative (bigger than Yahoo!) uses volunteers to describe and categorize online content. The content contributed by average people is just as important (and as relevant) as the content created by paid researchers. So how successful has this project been? The directory sections of many of the large search engines are now powered by Open Directory.

Everything$_2$

There are also some truly original efforts, like Everything$_2$ <www.everything2.org>, a collaboratively filtered database whose contents are created by its users and a small army of volunteers. Users create 'nodes' that are heavily hyperlinked to other nodes onsite. The Everything$_2$ FAQ provides a motto for commonspace in general: 'you are the most important person here.' In the words of side administration team member 'dem bones' [all underlined words are hyperlinks],

Everything$_2$ is what you make of it, that's the bottom line. It's open-ended, open-minded and waiting for you. You can node your diary, CD collection, dreamlog, notes on the apocalypse or a recipe for fettucine alfredo. You can sit around and read what other people have written. You can recommend changes in the system. You can do almost anything you want to provide you spell it right...

Everything$_2$ is an ever-growing, pulsating database that moves through cyberspace like a death-borg... slowly collecting and assimilating information and nonsense until... until...

Until it knows all.

Currently it's impossible to link from within Everything$_2$ to external sites, because the site's creators didn't want to turn Everything$_2$ into 'just another portal.' But since the code is open source, there's no reason that anyone who knows how to code couldn't re-engineer it to link externally. However, this doesn't mean that you can't link into Everything$_2$ from outside. Slashdot has taken advantage of this fact to use Everything$_2$ as its official glossary. Terms that the editors feel may be unfamiliar to their readers

The audience is no longer a pool of receptive eyeballs. It is a connected, active group of people with both voices and ears.

are hyperlinked from a [?] that follows the term to the appropriate Everything$_2$ node. But this is just one possible application. Part of the excitement of new commonspace technology like Everything$_2$ is its potential to be turned it into something else by someone with a vision. Gentlemen, start your engines.

None of the above should be taken as suggesting that movies or TV professional journalism are dead. But we are saying that in online culture, the distinctions between author and reader are disappearing. The audience is no longer a pool of receptive eyeballs. It is a connected, active group of people with both voices and ears. They are singing and playing together, like a roomful of musicians riffing off of each other, playing deep into the night.

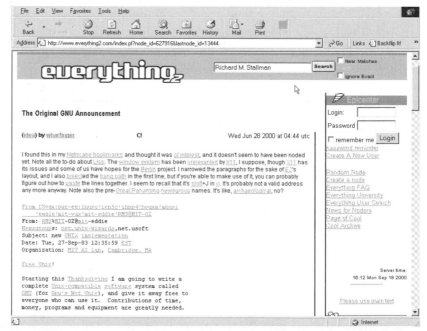

The collective mind at work: Everything$_2$ presents a heavily hyperlinked version of Richard Stallman's original GNU announcement. This sort of information resource makes researchers wet themselves with joy.

As markets, we see each other

The Internet is turning markets back into conversations.

While we all make fun of plaid-jacketed, pompadoured hucksters and hard-sell infomercials, buying and selling is not an inherently bad thing. After all, we need the basics of life and a few opportunities to throw our money after things that thrill us. But the problem with the soon-to-be-extinct industrial media marketplace of the last century was precisely this: it didn't produce things to meet our needs or even to thrill us. It has simply produced — and expected us to consume what it produced. In short, it hasn't listened to us.

But some companies are trying hard to listen now. While many factors have influenced this change, the Internet is one of the biggest. As the authors of *The Cluetrain Manifesto* point out, the Internet is turning markets back into conversations. This means that buyers are talking to each other, not just about what they want and need, but about what they don't like as well. Smart companies are listening to these conversations and joining in on them.

It's not hard to find examples. Just take a look at any of the epinions.com-style rating sites. Or on mailing listings. Or on discussion boards on Web sites. Or, in the granddaddy of them all, USENET. Here's a recent conversation about United Airlines that we found in the UseNet group <rec.travel.airlines>:

```
Subject: What's up with United?
Date: 07/11/2000
Author: xxx@wenet.net

I just had a fairly lousy return trip ORF -> ORD ->
SFO. on Sunday 7/9.

[snip]

My question, rta-ers, is what have you heard of ru-
mors that UA is having a work slowdown, hence lots of
minor mechanical problems and severe schedule disrup-
```

tions? The ground staff had an OK attitude and seemed
to do there best but I fee like booking my next
flight on CO.

—

Subject: Re: What's up with United?
Date: 07/14/2000
Author: xxx@spammindspring.com

Strange indeed.

What are the odds that the two United flights I took
ten days apart would both suffer instrument failure
that delayed both your flights.

I flew on June 19 out of SMF, June 29 out of ORD.

—

Subject: Re: What's up with United?
Date: 07/15/2000
Author: xxx@my-deja.com

UAL has the lowest on-time rate in the industry right
now...far worse than even America West. They also
have the highest cancellation rate, most complaints,
and most lost luggage per 1,000 passengers.

But, they claim they are reducing their schedules in
order to combat these problems. All I can say is, I'm
staying away from them until they get through their
labor negotiations.

—

```
Subject: Re: What's up with United?
Date: 07/15/2000
Author: xxx@webtv.net>
```

That's one of the questions Congress has asked about
the UA/US merger: If UA can't arrive on time now, why
let them gobble up another carrier?

As the dialog demonstrates, customers are no longer isolated from each
other, wondering whether other people are also pissed off with a company's service, reduced to venting their frustrations through rants in the coffee shop. Now they can go online to check in with others. And the
conversation is not just limited to service concerns. Everything from labour
relations to honesty in customer communications to regulatory review is
up for discussion. This changes things for business — dramatically.

But it doesn't mean that companies (and governments and non-profits)
need to become nervous nellies watching their every word. In fact, it means
just the opposite. When customers start to see each other and talk to each
other, they start to demand a higher degree of honesty and forthrightness
from the companies they patronize.

What connected customers want is for companies to stop dribbling treacly sentiments and join in the conversation.

Dear users...

Making this switch can actually turn a company around in commonspace.
Back in 1997, AOL was coming close being declared Public Enemy Number
One by its 8 million subscribers. It had drastically oversold its unlimited
pricing plan, and massively underestimated demand. The result was busy
signals for everyone. Sure, the accounts were unlimited, but you couldn't
get online to use them. People were pissed.

AOL CEO Steve Case turned the situation around with a series of apology
letters. In these letters, he both admitted that AOL was wrong ('We clearly
didn't go far enough in preparing for this') and provided a detailed description about how he was planning to fix the problem.[6] What's as-

What connected
customers want is
for companies to
stop dribbling
treacly sentiments
and join in the
conversation.

tounding is not that Case wrote an apology letter — this is par for the corporate course. Rather, it's the honesty and speed of his response that was impressive for the time. He was right there when the problems began. He was right there with refunds and a clear and honest explanation of what was going on inside the company.

While none of this makes AOL a paragon of virtue, it does say something about how companies need to react when their customers can talk to each other. They need to be engaged and responsive. The companies who do this well go far beyond the AOL example by freeing up their people to participate directly in the conversation.

Digital breadcrumbs

As we move around online, clicking on things, buying things, filling out forms, or simply loading a page into our browsers, we leave 'transparent data trails' behind us, the traces of where we've been and what we've done. This data includes such information as the IP address of your computer, the URL of the page you're viewing, and the type and version of browser you used. More importantly, it records what links you clicked on, how long you stayed on a page, and what you bought. These 'digital bread-crumbs' provide clues about who you are, where you've been, and where you're likely to go next.

The ability to gather this kind of information may seem commonplace now, but it would have been mind-blowing five years ago. Companies used to spend hundreds of thousands of market research dollars to collect such data, and, for that reason, it would have been treated as a highly guarded secret. Now, it is automatically collected, sorted and (when the business in question is ethical) made available to customers — and even competitors.

Of course, most companies, even those that are online, still treat this kind of information as their own corporate property and do with it what they want. They keep their customers in the dark, cut off from each other. The question is, under such circumstances, how long will those customers remain customers — especially when competitor companies are opening up?

In November of 1999, Real Networks was hit with a class-action lawsuit because its RealJukebox assigned a personal ID number to users and uploaded information about their listening habits to Real.com's servers. Not that the lawsuit seemed to have much effect on their corporate policy. The Privacy Forum Digest for May 18, 2000 < www.vortex.com/privacy/priv.09.15> reports that the Real Networks/Netzip 'Download Demon' (recently renamed 'RealDownload'), a utility that automates and improves certain aspects of the downloading process for users, also links itself to all browsers on a system and sends file names and URLs for all files a user downloads back to the Real servers. Think about that one for a minute. Such cavalier handling of privacy can only result in the alienation of customer bases that took years to build.

On the other hand, if a company keeps user data anonymous, aggregates it into general statistics, and makes it transparent to users, it can help us 'see each other' in new and useful ways. Amazon.com provides a positive example. Amazon uses the data trails generated by its customers to tell us how popular a book is among other buyers, what other titles have been purchased by customers who have bought the book, and what other people (sometimes including even the author and publisher) have thought and said about the book.

This application of anonymous aggregated data is useful to all of Amazon's users, without violating anyone's right to privacy. It also helps us see each other as we move through commonspace.

Resistance is futile

Understanding the connections between people — customers, collaborators, partners and anonymous supporters — is now crucial to the success of any online activity. The world of the captains of industry and ignorant masses is being left behind. The 'masses' are becoming individual people,

If a company makes data anonymous and makes it transparent, we can 'see each other' in ways not possible before.

creators in both name and fact. Because we're unable to avoid each other any longer, 'we the people' are joining forces, in explicit (online conversations) and subtle (transparent data trails) ways. The nature of media, communication and business for all parties involved has changed, for good or bad.

Like it or not, we are no longer in the age of the hierarchical corporate army. We are entering the age of the collective. And even your matinee idols will change.

The Power Ranger principle

You don't invent the future, you unleash it by leveraging the global community mind.

JOHN SEELY BROWN, XEROX PARC

Our heroes change along with our technologies. The Lone Ranger has long since ridden off into the sunset, but even if he hadn't, he could never have survived as a hero for the kids of the Internet age. He was, well, lone. Sure, he had a big white horse and a subservient, racial stereotype of a sidekick. But it was really the kemosabe himself that made all the decisions, saved all the days, and performed all the heroics. Just like the captains of industry, generals and other rugged individuals of his time, the Lone Ranger didn't need anything except his horse and his six-shooter. Hi ho!

But the terrain on the digital frontier is different from the Wild West. There's really no place for the loner, because the wagons are already circled, the towns are well under construction, and the fields are already planted. Online, the collective is already here.

In the age of the collective, we need new heroes: Power Rangers. The Power Rangers may be a lot of things, but they are decidedly not lone. They are the epitome of collective action — at least, to as great an extent as is possible in the two-dimensional world of kids' TV reruns. Alone, the Power Rangers are ordinary, even bland, kids. Sure, they can 'morph' into individual superheroes, who happen to look a lot like the Lone Ranger wearing a motorcycle helmet instead of a Stetson. Sure, they ride mechanical Zords rather than trusty steeds named Silver. But morphing has its limitations. When Power Rangers fight their enemies all by their lonesome, they inevitably get their pimply asses kicked.

On the other hand, when Power Rangers put their individual failings behind them and pool their talents, skills, personalities and technological assets together, they form the MegaZord, an unstoppable technological colossus. Collectively, they can whip the stuffing out of all the rubber-suited monsters (always loners!) that their nemeses Rita Repulsa and Lord Zedd can throw at them. Alone, they're just kids in candy-coloured spandex. Together, they're the Power Rangers — and they're invincible.

As the collective defenders of the commons (a.k.a. the town of Angel Grove), the Power Rangers are the perfect superheroes for the common-space era. They show how ...

Internet Super Ingredient #1
PEOPLE

combines with

Internet Super Ingredient #2
WORKING TOGETHER

to create

COMMONSPACE
(+ digital collective-ness)

With this gestalt comes a comprehensive shift in how everything around us works, looks and feels.

The Lone Ranger has slunk out of town, broken-down mythology trailing behind him in the dust. The Power Rangers have ushered in a world of collective superheroes. We are now living in the world of digital gestalts, where everything connects, merges and becomes MegaZordish. Excellent.

Your new superpowers

Congratulations. You're now an official commonspace Power Ranger. When you choose to work collectively online, you can accomplish some amazing things because you have the following superpowers:

- **Speed.** You can move faster than people who aren't online. The small, fluid, Internet-enabled project/idea/enterprise/meme moves faster than the majority of bloated corporate processes.

- **Creativity.** You can come up with astounding new ideas and solutions. There's no need to think outside the box, because the box is gone.

- **The MegaZord Effect.** Like the Rangers melding into the MegaZord, you can use collective action and synergy to create products and services far more impressive than the resources and time that went into creating them. The collective gives you the leverage to move mountains and kick rubbery monster butt.

Fortunately, doing things quickly and effectively has another side-effect: it allows people to be people without being dehumanized, restricted or circumscribed by their work. The collective power of the Internet is not important simply because it flattens hierarchies. In many respects, it also helps to create a more humane work environment.

A penguin is born

What does the MegaZord look like online? Well, despite the sorry lack of a Ranger who rides in a mechanical Penguin Zord, the online collective looks a lot like Linux.

Think back. About 10 years ago, an unknown Finnish university student started working on a home-made operating system that worked much like the Unix systems that ran huge corporate and academic networks. Once he'd created a reasonably stable version of his software, he started distributing it for free online. Moreover, he invited others to hack around with his source code and share their changes and fixes. The operating system grew. The number of users grew. The MegaZord grew. Together, Linus Torvalds and his users snatched a huge market share from Microsoft and Sun and other 'monster' software companies and created something that really worked. Something called Linux.

Sure, it's a story that we've all heard a million times by now. But it's still astounding. Linux happened, and is still happening like wildfire. The software is free and so reliable that many IT professionals consider it to be more powerful and more reliable than the commercially produced alternatives.

The crux of the matter is that Linux and other open source packages were evolved by self-organizing, reasonably 'flat' collectives. For those who've never been involved in one, an open source project works in a substantially different manner from other types of authoring. Eric Raymond's classic essay 'The Cathedral and the Bazaar' <www.tuxedo.org/~esr/writings/cathedral-bazaar/> provides, among other things, a kind of approximate flowchart for open source development gleaned from his experiences

Tux, the official Linux mascot, as
designed by Larry Ewing

developing Fetchmail. If arranged in a chronological order, the steps involved would look something like this:

- Begin with a project that's useful to you, and enjoy your work.

- Plan your data structures well.

- Establish what to recycle from other projects.

- Be ready to start over at least once… but don't throw anything away.

- Develop a base of users/beta-testers/co-developers to facilitate debugging.

- Release early, release often.

- Listen to your customers/users.

- If you get tired of your project, hand it over to someone who cares about it.

Some of these stages are merely the extension of good planning. But some of them highlight the essential differences between open source philosophy and other approaches to development and authoring.

First of all, nothing in open source is garbage. If you can't find a use for a given piece of your project, there may well be someone else who can. Accordingly, everything should be archived somewhere. When storage is as cheap as it is now, there's absolutely no reason not to save everything for posterity.

Secondly, customers and users are an important part of the creation process, because they will often catch bugs and other types of problems that you've missed. As soon as your product becomes stable and usable, send it out into the world, and be industrious about soliciting opinions from your client base on how to improve it. This allows you to take advantage of what Raymond calls 'Linus' Law': *Given enough eyeballs, all bugs are shallow.* In an open source environment, more releases means more corrections, and the result is a better product.

The third major difference in the open source approach has to do with intellectual property. If you have no interest in maintaining something, give it to someone who does. In an era of domain-name speculation and other forms of unleashed capitalist greed, this may seem like an astonishing demand. But the benefits of this approach are demonstrable from the success of the open source model. And if the property you've donated to the common pool develops some sort of second wind, it'll only look good on you.

Raymond also takes on conventional project management strategy by the horns and wrestles it to the ground. In 'On Management and the Maginot Line,' one of several 'version upgrades' that have been made to his paper over the years (even prose can benefit from the adoption of open source practices), he points out:

Traditionally-minded software-development managers often object that the casualness with which project groups form and change and dissolve in the open-source world negates a significant part of the apparent advantage of numbers that the open-source community has over any single closed-source developer. They would observe that in software development it is really sustained effort over time and the degree to which customers can expect continuing investment in the product that matters, not just how many people have thrown a bone in the pot and left it to simmer.[1]

But Raymond points out that EMACS, the standard text editing software in Unix/Linux, 'has absorbed the efforts of hundreds of contributors over fifteen years into a unified architectural vision, despite high turnover and the fact that only one person (its author) has been continuously active during all that time. No closed-source editor has ever matched this longevity record.[2] And the effect of this continuous focus is evident in Linux's continued success and growth. Almost a decade old now, Linux has weathered technological changes such as the migration from 16-bit to 32-bit with a much greater degree of ease and stability than competing systems such as Windows.

Open source development makes the traditional functions of software project management 'strangely irrelevant'. To understand what's changed, Raymond examines the factors that define the traditional manager's role:

- Managers define goals and keep everybody pointed in the same direction.

Raymond accedes that this function might be necessary to some extent. Every project has to have some sort of long-term direction if it's going to be of continued use. But he objects to the notion that middle managers can do this better than the 'tribal elders' of the open source world.

- Managers monitor projects and make sure that crucial details don't get skipped.

According to a story on ZDNet <www.zdnet.com>, an internal Microsoft memo viewed by Sm@rt Reseller revealed that the first release of Windows 2000 was shipped with 65,000 bugs. Crucial details don't get skipped? There's no point in even debating the merits of the open-source model over monitored workflow in terms of product quality. Decentralized peer review clearly kicks the tar out of all the prevailing traditional methods for debugging.

- Managers motivate people to do boring but necessary drudgework.

What interests Raymond here are the underlying assumptions: that without someone dangling a big bag of money in front of them, programmers in an office environment will turn in substandard work, and in fact, that this form of management is useful only in circumstances when work is perceived as 'boring.' But the moment that a competing open source solution for a 'boring' problem appears, customers are going to know that the problem was solved by a highly motivated person who tackled it because they enjoyed the process. Any guesses which product the customer will see as superior?

There's no point in even debating the merits of the open-source model over monitored workflow in terms of product quality

- Managers organize the deployment of people for best productivity.

Raymond's argument becomes unabashedly elitist here, claiming that open source productivity is a result of the community's 'ruthless self-selection' for competence. Office workers, by implication, are slow and feebleminded. Whatever you think of this contention, consider 'that it is often cheaper and more effective to recruit self-selected volunteers from the Internet than it is to manage buildings full of people who would rather be doing something else.'[3]

- Managers marshal resources needed to sustain the project.

In an office environment, where people, machines and spaces are limited and in constant demand, the need to pull the wagons into a circle and defend a project's resources is a sad fact of life and the subject of many Dilbert cartoons. But in an open source world, where there are no offices, and everyone is a volunteer, there's no 'enemy within' to fend off. Hence the only limited resource is skilled attention.[4]

Raymond's parting shot on the issue of traditional management vs. open source development is a rhetorical zinger: 'if the open-source community has really underestimated the value of conventional management, why do so many of you display contempt for your own process?'[5]

The cynicism of office culture is omnipresent, from movies like *Office Space* to the tales of worker alienation in zines like *Processed World*. If Raymond was correct in his assumption that 'It may well turn out that one of the most important effects of open source's success will be to teach us that play is the most economically efficient mode of creative work,'[6]

And, well, that wouldn't be such a bad thing, now would it?

The aggregation nation

As the notion of collective work builds steam, the walls between organizations are beginning to topple. Lines are disappearing — between inside and outside, customer and partner, supplier and buyer. Amid the rubble, astounding pools of collective information and ideas are emerging.

Just think for a minute about how companies have changed their tune about 'links.'

When the Web first appeared, most companies feared links. Linking offsite: Don't do it, it's like giving away customers. Linking in: We don't want it, unless you are linking to our majestic homepage. 'Please, please, please Mr. Internet MegaZord, don't deep-link to the individual stories within our site' was the plea of the marketing wonks. Most companies were afraid that the connections the Internet provided would ruin their business. They believed that they'd be fine if they could just corral people inside their sites as they could in the mall.

The situation has changed drastically in the last five years. At least at the basic level of links, most companies have realized that their Web site doesn't amount to squat if it's not linked to the larger collective resources of the net.

The emergence of Rich Site Summary (RSS)-based headline sharing is clear evidence of this shift. Sites as diverse as HotWired, Slashdot and CNN have all started broadcasting their headlines and links for free to the rest of the Internet. As a result, anyone can easily and automatically pick up these headlines and incorporate them into their site's contents. Not only has this aggressively encouraged the practice of deep linking; it has also led to more off-site linking, because it ultimately generates more traffic.

The copyright-obsessed corporate media world has finally twigged to the fact that online, links are life itself. Of course, what they have really discovered is something more revolutionary than 'links.' They've discovered the power of content aggregation, a phrase that means exactly what you think it does: bringing content from a variety of online sources into one place (literally or metaphorically). With headline sharing, information becomes a huge pool from which anyone can draw the pieces they want. This kind of aggregated data pool — and the opportunity to take what you want from it — is one of the most powerful forces in commonspace.

Sites as diverse as HotWired, Slashdot and CNN have all started broadcasting their headlines and links for free to the rest of the Internet.

When most people say 'content aggregation' they mean 'portal.' For several years now, becoming a popular content aggregator (or portal) has been the Holy Grail of Internet business. Building an aggregation site like Yahoo! or MySimon has meant lots of traffic, lots of eyeballs, and the potential for lots of advertising dollars. It was (and remains) a quick way to create a Big New Media Brand.

A portal is also a *centralized* pool of information. Anyone can come to draw on it, but only within the confines of the rules and categories imagined by the people who created the site. Anyone can provide content to the pool, but they have to accept that users will only find their content through the rigid filter provided by the portal. Of course, portals are useful in the same manner that the Yellow Pages are useful. But despite their helpfulness, they're also boring, over-regulated and frequently out-of-date.

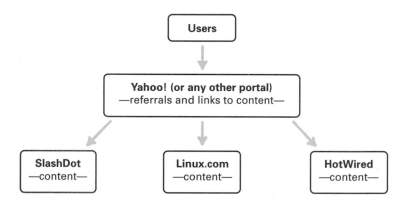

Figure 3: Traditional portals put themselves between people and information.

The standard portal is not that different in structure from the hierarchical one-to-many media models that we are hoping to leave behind us. Despite the shiny technological trappings, it's still one site, one brand, one group of editors and webmasters pushing content out to the masses.

The now zodiac

Isn't there a way to draw on the power of content aggregation that is more creative and interesting than the Yellow Pages? Is there a way to that takes better advantage of the collective power of the Internet than a one-to-many portal?

Of course there is. In fact, there are many.

The most recent approaches to aggregation are more collective in structure than their predecessors. They recognize that people online want constant access to filters, context and opinion. Such approaches blur the lines between producer and audience and between organizations. They provide X-ray vision that lets you see through the cubicle walls and super-strength to break down the gates around carefully hoarded data and to open up an omni-directional flood of information. Most importantly, they recognize that the Internet works best when we all contribute to and draw from collective pools of aggregated information.

These emerging models look less like the Yellow Pages and more like the chaotic headline-sharing that content providers are starting to embrace. The closest analogy would be a networked, many-to-many version of the old media concept of 'syndication.' By sharing headlines freely across the Internet, information pools feed the diverse needs of the network and its users.

The result of these linked information pools resembles a constellation more than a portal. Vital pieces of information flow freely within the network. Just as in a constellation, information appears bigger/more important or smaller/less important depending the location and orientation of the viewer. For example, on Slashdot, the 'Slashback' section (a summary of commentary on important current stories) appears in large type with a long summary. But stories from other sites such as Salon or Blue's News appear as small headlines in the margin column of the page. The opposite would be the case if your were on Salon or Blue's News.

These linked information pools resemble a constellation more than a portal.

The traditional portal is still too much like a firewall between the user and the content provider.

The collectivized constellation model — the MegaPortal — is more useful to both content providers and users.

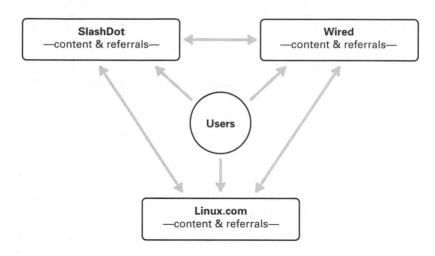

Figure 4: Constellations connect users directly to content, drawing traffic away from traditional portals.

These are considerable advantages. The traditional portal is still too much like a firewall between the user and the content provider. It benefits the portal owner in the short term, as the site's large size generates a lot of ad dollars. But the trade-off is that the content provider is isolated and disconnected, and the user has to dig for related content across disconnected sites.

In contrast, the collectivized constellation model — the MegaPortal — is more useful to both content providers and users. Content sites receive traffic and additional material from related sites. Users discover links to material they wouldn't otherwise have found. The constellation model gives every site the potential to be the know-it-all — the expert in their field. Sites become more vibrant and users find content more easily and intuitively.

This is not to say that there is no need for aggregator sites. They still provide the road maps and the ability to pinpoint specific information. But over time, aggregator sites will simply become players within larger constellations. Often they will aim to fill a particular niche, acting as the main aggregator for a constellation focussed on a particular topic.

COMMONSPACE

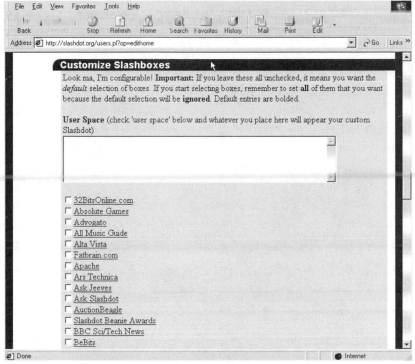

File Edit View Favorites Tools Help

Back   Forward   Stop   Refresh   Home   Search   Favorites   History   Mail   Print   Edit

Address http://slashdot.org/users.pl?op=edithome   Go   Links »

Customize Slashboxes

Look ma, I'm configurable! **Important:** If you leave these all unchecked, it means you want the *default* selection of boxes. If you start selecting boxes, remember to set **all** of them that you want because the default selection will be **ignored**. Default entries are bolded.

User Space (check 'user space' below and whatever you place here will appear your custom Slashdot)

☐ 32BitsOnline.com
☐ Absolute Games
☐ Advogato
☐ All Music Guide
☐ Alta Vista
☐ Fatbrain.com
☐ Apache
☐ Ars Technica
☐ Ask Jeeves
☐ Ask Slashdot
☐ AuctionBeagle
☐ Slashdot Beanie Awards
☐ BBC Sci/Tech News
☐ BeBits

Done   Internet

Everyone's fave RSS-based Web site, Slashdot, is highly configurable, allowing users to select the particular 'Slashboxes' they want to appear on their home page. There's even room for URLs of your own in the 'user Space' section.

One World <www.oneworld.net>, a human rights network, is already playing this kind of role. At first glance, One World appears to be a slick on-line magazine and portal with a strong focus on human rights. The front page is a tight mix of well-written headlines, photos and links that push through to an eco-friendly, people-friendly shopping mall. While it isn't the New York Times, it's a pretty impressive site by non-profit Web standards.

What's brilliant about One World is that it's really a collectively written digital media product and knowledge base. All of the content comes from One World Partners — non-profits who pay a membership fee to be listed in the search engine. Partners push content to the One World editors, who pick up the best content for their front pages and sector-based theme sites.

Many businesses
don't see the
constellations,
only individual
stars, cold and
lonely.

Essentially, One World is a traffic co-op for its members and a great magazine for its users. Professional-quality media, created by the collective. Amazing.

Internet syndication and content co-ops like One World and Slashdot are creating a collective media universe that is more flexible, configurable, and responsive than analog media models, and even first-generation digital models. Small players can instantly become a part of something much larger — and bootstrap themselves in the process — by contributing to the syndication pool and picking up headlines from others. Constellation members can provide their own editorial take on information. Users can quickly and easily find what they need from anywhere in the constellation. In content syndication, everyone contributes a little, and the result is a media universe that is much, much bigger than the sum of its parts.

And so publishing, the bastion of the copyright, becomes an act of sharing rather than hoarding. Small players leverage off each other, and everyone gains in the process. Hucksterism wanes as publicity becomes dependent on high-quality writing and content-sharing.

Of course, such growth is impossible for businesses that retain outmoded, silo-style organizational thinking, where information only gains value from being stockpiled. Constellations require mutual access to yield mutual success. Businesses have to be willing to see the benefits of their information appearing on Web sites run by their partners and even their competitors. Getting over this conceptual hump is going to be a huge challenge for many. In fact, some people just don't get it no matter how many times you show them or tell them. They see their Web site as their outpost in a vast and chaotic universe of information. They don't see the constellations, only individual stars, cold and lonely.

But once they do .... bang! It's time for fireworks.

Frequently answered questions

The fireworks of collective media aren't being created solely by professional media-makers and people consciously seeking to 'get their message out.' In fact, amazing new kinds of collective media are being produced by all of us every time we open our metaphorical mouths online. Our words, our ideas, our complaints are transforming into self-generating knowledge bases and information resources that we could never have dreamed of ten years ago. Unconsciously or consciously, we are all becoming a part of the collective mind.

Collective minds begin to form when online communities, discussion forums, listservs and other ongoing digital conversations turn into searchable archives. As in the real world, online discussions often contain much wisdom. But unlike real-world discussions, online talk is recorded more often than not. Once recorded, discussions can be searched, analyzed and referred to by others. It's as if every community meeting, kaffeeklatsch and bull session down at the pub or around the cooler had a set of written minutes.

In the majority of cases, the response to all this recorded chatter might justifiably be 'So what?' The minutiae of daily life online is usually as tedious and banal as it is in the real world. But because the archives exist, and because we already have sophisticated search tools that alleviate the gruntwork of having to sift through mountains of hay for the digital needle, online communities and other kinds of discussions have the potential to be knowledge bases and answer pools of unprecedented power.

The first real example of a conversational archiving form was the USENET FAQ. For those who've never stumbled across it, USENET was (and is) a vast Internet-wide discussion system that contains thousands of different 'newsgroups' and has been in constant use since 1979. Each newsgroup focusses on a particular topic — Java programming, stamp collecting, bondage, you name it. Before it became a high noise haven for pranksters, trolls and spammers (around 1995), USENET was a place that people could turn to for useful answers from their peers.

In order to capture the essential knowledge generated by a given newsgroup and to avoid having to answer the same questions repeatedly (not suprisingly, telling potential new users to RTFM — Read The Fucking Manual — tended to alienate them), people in these mini-communities started developing documents containing the answers to 'Frequently Asked Questions'. These collectively generated documents became known as FAQs. Many FAQs are available at AskJeeves <www.ask.com> in their Internet FAQ Archives, if you're curious.

It's something of an exaggeration to call a USENET FAQ a knowledge base, because FAQs only skim the tip of the USENET knowledge iceberg. But they do serve a valuable purpose as the distilled core knowledge contained of any given group. Think of them as the Cliff's Notes of community knowledge.

Once the practice of mining USENET for information had developed, it didn't take long for people to start digging deeper — and more broadly. Enter Deja News <www.deja.com>. Deja's great revelation was that USENET could become a hugely more powerful information resource if someone just pointed a search engine at it. So they did. They didn't really know what else they would do with their site, or how it would make money; they just hoped that people would search. And they did. In droves. They searched for solutions to their technical problems, for feedback about what laptop to buy, for hints on where to find stolen software or what to feed their iguanas.

Over time, the patterns and the opportunities became clear. People were searching for the opinions of others. Building on this knowledge, Deja News became Deja.com — a collective opinion pool. Over time, the site began to organize information from newsgroups most likely to include opinions on consumer items, such as laptops and camcorders. It also started adding proprietary content-gathering tools to supplement the opinions generated through USENET. For example, product-rating polls were added to collect — and reflect — the opinions of searchers. Every time you searched for 'laptop,' you'd be discreetly asked for your opinion on various laptops models. The aggregated opinions of other Deja users began to supplement the information available from USENET. And so the 'collective opinion mind' was born.

The sad part of the story is that the collective mind is still kind of an idiot savant. The commercial side of Deja has gradually swallowed almost all of the site's original purpose, Jekyll-and-Hyde fashion. The USENET search engine is still there, but you have to do a bit of tunneling to find it. In any event, the Deja archive only extends back to 1995, so it's hardly a comprehensive research tool. But we can always hope that some day the archive will be extended to cover earlier years as well, by Deja or someone else.

In some respects, opinion sites take on the same role as Consumer Reports or Edmunds used car guides. They provide feedback on the quality and usefulness of products we might consider buying. While the collective Internet mind lacks the objectivity and rigor of such publications, it offers a kind of information that could never come from a print publication or even from top-down Web publishing: current, dynamic and unmediated.

Together we compute

For the most part, the power of the collective comes from some sort of active participation, such as words, ideas or code. But slowly, collective work is beginning to extend from ideas to resources, such as spare CPU cycles.

'Community computing' used to refer to the setting up of a FreeNet or some kind of socially-minded online community. But increasingly, it's come to mean sharing your spare computer resources with a large project that needs extensive computing power. Small computing tasks are divided up and sent out to participating computers across the network by a central server. Once the 'work' on each little packet has been completed, it is sent back to the central server for integration into the main data pool.[7]

SETI@home <setiathome.ssl.berkeley.edu> was the first to try this 'voluntary collective processing' on a large scale. In the SETI (Search for Extra-Terrestrial Intelligence) project, over two million users worldwide lend their computers to aid in the search for alien life. The project gathers a huge pool of galactic surveillance information with the project's telescopes. Then, using a little program disguised as a screen saver, it sends small amounts of this data to the each of the users' computers for processing. The computers, in turn, send back the processed data. This huge network of regular desktop computers gives SETI the equivalent of a powerful super-computer that would be far outside of their budgetary constraints.

SETI@home has proven so popular that it's even inspired Internet hoaxes. A group of young programmers posing as a Russian computing company

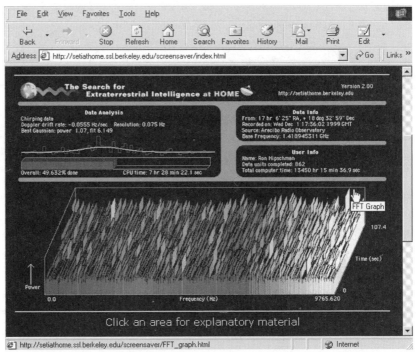

The SETI@home screensaver not only signals the advent of a new type of networked parallel processing, it also looks really, really cool.

COMMONSPACE

posted a notice claiming they'd developed a computer accelerator board designed exclusively to speed up the SETI@home software. They were deluged with so many inquiries from people interested in acquiring this nonexistent product that they were forced to reveal their spoof almost immediately and subsequently removed their Web site.

At one level, the emergence of this kind of networked parallel processing is a useful yet boring development. The most obvious applications for it will probably involve the sharing of processing across unused machines on large corporate networks. Who really cares if Shell can speed up the analysis of geological data by farming the task out to idle computers in the secretarial pool? It's certainly a nifty technical feat and an efficient use of resources. But it's not commonspace.

The really interesting applications are in projects like SETI@home, where huge numbers of people can pool their spare resources to support a project that inspires them. The participants in SETI@home aren't really giving up anything they'll miss, but they are giving something nonetheless. In doing so, they are creating a collective supercomputer, a computer that is literally bigger than the sum of its parts. Who knows how far these kinds of projects will go? What if SETI really discovers some extraterrestial life? We are on the verge of a huge shift in how we share resources and participate in large-scale projects.

We are each other

Human beings have always needed each other in order to grow and thrive as individuals. For a long time, we'd forgotten that. But it's possible once again to work together in short-term, non-hierarchical groups in order to accomplish highly specific goals with very little individual work.

People always have varying degrees of interest in any project. The beauty of collective work is that it doesn't require everyone to contribute all of their resources, so long as some people contribute some of their resources.

And everyone benefits from these casual moments of philanthropy. Collective synergies yield results that can never be produced deliberately and mechanistically, no matter how large the project budget.

This is not wide-eyed New Age optimism. It is clear and present reality. Hierarchies and other structures that traditionally drive collective work are dying out. Now success demands flat systems and commonspace:

In practice, this means 'think open source' and 'contribute to the collective data pool.' You need to put your ideas into the collective to benefit and thrive.

And here's the dirty little secret about joining the collective: your work doesn't just get more powerful... it gets easier.

The infinite unbirthday party

*These business models presume generosity — or at least
some basic drive to share. Why not? Some anthropologists
and evolutionary psychologists argue that humans are
hardwired for generosity, that our propensity for sharing
was inherited from our primitive ancestors. The economist
Mancur Olson came to the same conclusion in his
consideration of the rich man who provides a coastal
community with a lighthouse: Even though it isn't in the
interest of an individual to pay for a public work, the
benefactor is indirectly compensated through a boost in
status.*

MARK FRAUENFELDER, WIRED 8.07

Online, the only way to win is to give away as much power as you can. As
fast as you can.

More specifically, you need to give power to your users, your community
and your partners. You need to help them reach their goals. Help them
make money. Help them find each other. You need to empower these people, and, in doing so, empower collective action. In turn, you'll get the
kind of respect, support and (yes) revenue you need to make it on the
Internet.

The atmosphere
of a gift economy
in full gear
is chaotic, noisy,
and exuberant.

For traditional organizations and businesses, this is the most confusing and scary rule of commonspace. Business, politics and even community building is about consolidating power, controlling what happens, and being in charge — isn't it?

Not any more.

We all have the drive to be creative, to contribute and to succeed. As we leave our roles as drones behind, we realize that we can have all of these things and make a living. Having a job, participating in a community and reaching your goals isn't about conformity anymore. And for more and more of us, it's possible to pursue our passions as more than a sideline.

In many respects, the network makes this possible. It gives us the tools that make it cheaper to do what we want to do. It makes smaller, more focussed markets and communities possible. Most importantly, it gives us each other. In a flat, accessible networked world, you don't have to fill out a form or worm your way up through the bureaucracy to start selling your online game or networking with solar energy enthusiasts. You just do it.

Not to say that it's easy. We all need the right tools to make the network dance. Helping each other to grow while simultaneously nurturing the collective requires the right context and a solid platform. This is where the 'give power to get power' rule comes in.

We talked briefly about the gift economy in Chapter 2 and pointed out that the most innovative parts of Net culture operate at least in part as gift economies. And we explained that even though gift economies and restricted economies are opposites in many respects, they always co-exist. The atmosphere of a gift economy in full gear is chaotic, noisy, and exuberant. A good analogy is the Mad Hatter's unBirthday Party in Lewis Carroll's Alice in Wonderland. People think they're animals, animals think they're people. (If you don't see what this has to do with the Internet, do a search on 'Anthromorphics' sometime.) Everyone talks and sings at once, often in bizarre argots of their own devising. Blow out the candle and make a wish . . . but don't forget: if it's your party, you give out the gifts. Welcome to the Infinite unBirthday Party.

Eric Raymond contends in 'Homesteading the Noosphere' (the sequel to 'The Cathedral and the Bazaar' at <www.tuxedo.org/~esr/writings/homesteading/>) that 'it is quite clear that the society of open-source hackers is in fact a gift culture. Within it, there is no serious shortage of the "survival necessities" — disk space, network bandwidth, computing power. Software is freely shared. This abundance creates a situation in which the only available measure of competitive success is reputation among one's peers.'[1] But elements of gift cultures exist in other parts of the Internet as well: file-sharing networks and opinion sites are relatively pure gift cultures. Many online communities and some types of gaming networks also exhibit these characteristics.

The failure of greed

In a recent editorial on The Silcon Alley Daily <www.siliconalleydaily.com>, Jacon McCabe Calacanis writes the following: '[L]et's first look at the two lessons we've learned in the five years…. [W]e've learned that consumers want content for free, and that subscriptions don't work. Second, we've learned that banner ads are a miserable failure. Consumers have blocked them out, and more importantly, banner ads alone can't cover the costs of producing content.'[2] What Calacanis is saying is that many Internet businesses have never made any money in the way that they expected to (i.e. through metered content) and may never make any money at all. A new study from the Harvard Business School suggests that 58% of the 'Internet incubators' which fund other Internet startups are startups themselves, with the same cashflow problems, the same sketchy life-expectancy, and precious little success to show for their efforts.[3]

It's almost funny. The blind are leading the blind. Maybe it's time to round-file the whole greedy capitalist schtick and take another tack.

The entrenchment of gift economy ethics online may well explain why it's been so difficult to port restricted economy practices onto the Internet

58% of the Internet incubators which fund other Internet startups are startups themselves.

Rule #1: Never run your online service or community like a control freak. We learned this rule the hard way.

successfully. Many of the most astounding Internet successes have been the result of creating tools and environments that empower others. Sometimes success has been the result of creating a platform that allows the magic sparks of community to fly (The WELL). Other times it's the effect of creating basic tools that allow collective interactions to spread like wildfire (Netscape). Success has also been about giving away what's rightfully yours so that it'll come back as something better (Linux). Whatever the case, those who have empowered others as much as themselves have thrived on the Internet.

This seeming selflessness can come from many different sources:

- Hackers and programmers who are driven more by vision than by profit;

- Companies that are trying to empower their users and customers;

- Managers who realize they'll increase quality if their employees are pursuing their passions;

- Activists who are trying to change the world.

The common thread among these disparate groups is their understanding of the need to invigorate, excite, hook, create benefit for and empower others to succeed in the commonspace world. And, as we have suggested, this approach works a hell of a lot better than 'business as usual.'

The last of the control freaks

Rule #1: Never run your online service or community like a control freak. We learned this rule the hard way.

In 1994, one of us (Mark) was part of a team of people who were running Web Networks <www.web.ca>, a small but successful online community in Canada. Starting in 1988, it offered international e-mail and discussion groups for environmentalists, peace activists and others with burning causes to champion. In its first six years, Web built an astoundingly loyal following. Web members did everything community members are

COMMONSPACE

supposed to do: they fostered relationships, built libraries of documents, engaged in passionate debates, and started new mini-communities. Most importantly, the users kept the community lively and covered costs by paying a monthly fee. Unlike most Internet companies today, Web almost always broke even.

And then, around 1995, the Internet exploded as a commercial phenomenon. Suddenly, our loyal users were presented with a whole new set of products and opportunities. Out in the open market, they could get cheaper e-mail and connectivity. With the advent of Netscape and the availability of cheap, fast modems, the World Wide Web began to grow at such a phenomenal rate that many people thought that the WWW was all there was to the Internet. Web Networks users started to see the advantage of having their own WWW sites, whether they were hosted by us or other providers. This was a real revolution, because our members produced a lot of documents. They'd seen our online community as a great distribution channel for their documents, but now they had the WWW, which was even better.

This is where we screwed up. Big-time. We were so full of ourselves, and so full of the success of our online community, that we ignored the 'give power to get power' rule that had worked to our benefit for so many years. We tied our pricing and services to our online community. To post information, you had to be a member. To read information, you had to be a member. We were the gatekeepers. 'Join our text-based service and see the best activist information! Avoid the noise of the Web and USENET!' That was our message. Clearly, people would see the advantage of making us the gatekeepers. And the advantage of paying us to post and read each others content. Right?

Nope. Not on your life.

Our once-loyal users saw these misguided efforts to bolster community as damage, and routed around us. The postings that once made our community so valuable quickly scattered across this Web page and that. Understandably, our users were more interested in creating an information resource that they controlled than they were in paying money to be a part of a generic information pool run by someone else. They wanted independence, power and control over their own information. We didn't give it to them. And we lost.

But we weren't the only ones. Compuserve, Prodigy, The Source, Delphi, even AOL — all of the early big daddies of online community — made the same mistake. All of the early online services spent the mid-1990s thinking that their gated communities were more valuable than the World Wide Web. They thought they could win by mediating the user experience rather than cracking it wide open. They were wrong. With the exception of AOL, which rescued itself by offering cheap, unlimited Internet access just in time, all of these online pioneers are either dead or buried in someone else's company.

Power that shares: Action applications

The 'give power to get power' lesson was one that Web Networks learned the hard way. We saw why users were leaving and starting looking for a solution. But we also saw that there was a real market niche for a content aggregator focussed on non-profit organizations in Canada. We learned that the only way to grab this niche was to empower users — to put them in charge.

What Internet users want most is freedom and control over their own content. For all but hard-core geeks, this usually translates into the ability to easily update their own Web pages. The non-techno-savvy community organizers using Web Networks wanted to be able to press a button to put their information online without hiring an expensive teenage nerd to help them. This seemed reasonable enough, so we started thinking in that direction.

A few programmers and content people at Web Networks began the process by building little databases called 'Action Applications'. These tools were designed to manage the kinds of information that many organizations post to Web sites: events listings, press releases, lists of links, and descriptions of resources. The Action Applications were simple tools that were easy to customize and replicate. Add a few extra HTML tags and graphics references and voila: a user had a new events calendar for their Web site.

While this was no big deal to us, it was a big deal to our customers. They ate the Action Applications up, because these tools helped them move a step closer to controlling their own communications destiny.

More interestingly, these tools also helped us launch the concept of constellations and to feed commonspace. Every time we gave an Action Application events calendar to one organization, we made it possible for that calendar to share content with the dozens of other organizations using the same software. In the non-profit arena, where resources are scarce and shared campaign work is a way of life, this technology was a tremendous boon. Like-minded groups could leverage each other's content, build collective newsletters, and share the load of developing communications campaigns. Among organizations where this worked well (and where it hopefully will spread to other groups), organizational boundaries began to leak, and constellations of content began to emerge.

Creating these tools made users happy, because it empowered them. But they also kept Web Networks alive as a content aggregator for longer than it would have survived as an ISP. Web was able to take the best of the material from its user databases and promote that material on its 'community.web.ca' site, which in turn drew more traffic to the users' sites. It was a win-win-win-win-win situation.

While the Action Application idea is still in its infancy (it's been up and running in various iterations since early-1999), the idea seems to be catching on. The constellation idea combines the best qualities from Web publishing and the best ideas from USENET, connecting the strong voices of individual users to a networked community of ideas. With the hope of expanding the use of these tools, Web Networks has handed off Action Application development to the Association for Progressive Communications (APC) — a consortium of 25 non-profit Internet solutions providers from around the world. The APC is rewriting the Action

What Internet users want most is freedom and control over their own content.

Applications software and will release it as open source. Once that happens, who knows how large the constellations will become?

The group mind: Slashdot

The convergence between online community (which has always been associated with many-to-many, omni-directional discussion) and the Web (which is usually associated with one-way document delivery) is a fascinating one to watch. In many cases, the two styles blend like oil and water. Many organizations think they can simply graft the appearance of many-to-many discussion onto their service while still retaining the advantages of one-way selling. But it doesn't work. What does work is to give people real power over your Web site, to merge the conversation and the document so they become one.

And nobody does this better than Slashdot <www.slashdot.org>.

Focusing on open source and tech news (their masthead reads 'News for Nerds. Stuff that Matters'), Slashdot is a conversational-living-document-group-mind. There is a thrilling blur between documents and discussions, writers and readers. The writing on Slashdot is a form of collective authorship as unique to the Internet as the concept of open source software itself.

Here's how it works. Anyone can submit a story to Slashdot using its Submissions Bin. There are hundreds of submissions per day. Anonymous submissions by non-registered users stand the same chance of being published as those of members; but as the site's FAQ states, 'We do, however, reserve the right to refer to you as an Anonymous Coward, and mock you mercilessly.' Submissions are sorted and judged by four to six of the site's core authors, and those deemed of interest to the community appear on the front page.

What's of interest to the community? Rob Malda, (a.k.a. CmdrTaco) the site's administrator, describes it as an 'omelette':

Over the years, we've figured out what ingredients are best on Slashdot. The ultimate goal is, of course, to create an omelette that I enjoy eating: by 8pm, I want to see a dozen interesting stories on Slashdot. I hope you enjoy them too. I believe that we've grown in size because we share a lot of common interests with our readers. But that doesn't mean that I'm gonna mix an omelette with all sausages, or someday throw away the tomatoes because the green peppers are really fresh.

There are many components to the Slashdot Omelette. Stories about Linux. Tech stories. Science. Legos. Book Reviews. Yes, even Jon Katz. By mixing and matching these things each and every day, we bring you what I call Slashdot. On some days it definitely is better than others, but overall we think it's a tasty little treat and we hope you enjoy eating as much as we enjoy cooking it. [4]

Once a story has been posted as part of the Slashdot omelette, it's open to comment from the site's users. Thousands of comments are posted a day, tens of thousands each month. At any given time, the site's database holds over 40,000 of them. Meanwhile, Slashdot offers the users a wide variety of options for viewing these comments, so that each person can decide exactly how involved they want to become in any given discussion.

Why does this system work so well? And how did it become one of the most read and respected news sources in the hacker world? By giving power to the users.

On Slashdot, the users run the site, creating almost all the content. Slashdot exists by giving power and a platform away to people with nothing more than an urge to say something. Fortunately, many of these people are stratospherically smart, and even most of the ones that aren't have internalized some sort of community standard for what constitutes a good post. And of course, not all postings get approved; there is a sophisticated filtering process that determines what appears on the site. By giving people a high-profile place to articulate their interests and concerns, Slashdot gives its users a kind of power they don't have own their own Web site. This kind of empowerment builds loyalty and trust.

How did Slashdot
become one of the
most read and
respected news
sources in the
hacker world?
By giving power
to the users.

Looked at cynically, empowering your users also builds a brand. That's why VA Linux bought Andover.net at a cost of almost $900 million in cash and stock. Andover owns Slashdot and Freshmeat.net (a Web newsletter that tracks the latest releases of open source software), among other things. Supporting sites like Slashdot and Freshmeat brings VA Linux closer to its the users. At least that's the theory.

Hotwired.com ran a column in February 2000 titled 'Et Tu, Slashdot?' <hotwired.lycos.com/webmonkey/00/06/index2a.html> suggesting that this purchase will inevitably prejudice Slashdot's commentary in favour of VA Linux over other Linux distributions, and thereby cause a loss of credibility in the open source community. However, the snipe that the author took at Jon Katz in the same article suggests that it has more to do with Wired/Hotwired staff's insecurities about their own decaying reputation than with any real threat to Slashdot's integrity. (Katz is the author of *Geeks*, *Media Rants* and other important books about the Internet explosion, and a former writer for the original — read 'relevant and interesting' — *Wired* before its purchase by the Condé Nast news empire.)

In any event, there really isn't much else like Slashdot in cyberspace today. But there could be.

The big friend of the little guy

The most impressive feature of the 'give power' rule is that it applies in even the most crass of online arenas: retail. (Okay, maybe porn and gambling sites are more crass. Maybe.) The phenomenal rise of eBay and online auctions in general have built solid businesses by empowering the 'little guy' to become a retailer. This may seem trivial, but it is a significant shift in the balance of power.

Think about traditional retail. From Sears Roebuck to Barnes and Noble to Home Depot to Starbucks, BIG has always been the name of the game. Get BIG and sell mountains of stuff. How do you do this? Have a good selection of products. Set up outlets in as many places as you can. Control the supply chain as tightly as possible (including establishing private brands). In other words, spend as much money as you can to control as much of the turf as you can.

The eBay business model takes most of these principles and flips them upside-down. eBay is about giving away turf, giving other people a place to sell and letting go of the supply chain.

This inversion of retail power relationships applies not only to the sellers, but also to the buyers. The eBay discussion forums and approval rating system allow buyers to tell each other what they think about a particular vendor. Whether they have something good or bad to say about a vendor, eBay gives buyers a space to share their opinion and gives other buyers transparent and immediate access to this information. This would be akin to Sears, or at least the mall that houses Sears, providing consumers with a place to rant and rave about what a great (or crappy) place Sears is to shop. This kind of openness is unheard of in the offline world and is even uncommon in big-time online retailing. But it is standard fare on eBay.

The only part of eBay that reflects the rules of traditional retailing is its product selection, and even here there's no real grounds for comparison with a bricks-and-mortar store. eBay has ratcheted up the selection quotient beyond belief. People can buy anything from coins to motorcycle gas tanks to Swiss watches to shoes to online role-playing-game characters to computer RAM. You can get anything. (Well, almost anything, though people have posted hoaxes on eBay advertising sales of everything from cocaine to human organs to their own virginity.)

In a way, providing small-time vendors and buyers with a platform makes eBay an empowerment company. It makes its money by helping others succeed financially. It keeps its credibility by listening to buyers and shutting down abusive vendors. The result is a business that is low in overhead and potentially very high in profit. With the advent of software such as PayPal <www.x.com>, the #1 payment service on eBay and fast becoming a Web standard for e-commerce, online transactions are becom-

Providing small-
time vendors
and buyers with
a platform
makes eBay an
empowerment
company.

ing more transparent, more closely linked to everyday life, and less in-convenient, which is the ultimate goal.

eBay's largesse with its power has created a brand — maybe even a com-munity — that people love enough to transfer from their computers into the real world. 'eBay Anywhere' is a system of pagers, Internet-enabled Personal Data Managers (PalmPilots, etc.) and WAP-enabled cell phones that ensures that the most fanatical eBay users never have to worry about being outbid because they didn't have constant access to their transactions.

It will be interesting to see how the eBay 'empowerment model' and other systems that allow the 'small guy' to successfully sell online will fare over time. Certainly, there is a lot of money in big Business-to-Consumer (B-to-C) operations like Amazon. But is there enough to make them consis-tently turn a profit? Such operations combine many of the advantages of traditional retail (quality, selection, reliability, predictability) with some of the advantages of the Internet and commonspace (user input, aggregated preferences, timelines). But they also have disadvantages. Internet retail is expensive to operate and requires huge turnover; inventory manage-ment is difficult; brand-name recognition is lower than it is with established bricks-and-mortar companies, and when the venture capital runs out, Internet stores actually have to turn a profit (a harsh fact of life with which many e-tailers just can't cope with).

In order to handle the just-in-time process of ordering items from suppliers and then re-shipping them, big B-to-C operations require stock and com-plex inventory management systems . And therein lies the secret that Amazon and other companies hope that the average Net user never real-izes: on the Internet, Big B-to-C is an unnecessary middleman. There's no reason to shop at a Big B-to-C site for something that the manufac-turer's Web site can provide more cheaply and more rapidly. The only purpose of Big B-to-C's is to be a one-stop shopping source. Because com-parison shopping engines are becoming more available and more power-ful, finding the Web sites for the manufacturers of even the most obscure products is becoming much less difficult.

Big B-to-C strategies may be successful in the short term, but they're just marking time. The values of Amazon and Canadian equivalent Chapters <www.chapters.ca> (which runs the biggest bricks-and-mortar book retail business in the country) are dropping like stones. Adding insult to injury, their independence as online businesses is also waning. Just as bricks-and-mortar stores with good brand-name recognition are finally establishing a strong online presence, the big Internet equivalents are finding that they have to strike alliances with them in order to keep on top of their wholesale costs and inventories — something that would have been anathema to them only a year earlier, when many online businesses were smugly proclaiming their independence from the physical world of storefronts.

There's no reason to shop at a Dig B-to-C site for something that the manufacturer's Web site can provide more cheaply and more rapidly.

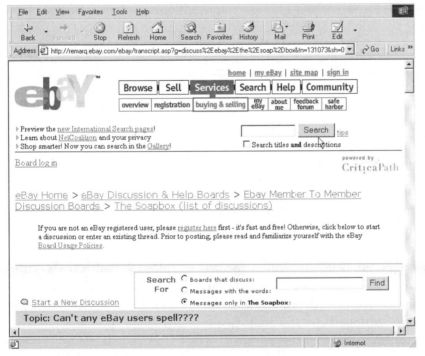

Through its auctions and discussion forums, eBay has given power back to the small vendors — even the ones that can't spell.

In many markets, consumer-to-consumer or small-business-to-consumer businesses may just be able to carve out the niche they need to erode the market share of these big Internet players. If enough niche-carving happens, the game will change forever. What's more, there is a whole hayrack of new technologies coming down the road that do their untmost to make that change happen.

The end of hierarchy? Peer-to-peer networking

Napster is currently in the process of discovering just how scary championing new technology can be. Facing suits filed by everyone from the RIAA to Metallica and Dr. Dre, they are the heat-sink for a societal feeding frenzy over intellectual property. Current copyright laws reflect the conditions in which they evolved: a hierarchical restricted economy, where media content could be cut into chunks, packaged and sold for whatever price the distributors wanted. But the Internet has eliminated the need for physical chunking and packaging. Any form of content — music, video, text, computer games, spoken word — can be digitized. Once it is, the choice of packaging — CD, cassette, videotape, hard drive, DVD, CD-ROM, encrypted file — is irrelevant and even unnecessary.

This is not a manifesto; it's a statement of fact. We're skeptical of that hoary old saw of Internet folk-wisdom, 'Information wants to be free.' Information doesn't 'want' anything. In fact, data doesn't become information until someone wants it. Beforehand, it's just noise. There are plenty of people on the Net who don't give a rat's ass about MP3s, and to them, file-sharing technology is merely a drain on server resources (noise) that makes it difficult for them to get their e-mail, play Quake, or check the stock market. But the implications of a fluid information medium like the Internet are immense: due to its very structure, the Internet causes the eruption of gift economies into mainstream life and the temporary inversion of the rules of business-as-usual.

Napster isn't the only peer-to-peer network (P2P) out there, just the one that's likely to be martyred for the cause. Services such as Hotline

<www.bigredh.com>, Publius <cs1.cs.nyu.edu/waldman/publius/>, Freenet <freenet.sourceforge.net> and Gnutella <gnutella.wego.com> have also garnered huge followings by giving Internet users exactly what they want — the unbridled ability to connect to each other, to run projects, to build community… and to swap contraband files: porn, MP3 music files, full-length feature films that haven't been released on video yet, pirated fonts and cracked software. 'Giving away power to get power' at this level is scary to most companies, perhaps with good reason.

For some people, that translates into carnival, dancing in the streets, unBirthday parties where stuff that normally costs something is available for nothing. For others, it's just a big group of idiots blocking traffic.

Son of Napster

But even if the metaphorical cops do manage to clear off part of the infobahn by shutting down Napster, P2P isn't going to disappear. The gift economy can't be suppressed any more than it can entirely replace a restricted economy. If Napster goes down, something else will take its place — quickly. People who get all hot and bothered about file-sharing always forget about the existence of the USENET alt.binaries groups, which have been around for many years more than Napster and are still going strong. Napster wasn't the first place to find contraband content on the Net, and it won't be the last.

When Nullsoft released the first beta copy of Gnutella, it only took parent company AOL a couple of hours to notice and to rip the software off the Web. The ramifications of such a tool scared AOL poopless. But even a couple of hours was too late: thousands of copies had already been downloaded. Gnutella was out and replicating like wildfire. Dozens of Gnutella clones and alternate distributions popped up almost overnight. Yet because there's no central Gnutella server, there's no one to sue. And after Gnutella, there will be other forms of P2P and technologies that we can only imagine. Try this on for size: hordes of kids with wireless Linux-powered digital sound-and-video recorders, scooping new-release movies straight off the theatre screen; ditto for sporting events, live concerts, and stuff on

Napster wasn't the first place to find contraband content on the Net, and it won't be the last.

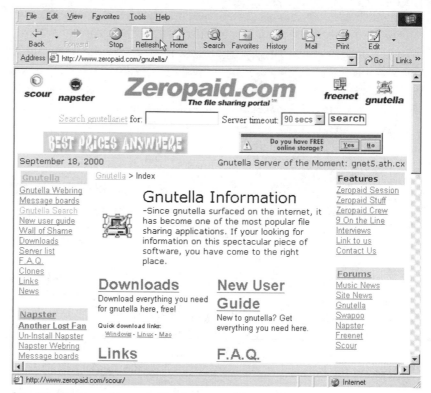

Son of Napster: Zeropaid.com, the file-sharing portal, keeps a close eye on the various technologies that are eager to take up the torch if Napster falls.

their friends' stereos and TVs, hitting a button and their wireless omnicorder immediately dials into the Net and is connected by Gnutella Mark VII to millions of other devices just like it, whose users then pick and choose from what what they want to view next; microwave uploads and downloads occurring at blinding speed, and no one is ever connected to the network long enough to even be identified, let alone caught. Cool.

It's ironic: shutting down Napster will simply create a worse nightmare for the RIAA than the one that already exists, because the copyright violators will be much harder to track down. With Napster intact, there would be at least the possibility of extracting some sort of licensing fee from its users to pay artists their royalties.

P2P raises more questions than it answers, but that's what new technology always does. Thomas Edison thought the chief use for the phonograph was going to be storing the voices of dead relatives for nostalgic value. Modern typewriters had been around for about fifteen years before someone invented touch-typing. The major gift-economy question for business is, what do you get when you give this kind of power? Part of the picture is notoriety, support and even loyalty. For some people — some *heavy* people — evidently that's enough for the time being. Venture capital loves file-sharing this year, pumping $15 million into Napster despite the apparent lack of any business model and the court cases to contend with.

So where is the business model in all of this? Well, there's always the development of new encrypted file formats to consider — a growth industry because there will always be clever 15-year-olds who figure out how to crack them. Or businesses could take their lead from Gnute <www.gnute.com>, the first search engine to target the Gnutella network, and start building portals for the new P2P networks. And, for those with absolutely no shame, you can spam those new networks. Flatplanet.net, developers of a program called ShareZilla, have created a way of hijacking user queries and replacing them with advertising. Rob Smith, a FlatPlanet partner, says 'People are upset that they have to look at an ad because it gets in the way of stealing music. It's a little laughable.'[5] And it is. But there were enough complaints to FlatPlanet's ISP that they took down the Web site. The future is anyone's call.

The biggest currently unanswerable questions underneath all of the P2P hoo-ha are as follows:

- Will P2P change the structure and use patterns of the Internet as greatly as the Web did?

- What will happen to our notion of copyright and ownership of intellectual property?

Stay tuned. As with the majority of paradigm-shifting Internet plays, there needs to be some faith that the 'what you get' will shake out later. If the his-

Two developments
caused USENET's
downfall:
spam and the Web.

tory of unBirthday Party technologies is any indication, the answer will be, at least, entertaining.

Talking back to the Net

Empowering others is the idea at the very core of Internet philosophy. Long before the business world had even heard of the Napster or the Web, users, programmers and engineers were already doing what they could to spread control over communications into as many hands as possible. They believed in decentralizing power and giving it away. This is probably why the Internet has worked so well as a collaborative, many-to-many technology.

But it hasn't always worked. There are lots of examples of 'give power away' Internet ideas that went astray or ended up nowhere.

Take USENET, for example. Before the Web exploded, it was the major public medium on the Internet. Composed of thousands of completely public 'newsgroups' on all manner of topics, USENET was a democratic many-to-many medium. People said what they wanted. If others disagreed, they simply said so. If some one was spouting bullshit, they were challenged at the least, and in most cases, they were flamed by other indignant users. USENET was a thriving and often very noisy democracy. It was people media, not drone media.

But two developments caused its downfall: spam and the Web. By now, everyone knows what spam is. But it came as a rude surprise to the long-term USENET community when unscrupulous capitalists came stomping through USENET like a herd of elephants across a well-tended flowerbed (The first really serious spammers were a pair of shameless lawyers based in Arizona named Canter and Siegel, who, in early 1994, posted ads for their firm in virtually every unmoderated newsgroup in USENET). There were many valiant attempts to stop spam: the CancelMoose, the RealTime Blackhole and the Spam Hippo all struck blows for justice. But the flow of spam continued, and ultimately didn't change the essence of USENET itself.

At the same time, the Web was becoming popular and was changing the public perception of the Internet. Suddenly USENET couldn't attract the numbers anymore. But when seasoned Internet users looked at the Web, they didn't see a many-to-many democracy. They saw a network based on one-to-many publishing because the Web didn't including any inherent ability for readers or users to talk back, at least until Web annotation came along. USENET still exists and has some very loyal newsgroups. But nowadays, when people talk about the Internet, they're talking about the Web.

Swear words and fart jokes

In 1996, some early Internet users concerned about the Web's limitations started talking about creating a way to 'talk back to the Web.' They wanted to create a medium that would 'bring a little USENET to the Web' by allowing anyone to add comments to anyone else's Web page. The comments would be stored in a 'neutral' database and would appear when a user visited a site. The result was going to be a USENET-style dialogue between people who were currently visiting the site. Moreover, it would be completely outside of the control of the site's creators.

Web annotation was an important cause to its early advocates because it was seen as a way to prevent the Internet from becoming television. A friend of ours named Misha Glouberman — database programmer and early Internet prankster based in Toronto — wrote a paper on the subject in 1996. It started out like this:

It should be possible for anyone to add comments to any page on the Web. It's a single change that would make a tremendous difference to what our media will be like for years to come. Making it happen would be easier than you might think.[6]

Like many others, Misha believed that Web annotation was an essential political step if the Internet was going to continue as many-to-many people medium. So many Internet people held this perspective that the World Wide Web Consortium (W3C) set up a working group to discuss the development of a Web annotation standard.

Web annotation was an important cause to its early advocates because it was seen as a way to prevent the Internet from becoming television.

The constructive
debate that Web
annotation
visionaries had
hoped for never
emerged.

Web annotation advocates were right — adding comments to the Web was easier than we thought. Within a year or two, companies like Third Voice <www.thirdvoice.com>, Odigo <www.odigo.com> and Gooey <www.gooey.com> had appeared, providing the browser plug-ins and independent databases needed for people to comment on Web sites. They gave the plug-in away for free, and people started talking.

The problem was what they started talking about. Typical comments tended to be along the lines of Beavis and Butthead dialogue: 'This sucks' or 'Where's the naked chicks?'. The constructive debate that Web annotation visionaries had hoped for never emerged. Giving power to the people didn't create a more democratic Web. It created a schoolyard full of swear words and fart jokes.

To a certain extent, the shortcomings of conversation on Web annotators are inherent to the medium. Noam Chomsky has argued for years that it's impossible to stage an intelligent argument in TV sound bites, so why should anyone expect to be able to do so in a tiny thought balloon?

As of April 2000, Third Voice 2000 Beta 1 has been available for download. Unlike previous versions of the Web annotation software, which had used tiny triangular markers to indicate notes (markers which became infamous because they caused carefully aligned Web graphics to move out of their alotted places), the new Third Voice uses orange underlines to indicate hotlinks to specific words on a page. (Be careful: there could be ads lurking under some of those links. You've been spammed again, anarchist boy!)

But Third Voice committed one of the cardinal errors of the software industry when they implemented the new version: they made the new technology incompatible with its older versions. And users did more than grumble. Third Voice's chief opposition, Say No To Third Voice <www.saynotothirdvoice.com>, makes the following observation: 'Interestingly, the sites we visited with the new version have no excitement, acknowledgement or brouhaha over the new release. Are there any active Third Voice users out there?'

The limits of power

It's an organic thing. Some technologies work, some don't.

Why do Slashdot and Napster work so well, and why did Web annotation fail so badly? After all, they're all commonspace technologies that give away power online, and empower users to connect with each other, to create collective knowledge. Why the difference?

Clearly, just coming up with an idea that 'gives away power' or connects people isn't enough on its own. There are other factors that determine a product's success: timing, media attention, word of mouth, design, accidents of history. It's an organic thing. Some technologies work, some don't.

In the case of Web annotation, it was probably a matter of an overly complex solution to a simple problem, combined with the problems that result from attempting to convince a large, unruly group of strong-minded individuals that they should place their faith in a proprietary technology. The emergence of the Web didn't erase the ability of people to talk back online. In fact, USENET has grown a great deal since the advent of the Web. And people have found lots of other ways to feed comment on what's on the Web. They use their own Web pages to comment on others. They find appropriate discussion forums and mail lists. In the final analysis, a dedicated tool for talking about the content of specific pages probably just wasn't needed.

On the flipside, Slashdot and Napster have struck a chord at just the right time. They have given people a power they've been itching for. In doing so, they have built loyal user followings and demonstrated that you can win by giving away power on the Internet… as long as you're prepared to deal with the full implications of the abrogation of power.

6 | Success through selflessness

> *Philanthropist, n. A rich (and usually bald) old gentleman who has trained himself to grin while his conscience is picking his pocket.*
>
> AMBROSE BIERCE, THE DEVIL'S DICTIONARY

Why are people drawn to collective endeavours online? Why are they giving away crucial information and intellectual property for free? Why are they sharing and working with others, even competitors? Why are profit-focused, power hungry business people being so generous?

Because the age of crass selfishness is dead. The age of the common good is dawning.

Pollyannic fantasy? No.

Look around. Huge companies are being built on software that they not only give away for free, but that they let other companies copy. Rival companies are setting up innovative joint Internet ventures to make their whole industry run more smoothly. Smart companies no longer see their customers as buyers to be duped but rather as a contributors and co-developers in the creation of better products. There is an increasing awareness of the business and political value of pursuing the common good online and of cooperating with those we may have seen as competitors in the past.

Like a grain of salt with that? Fine.

People — and companies — are still motivated by self-interest. By money. By power. By prestige. But the terms on which we pursue what we need and want have changed. In a many-to-many network that emphasizes sharing, everything that you do for yourself has the potential to benefit everyone else. Likewise, anything anyone else does has the potential to benefit you. A piece of software that you write may be exactly what others in your field have been looking for. In a digital environment, sharing this software costs you nothing and earns you a great deal: respect, feedback, and good turns in kind.

Our increased reliance on networks means a new dependence on common infrastructure: tools, data exchange protocols, reference information, the network itself. Each of us needs these tools to succeed and to meet our own goals. But we also have a shared interest in making sure the network not only functions, but constantly improves. We have a common interest in efficiency and ultimately in the collaboration that creates commonspace.

Bring me the head of Ayn Rand

In the world of atoms, our economy and culture are driven by the notion of scarcity, where sharing means giving up a precious resource. This has been the reality since, well, forever. But with the emergence of open source and other bit-based commonspace phenomena, this reality is changing. The common good is starting to triumph over scarcity.

Garrett Hardin's 'Tragedy of the Commons,' which first appeared in 1968, describes the problem of sharing in an atom-based world.[1] We'll summarize it here, spiced it up slightly to reflect the wonderful world of the new millennium:

A village of farmers holds one field in common, which they use to feed their herds. Each farmer has a herd of equal size, and together, the herds eat exactly all of the fodder that the field produces. On day, one farmer, while thumbing through his dog-eared copy of *The Fountainhead*, gets the brilliant idea that he should exploit the other farmers by adding another cow

The self-interest
vs. common good
dilemma flips
upside-down in
an economy
driven by bits.

to his herd. After all, he'd only be paying the same as everyone else for his grazing rights, even if he had more cattle. While all of the animals will be a little skinnier when they go to market because of the overuse of the pasture, he'll still make a few extra bucks. And what the hell, he deserves it. Selfishness is a virtue. Ayn says so.

Meanwhile, the other farmers are losing money to their Objectivist buddy because their cows go to market with slightly less meat on them, and they have fewer animals to sell. What to do? Inevitably, they all decide that they too have to buy more cattle to stay competitive. The cycle repeats itself. The field becomes muddy and rank and bare of grass; the increasingly scrawny cattle are packed in like sardines. Eventually, all of the grass is gone, and one of the farmers (probably that bastard with the copy of *The Fountainhead*) decides that the only thing to do is to feed the living but scrawny cattle on the ground-up remains of the cattle who've died of starvation. Everyone gets Mad Cow Disease and dies a horrible, foaming, gibbering death. Not a pretty picture.

Eric Raymond to the rescue. In 'The Magic Cauldron' <www.tuxedo.org/ ~esr/writings/magic-cauldron/>, he uses the example of open source to demonstrate how 'The Tragedy of the Commons' disappears in commonspace. The self-interest vs. common good dilemma flips upside-down in an economy driven by bits.

Say you have a custom program for managing your farm. If you are willing to open the source code and share this software with your 'community' (the other farmers), you'll definitely build goodwill. But will it cost you anything? No! Will it make the software less useable for your business? No! In fact, sharing it (and contributing to the common good) may even make the software more valuable, because the farmers you share it with may have geeky kids who improve the software and then share the improvements with you. Instead of falling under a despotic communist dictator or being broken up into tiny little capitalist freeholds, the commons continues to expand. Freaky but true.

In a world without scarcity, there are often insufficient rewards to motivate the creation of new software. The result is under-provision, and it's a real issue. But as Raymond notes, this problem doesn't grow with an increase in the number of end-users: 'The complexity and communications overhead of an open-source project is almost entirely a function of the number of developers involved; having more end-users who never look at source costs effectively nothing. It may increase the rate of silly questions appearing on the project mailing lists, but this is relatively easily forestalled by maintaining a Frequently Asked Questions list and blithely ignoring questioners who have obviously not read it.'[7]

The fact that valuable things made out of bits can be replicated easily and at almost no cost is having a profound impact on our culture.

common good vs. self-interest

becomes

common good = self-interest

Of course, this fact doesn't mean that everything is free. We all still need a way to make a living. It also doesn't mean that things made of atoms are no longer scarce. The new economy is not going to magically create enough food to feed the world, or solve the global housing problem, or make sure that we all have enough clean water to drink. But it will change Internet-based business, politics and education is.

In the long run, this shift in the way we think — towards mutual self-interest and an appreciation for cooperative work — will have a profound impact on the world of atoms. Old-economy businesses will learn from successful Internet companies how to have their cake (self-interest) and eat it too (community and common good). They will see how helping and collaborating with others feeds success and the bottom line.

It's not that self-interest has disappeared, but rather that people are starting to see the synergistic nexus between the common good and their self-interest.

Old-economy businesses will learn from successful Internet companies how to have their cake and eat it too.

Figure 5:
Commonspace
makes it possible
to have your cake
and eat it too.

**Common
Good**

**Self
Interest**

commonspace
(mutual
self interest)

Communities
clans and
groups

Companies
and
individuals

*Luckily, our needs
are often the
same as the needs
of others.*

Self-interest drives smart individuals to collective work and collaboration. The common good serves everyone involved, creating opportunities for all to prosper. It's in this context that the industrial-age, Ayn Rand-style selfishness is dying. It's simply become unnecessary.

My software is your software

The prime example of mutual self-interest and common-good thinking in action is (surprise) in the open source movement.

Most open source projects are not driven by some abstract perception of what the market wants (and what you can sell). Rather, they start with the immediate needs of an individual or a small group, such as a tool to keep track of all the networks you connect to with your Linux laptop, a better Web server, a better application server, or a better operating system. All of these things were germinated by an individual or a small group driven by their own needs, wants, desires and vision.

Luckily, our needs are often the same as the needs of others.

This is one of the reasons that Apache is the number one Web server on the Internet. Many people need a Web server that provides the flexibility and control of an open source package. For that matter, many people just need a Web server, and a free Web server that is just as good or better than the ones you pay for is an obvious choice. And so it is that a solution designed

Bugs happen, even in Linux. Redhat's Bugzilla system helps to track and eliminate the pesky little critters before they do widespread damage.

to meet the needs of a small group becomes a solution for hundreds of thousands of others.

From the inside the walls of old-style business thinking, creating something that others want is an opportunity for exploitation. What do you do? Copyright it. Package it. Bundle it. Advertise it. Sell it. And make sure that people can't steal it. Make it proprietary. Create frequent incompatible upgrades. Release sequels. Keep it to yourself, and charge as much as you can.

The thing is, you will also see an opportunity for profit if you put on your open source thinking cap (comes complete with propeller!).

And we're not just talking about monetary profit. There is no question that you can still make heaps of money from support, consulting, and ancillary businesses while giving away your software. You'll also receive feedback, new ideas, upgrades and fixes written by your users. You may even

People will join
you and act as
shepherds for the
idea that you have
germinated.

get loyalty and community in the bargain. People will join you and act as shepherds for the idea that you have germinated. These things are just as valuable as money, and in the end may lead you to more economic profit than you would have been able to generate by staying strictly commercial.

Look at the differences between Microsoft and Red Hat, one of the major Linux distributors. Both companies face the same challenge: they need to build stable, useful operating systems that people will trust. Trust is key, as people are betting their livelihoods on the reliability of their systems. At the same time, both companies need to be constantly updating their software in order to meet new demands and respond to changes in the technology. This, in turn, introduces inevitable bugs and instability into their systems — a problem for both companies. However, the pressures of reliability and software evolution take a greater toll on Microsoft.

It's a Catch-22. Dealing with this reliability problems is a painful and expensive process for Microsoft. First, every upgrade or 'service pack' needs to be rigorously tested before release. This process needs to be more extensive (and expensive) than it is with other companies because Microsoft already has a bad rep for buggy software. (One hacker's Web site bears the following wisecrack: 'The software said it required Windows 95 or better, so I installed Linux.') But even when Microsoft manages to cover most of their bases, there will inevitably be bugs or security holes (65,000 in the case of Windows 2000… ouch!). If Microsoft is lucky, these holes will be discovered by a friendly Fortune 500 customer who will responsibly report the problem. Microsoft will then send the bug back to one of its development teams who will in turn come up with a solution in a month, or two, or three, and post a fix to their Web site. If Microsoft is unlucky, the bug will be discovered by teenage pranksters who will write a virus that will take down half the Microsoft-based servers on the Internet. Either way, bugs are an expensive embarrassment for a company like Microsoft.

For a company like Red Hat, the process is completely different. First of all, many of Red Hat's upgrades and fixes come prewritten and pre-tested as a part of other Linux releases. In an open source world, Red Hat can build on the work of others who are also committed to the 'common good' of growing Linux. When Red Hat actually does write its own upgrades (and it does so fairly often), it has a responsive and understanding testing community — Linux users. Linux users will not only report bugs, but they will also propose fixes. Doing so is in everyone's interest. As a result, bugs get fixed quickly and cheaply, often in a matter of hours. As Linus' Law states, the open source group mind makes all bugs shallow.

Mutual self-interest

It's worth noting that open source software often comes from places other than 'open source companies.' For example, people who aren't in the software business at all often write software to meet their individual business needs. This could be a custom tool to manage bookings for a hotel or an accounting system for an ISP. No matter how good this software is, setting up shop to sell it commercially would probably be folly for most people in this situation, for it would distract the company from its primary business. But this doesn't mean that the software isn't useful to others. To people who do similar work, it's probably very useful indeed. And the people who do similar work would probably be further ahead by putting their meagre software budgets into expanding something that's already written than on writing something new from scratch. This is a perfect opportunity for open source: share what you create for yourself with others, then get others to share their improvements.

This points to the key value of open source — sharing and collaboration. It's not the idea that the software is 'free' that is so amazing (in fact, some open source software isn't free). Rather, it's the collaborative development and shared ideas. You start something. I add to it. So does someone else. We keep swapping code. This kind of collaboration is the nexus of self-interest and common good. We all get something better by sharing and using our group mind.

The notion of the collective mind as it applies to the open source community needs to be qualified slightly, which is one of the reasons we emphasize the notion of 'self' in the phrase 'mutual self-interest.' (This is the

Linux users will not only report bugs, but they will also propose fixes. Doing so is in everyone's interest.

The open source
approach to
collaborative idea
production is
creating a
significant shift
in culture and
economics.

Power Rangers, not the Borg, remember?) The Orbiten Free Software Survey, released May 1, 2000 analyzed over 25 million lines of code and the work of over 12,000 authors in an attempt to provide some empirical data about how open source projects actually work. Their findings are interesting:

The top 1271 authors, 10% of the total, accounted for 72.3% of the total code base. The top 10 authors alone (0.08% of the total) are credited for 19.8% of the code base. Free software development may be distributed, but it is most certainly very top-heavy.

What goes for lines of code written goes for involvement in projects too. Only the top 25 authors (0.19% of the total) were credited with participation in more than 25 projects. The top 250 authors were credited with participation in over 5 projects, and the vast majority (over 77%) of authors were only involved in a single project. Our conclusion: Free software development is less a bazaar of several developers involved in several projects, more a collation of projects developed single-mindedly by a large number of authors.[3]

These findings don't invalidate the 'bazaar' model that contrasts open source development to traditional hierarchical organizations. What they do demonstrate is that at least in this early phases, community thought leaders don't disappear. The attitude people take toward their own work changes, and the relationship that they believe others should take to it as well. Over time, as the code base increases in size and years, and more people become involved, more projects will pass from hand to hand, and these statistics will change. But the initial gesture had to be made, and an example set.

The open source approach to collaborative idea production is creating a significant shift in culture and economics. People are excited about open source. It's real, and it works. But does its example map onto other industries and other parts of society? Do people other than idealistic anarcho-hippie programmers see the value of mutual self-interest? Yes. Of course.

The community and the common good

The other place where common good thinking is spreading rapidly is in online communities. This is especially true in the nexus between traditional business practice and virtual community building — the creation of 'communities of commerce'. By truly engaging in community building, smart companies are able to move beyond the rhetoric of 'improving relationships with customers' to something more real and tangible. These companies are dropping one-way media emptiness in favour engaging online communities. As they do, they become able to see their customers as true partners, or even as leaders.

Rick Levine provides a small but instructive example of this in *The Cluetrain Manifesto*.[4] When Sun first released Java, documentation was poor, and there were still major problems with the code. To 'help' developers with these problems, Sun set up a flashy, marketing-department-inspired support site that charged $100 'per incident.' This site was a money-losing failure. Almost no one from the developer community showed up, and when they did, they were costing Sun $110 for every $100 support incident. The site was both a business flop and a credibility flop. It was hard for developers to take Sun seriously.

Realizing it was going nowhere, Sun did a 180-degree flip. They set up a site that provided free support in discussion forums from Sun engineers, and that allowed developers to support each other. The result was a fast-moving information stream that built up the overall knowledge base among Java developers. With developers helping each other, the new system cost much less that the paper-pushing bureaucracy of the paid support site. Sun had created a valuable, self-sustaining resource that boosted its credibility with the development community.

What's the difference between the two Sun sites? The first site treated developers and their questions as opportunities to grab a little extra revenue. The new site recognizes that regular users are likely Sun's most

If you don't provide
this kind of
openness, people
will find a way to
route around you.

valuable resources as well as customers and treats them accordingly. It addresses them as collaborators. It asks for their opinion. It rewards them for using Java. Most importantly, it builds a community by connecting Java developers to each other. In turn, this helps Sun with its core business — selling computers and software.

Contrasting these two sites shows what works online and what doesn't. Services that are open, transparent, people-driven and based on principles of community building are the services that are increasingly in demand. Meeting this demand will be essential to the survival of businesses, governments and other organizations in the near future.

If you don't provide this kind of openness, people will find a way to route around you. They will talk about your lame-ass, tight-fisted attitude in newsgroups, Web forums, listservs and e-mail. They will complain about

The Sun Java Developers' Community Discussion area is full to the brim with useful information (including which discussion are currently the hottest).

your lack of responsiveness on ICQ and IRC. And together, because someone will have the answer, they will find companies who are responsive to their needs. Of course, this can also happen to those who are open, transparent and engaged in online community. But if you are engaged in an honest manner — if you are part of the community — people will laugh (and learn) with you. If you are a grumpy outsider, they will probably laugh at you, and they will definitely abandon your crappy, unsupported product in favour of something more, well, open.

Understanding and making this kind of shift is not always easy. In the Sun example, decision-makers were extraordinarily open and honest to themselves and their customers when they redesigned their support service. They also had to abandon a lot of tried-and-true business thinking. Even with dozens of business books and magazine articles out there touting the value of online community, being this honest and dropping old ways of making decisions isn't easy. But it has to happen.

Better markets for all

The Gartner Group, a large American consulting firm, says 'collaborative commerce' within the context of business-to-business (B2B) transactions is going to be The Next Big Thing.[5] Collaborative commerce is basically business-to-business Internet services plus community. It covers a wide range of applications designed to connect players within an industry and enable collaboration. These applications allow companies to place fluid bids on tenders, find pricing, work on joint bid proposals, manage their supply chain, and so on.

Systems that provide this type of automated B2B information exchange are not new. Large companies and governments have been trying for years to make their interactions more fluid by investing in huge Electronic Data Exchange (EDI) projects. These projects allow for the automated exchange of purchase orders, inventory information and other supply chain information between established business partners. But while these systems have made business more efficient, they neither work across a whole industry nor allow for flexible collaboration.

A better historical example of early collaborative commerce is Sabre — the travel booking system established by IBM and American Airlines in the 1960s and still in use today. Sabre provides a single marketplace for travel agents, where all airlines list their flights. By aggregating large volumes of travel information in one place, Sabre is a type of commonspace. It crosses the boundaries of individual companies and essentially encompasses the whole industry. As a result, the travel market becomes fluid, enabling buyers and sellers to find each other without much hassle.

But 'collaborative commerce' means something more than Sabre and EDI. It's about the Internet. A report by the consulting firm Bear Stearns states that the Internet is pushing industry well beyond EDI and Sabre and into a more collaborative world.[6] It not only provides electronic transactions and data aggregation, but also acts as a platform for open, interconnected marketplaces. It also lowers the cost of entry for smaller players. In some senses, it provides the potential for a more democratic world of B2B exchange.

Currently, the main form of collaborative commerce is the 'vertical marketplace' Web site. Popping up in almost every industry, these sites provide content and commerce tools focussed on a particular industry. For example, VerticalNet provides online marketplaces for the airline industry, wireless technology companies, hospitals and over 40 other industries. Each of VerticalNet's sites (i.e. <www.hospitalnetwork.com>) provides product information, industry news, requests for proposals, directories, job listings, discussion forums and auctions within that industry.

Another example is Covisant — an online auto industry marketplace announced in early 2000 and owned by General Motors, Ford and DaimlerChrysler. Covisant provides all the standard vertical market tools, such as auctions, catalogues and directories; but it also goes a step further by offering services like 'collaborative forecasting and planning'. In other words, Covisant members are actually sharing strategic information they would normally have compiled separately — and secretly. This joint venture between cutthroat competitors shows that even dinosaurs can see the value in shared infrastructure and feed the common good ... even if it is only the common good of the auto industry.

When — and if — these vertical marketplaces work, they will indeed bring some of the potential of online communities to commerce. Suddenly, one's scope and one's colleagues move beyond the boundaries of individual organizations and out to the industry as a whole. This provides the potential for overall evolution within the industry. It also jumbles up once-static relationships. Open RFPs and auctions allow for a constant shifting of suppliers. In turn, small players can more easily sneak into the market.

Of course, the potential scope for collaborative commerce goes beyond throwing the supply chain up in the air and connecting peers within an industry. There is also a great deal of hands-on intellectual collaboration going on between business. Software companies with related products need to agree on common protocols. Lawyers and accountants working on big mergers need to shuffle collaboratively authored documents. In other words, even the boring world of B2B work needs access to group mind tools.

While this more cerebral aspect of collaborative commerce has been ignored by most of the big B2B players, there are some companies experimenting with ways to meet this need. For example, Open Text spin-off b2bScene <www.b2bscene.com> currently provides rentable intranets and a 'trading community' platform to help knowledge workers cluster around a particular project. The tools provided include project management and workflow programs, document management software, and discussion forums. Moreover, the service is designed much more along the lines of traditional community-building tools. The result is an environment that can foster real and fluid communities of commerce. They appear. People collaborate. They shut down. The gears of industry grind on.

When — and if
— these vertical
marketplaces
work, they will
indeed bring
some of the
potential of online
communities
to commerce.

Trust-busting community

Can collaborative commerce projects really bring commonspace to old-style businesses, or will they simply replace industry associations? Will markets really become more fluid and democratic, or will they simply be sewn up by the big players who own the marketplaces?

Not surprisingly, the trust-busters at the U.S. Department of Justice are starting to ask some of these same questions about industry-backed e-marketplaces.[7] While it's likely that independent markets like those run by VerticalNet will provide the momentum to speed up and add efficiencies to the marketplace, the impacts of industry-backed exchanges are a little harder to predict. Will reverse monopolies form, allowing big players to bully their smaller suppliers? Will alternate markets be shut out of the game? Or will they be able to communicate with the more established markets through open standards?

These questions don't apply just to the world of spark plugs and spray paint. During the first half of 2000, industry-backed exchanges were announced in over 20 sectors. Everything from meat (Tyson, Cargill, Gold Kist, etc.) to rubber (Goodyear, Michelin, Pirelli, Bridgestone, etc.) to chemicals (Dow, Shell, Dupont, etc.) now has its own industry-backed exchange in the works. Given this trend, it's unlikely that any major business sector will be without a huge, jointly-run e-marketplace.

On the one hand, this bodes well for commonspace. Huge companies are starting to understand the value of collaborative infrastructure. They are putting their money on the table and opening the pores of their corporate membranes. This will no doubt have an impact on the way that people in these industries work. Work across company boundaries will become more fluid and transparent.

What has regulators worried is the impact of this kind of openness and transparency when it flows from systems run by the dominant players in a huge industry. In an effort to prevent the big guys from ganging up on the little guys, the U.S. Justice Department has undertaken preliminary investigations into Covisant and six other vertical marketplace sites. They have also held hearings on the subject. The likely outcome of this is some form of regulation. If this is indeed what happens, let's hope the regulators know about open standards — the factor that really will keep things open, and will allow the little guys to thrive.

Unfortunately, some of the new digital juggernauts are still too big and too flushed with their own power to care too much about minor details like senate committees and regulation. While the Microsoft antitrust case was still being heard, AOL was purchasing Time Warner and creating a huge vertical monopoly including everything from the content itself (AOL, movies, magazines, TV) to the software to view it (Netscape, AOL, ICQ, WinAmp) to the actual cable networks to carry the content to the users. Although AOL Time Warner signed a 'memorandum of understanding' in March 2000 promising to allow rival ISPs access to their cable networks in order to ensure a competitive market, the members of a U.S. senate panel investigating the merger were skeptical. Committee Chair Sen. Orrin Hatch went on record as saying 'Given that this [agreement] lacks both enforceability and specificity, this committee remains to be convinced of its value beyond the boardroom and public relations office of AOL Time Warner.' The senators also inquired why 'AOL's Version 5.0 software appears to hijack users' computers and prevent them from accessing competing services.'[8]

All this power in the hands of a company that tried to sue AT&T in 1998-for the use of common Net phrases like 'You Have Mail' justifiably makes legislators wary. After the judge threw that case out of court, AT&T's counsel stated that 'we feel this sort of overreaching by one company raises serious concerns about whether AOL is truly committed to keeping the Internet an open platform, or whether it intends to leverage its dominance to make the Net more proprietary.'[9]

Clearly, commonspace has some major competition. What's more, its techniques and powers can be used by players on both sides of the field.

Clearly, commonspace has some major competition. What's more, its techniques and powers can be used by players on both sides of the field.

Giving away the store

It's not always easy to convince people to open up their electronic barn doors and embrace the common good. In fact, even we were a tough sell for a while.

Back in 1999, one of us (Mark) was starting up a Web publishing software project for a group called the Association for Progressive Communications <www.apc.org>. The project proceeded as one would expect. We laid out all the criteria. We described the desired features for our software. We brought a bunch of techies to the table to look at our options. At the end of all this, we took the predictable steps that might have come out of an IT management textbook from an MBA program — we picked out the best commercial software and started building our tools on top of them.

Quietly at first, and then more loudly, there was a chorus of people in the background asking, 'Why don't you use open source tools?'

'Because they aren't as good as the commercial tools', we answered.

'Why don't you pick the best open source tools and make them better, to fit our needs?'

'Because we're in a rush', we said.

'But others will help you if you just share the code!'

But my gosh, we couldn't give away our smart, amazing, unique code. 'We'd be giving away the store!' we said. And so we went on our merry way, testing and customizing our commercial tools.

Then six or nine months into the process, we realized that the chorus had been right (the chorus is always right in tragedies). It was much harder to make the commercial software do what we had wanted it to do, despite the grand marketing claims to the contrary. In addition, users were telling us that they wouldn't adopt what we were developing since it was too big and complex. And as we looked around, the open source world was passing us by with a smug smile on its face. The tools that hadn't been good enough six months earlier had become much better. Other open source tools were emerging that could do the same Web publishing functions we were planning to provide. Clearly, we had made a terrible mistake.

Luckily, we hadn't missed the boat altogether. The voices calling for us to take a more open approach kept up their song (which often sounded like an angry mob of bald kids screaming hardcore punk lyrics). We started listening, dragged the project back to the drawing board, and redeveloped it with open source tools. This changed the project tremendously, forcing us at once to scale back our ambition and to see the real opportunities. Instead of regarding ourselves as the ones with the solution, we saw ourselves as a useful piece of a much bigger constellation. We eventually released our code under the General Public License (GPL) with the hope that others would find it useful and help it grow.

While this story doesn't reflect well on us in some respects, it does make a point. We are all too easily stuck in our do-it-for-ourselves-and-keep-it-to-ourselves attitude. Despite years of involvement with cooperative projects both on- and offline, we just couldn't get out of our mental straightjacket when it came to software development. And then, when with did, kablooooeeey! It all became clear. The connections between the common good, community building, iterative development and cooperative crystallized. Through this process, we learned that it was possible to reassess our initial positions and to 'switch sides' as a result.

Common good culture

The whole process of selling and learning to understand the simplicity and power of common good projects is like peeling an experiential onion. In order to have that eureka moment for yourself, you really have to see each layer of the onion being peeled away. You have to recognize each problem and deal with its results. Hopefully, you'll find your answers sooner rather than later, and you'll still have some onion left to garnish your burgers.

Instead of regarding ourselves as the ones with the solution, we saw ourselves as a useful piece of a much bigger constellation.

The fact that it is hard to get people's heads inside the core ideas of commonspace doesn't mean we aren't pushing for them all the same. We are committed to them because they work, which is unfortunately still a rarity in the world of networked computing. Whenever we're asked for advice on Internet projects, we look for the commonspace opportunities. We look for connections. We look for the nexus between the interests of the project participants and the common good. Trying to hook people on these ideas has provided some real opportunities for learning. We've come to see how people's attitudes and understanding of the power of the network impact the projects they undertake.

One of us (Mark) does a lot of consulting for the Government of Ontario regarding grants for non-profit Internet projects. Of the dozens of projects every year, there are always interesting opportunities for collaboration. One such opportunity arose in 2000, when almost 25 different groups came forward at the same time asking for money to write volunteer-matching software. Our eyeballs popped out. Were they all really asking for something different? Was there really no existing solution for the problem?

We brought together all of the folks interested in this kind of software and said: 'While we can't force you to work together, it seems like there is a real opportunity here. Why don't you write the software together?' A look of horror immediately appeared on some faces. Work together? Give other people our ideas? Screw that. But there were a few in the room whole smiled. They got it. They saw commonspace in front of them, and the opportunity to create something better, cheaper, and faster. [Place Bionic Man sound effects here, minus the six million bucks.]

Of the groups in that room, three decided to create their own software with the promise that they would make it available to others for a fee later on. One of these groups hasn't completed their software yet. Another has completed the software for themselves but has not yet succeeded in rolling it out for others. The third group has created an expensive monstrosity of an application in Oracle and put it up on their Web site. While it's too big and cumbersome (and proprietary) to share the code, others can supposedly 'share the wealth' by logging in to the group's Web site and using the tool there. Understandably, nobody seems to have shown up.

In contrast, the three groups that banded together at the meeting went on to create a piece of software that they could share. The results have been astonishing. Not only is the software up and running in the three communities that came to our meeting, but groups in 20 other communities have also adopted it. In some cases, the software has been shared and set up 'as is.' In others, the local community has added new features or tools to the software. These in turn are shared with other users of the package.

By jumping on the common good bandwagon, all the groups using this software have benefited. They have a solution to their needs that is cheaper and better than the packages produced by those who went it alone. They also have something that will grow over time. Additions to the software continue to be created by the Ontario communities using the program. Now that the software has been released as open source, it's likely that others from even farther away will begin to contribute.

This story drove home the common good message for everyone involved — and for many who were watching the process. Real success in the Internet age comes when you trash the walls of your organization and embrace commonspace culture. Championing mutual self-interest and taking a few risks is what makes the sparks fly. And, while your Ayn Rand library burns, you can roast marshmallows and sing campfire songs all night long.

By jumping on the common good bandwagon, all the groups using this software have benefited.

7

Reputation as reward

Success is nothing but being a quote.
ANDY PARTRIDGE, XTC

The Internet allows anyone to become a communicator of unprecedented power… or at least a communicator who gets some heartwarming recognition. Take your pick: you can be a USENET guru with answers for everything, a day-trader with 'badges of Foolish Achievement' from the Motley Fool for your consistently hot stock tips, an IRC celebrity with the gift of the gab, a DJ on Scour with your own netradio station, an ace Noder on Everything$_2$, the most trusted person on ePinions or eBay, a master hacker in the open source community, or a high-ranked ladder player on Battle.net or Kali. All you have to do is find your niche or niches, and work like a crazy person to add the most interesting and innovative ideas you have to the group mind. Sounds like a lot of work? It is. But it's the kind of work that can also be an incredible amount of fun.

Moreover, if enough people pick up on your post/signal/Web site and tell their friends and colleagues about it, the result is a geometric cascade effect that far exceeds the range and speed of traditional media. Intriguing ideas and cool links spread like wildfire across e-mail and ICQ networks. There are 'weblog' sites like the Haddock Directory <www.haddock.org> and Memepool <www.memepool.com> that do nothing but post links to the most engaging Web sites they can find. These sites are part of commonspace too, assembled by groups with similar interests working together to create knowledge pools for, well, whoever chooses to use them. And many people do on a daily basis (especially to Memepool, which syndicates its headlines to other sites using RSS), including both print and digital journalists. Where did you *think* the writers on HotWired found their stories, anyway?

15 minutes of fame

Attention is a powerful drug. People crave it, sometimes for the wrong reasons. And sometimes they bestow it on things that are frivolous or silly as well as those that have integrity and style. Increasingly prevalent are the people and Web sites we might call Net celebrities, who are just as famous — or more famous — than the geeks who actually accomplish real tasks. But only for their 15 minutes. Then, before you can say 'Spice Girls,' they're gone.

Mahir 'I Kiss You!' Cagri, the Turkish Forrest Gump of the Internet, is (or was) a Net celebrity. After Mahir's quaintly antiquated personal Web site <members.nbci.com/primall/mahir> went up in 1999, featuring snapshots of the mustachioed Turk sporting a red Speedo, playing the accordion and describing his hobbies in broken English — 'I like to take foto-camera (animals, towns, nice nude models and peoples),' the site received millions of hits simply as people circulated his URL through their e-mail, USENET and weblogs. Mahir fan clubs appeared all over the world (we've seen more than a few snapshots of groups of smiling office workers holding hand-made 'We Love You Mahir' banners above the walls of their cubicles), as did a number of parody sites, including the Bill Clinton 'I Kiss You' page (Slick Willie and Mahir have a lot in common. See for yourself at <www.geocities.com/Athens/Ithaca/4637/kissyou.html>.) A year after all the fuss, Mahir started the official 'Mahir tour of Turkey,' which allowed those willing to fork over the cash to see the sights and even have dinner with Mahir himself. ('Istanbul was okay, but man, you should see Mahir play 'In a Gadda da Vida' on the accordion! He's a party animal!')

Mahir Cagri and others like him are like the cartoon section of the newspaper . But the headlines and and front page go to the geeks and netheads

Even the most banal sites can capture the collective imagination — and someone will eventually figure out how to make money from that attention. The potential for this kind of instant, concentrated attention is a powerful motivator for participation in commonspace.

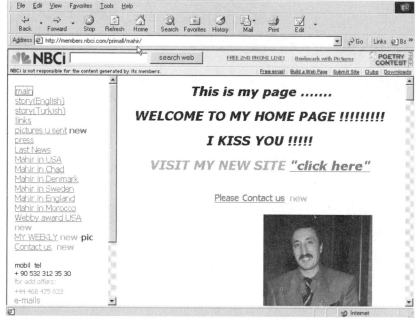

Mahir 'I Kiss You!' Cagri: if you ever thought online fame had anything to do with merit, think again.

Credibility and egoboo

In the world of serious Internet users, Mahir Cagri and others like him are like the cartoon section of the newspaper. But the headlines and and front page always go to the geeks and netheads — people whose posts have an extremely high *signal:noise ratio*. Long-time netheads whose posts are consistently interesting and useful have credibility. And on the Internet, that means more than anything.

On the Internet,
reputation is a
worthy goal. For
some people,
it's the only goal.

Take Bruce Sterling as an example. The noted science fiction writer and journalist (author of *The Hacker Crackdown*, *Globalhead*, *Islands in the Net*, *Holy Fire* and other fine books, 'Chairman' of the cyberpunk SF movement in the '80s, and regular feature writer for *Wired* and other magazines) is a nethead from way back. He has been a tireless propagandist for the potential of the Internet for the last decade. The transcripts of many of his speeches and articles are available online. In fact, the text from his book *The Hacker Crackdown* was posted to the Net in its entirety, for free, shortly after its publication, a good seven years before the current brouhaha over 'electronic books.' The Mirrorshades List <www.well.com/conf/mirrorshades/>, Sterling's forum on The WELL, has spun out a plethora of Web sites based on the writer's ideas (including cyberpunk science fiction; the Dead Media Project — an attempt to list as many of the various types of media used throughout history as possible, and the Viridian movement — a radically pragmatic strain of environmentalism.) Sterling's good reputation among Net users is based on his consistently interesting and useful hypotheses about the effects of technology on culture.

In *The Cathedral and the Bazaar*, Eric Raymond states that the open source movement has rechanneled the selfishness of individual hackers to focus on difficult goals that can only be achieved by sustained cooperation.[1] The fuel behind this rechanneling is 'egoboo'– the satisfaction and ego boost gained from doing something well and knowing that others know that you did it well.

Egoboo is a suprisingly powerful motivator. Skeptics would expect a culture like the open source community to be fragmented, territorial, wasteful, secretive, and hostile. But it's not. Open source hackers, for example, produce copious amounts of documentation for Linux — even though it's well-known that programmers hate documenting. In contrast, the carrot-on-a-stick motivation practices of corporate documentation sweatshops produce the barest minimum of documentation. And most of it is lousy.

On the Internet, reputation is a worthy goal. For some people, it's the only goal. They want it for three compelling reasons:

- Good reputation among one's peers is a reward in itself, period.

- Prestige not only attracts attention, but also it helps to assure the co-operation of others.

- Reputation in a gift economy may carry over into the off-line world and earn you higher status.

John Seely Brown, the former director of Xerox PARC, argues that it's even an indirect part of 'community hygiene', because gaining reputation, say, in the open source community, involves writing code that others have to be able to read and want to use.[2] This means that the product of one's work is circulated, talked about, and used as a springboard for all sorts of unexpected ideas. The community grows, and you get a little credit for playing a part in it. However, establishing a good rep isn't always a straight-forward process.

The signal: Noise ratio

Back in 1993, journalist and culture jamming commentator Mark Dery was receiving a cranky, flame-ridden reception on The WELL. One of us (Darren) took pains to explain to him why this was happening. He was making the kinds of mistakes any newbie makes when they post without doing their research first: asking questions that were answered in FAQs, writing long, off-topic posts, misinterpreting in-jokes and the particular conventions of local conversations.

Anyone who plans to spend time online has to grow a few psychic cal-luses. Dery listened and persisted in his explorations in online culture long enough to make a career out of it. (Dery went on to edit *Flame Wars* and to author *Escape Velocity: Cyberculture at the End of the Century*, both of which drew heavily on information he gleaned from The WELL.) But even in 1993, there were guidelines available that would have eased his entry into the online community, if he'd bothered to look.

Everyone thinks their ideas are interesting, even when there's ample evidence that they're not. Some people are unfortunately aggressive with boring, irrelevant and often offensive assertions, sometimes at the expense of the participation of other users. The term for such individuals is *floodgaters*, because of their tendency to flood lists and forums with irrelevant posts and other crap. There are also *flamers*, who rant and rage about the posts of others, and *trolls*, who write incendiary and insulting posts calculated to rouse the ire of other users so that they can respond with their own flames (posting barbecue recipes to a USENET newsgroup frequented by People for the Ethical Treatment of Animals is a classic troll). *Flame wars* are a frequent occurrence in online forums and are always a huge waste of time, energy and emotion for everyone involved, and even for those who have to watch from the sidelines.

The set of rules called 'netiquette' evolved in the early 1990s as a response to flaming, floodgating and other forms of online noise. Netiquette specifies the minutiae of good online conversational style and indicates that the brief post, preferably with hyperlinks to a longer text located elsewhere, is the ideal communique. There are some variations to this rule, because every community has its own netiquette standards, but in general it holds true everywhere. Some good general examples of netiquette FAQs can be found at <www.faqs.org/faqs/usenet/emily-postnews/part1/> (the Emily Postnews newsgroup netiquette FAQ) and <http://www.faqs.org/faqs/net-abuse-faq> (FAQs of online Thou-Shalt-Nots and how to respond when others do them anyway).

In general, the goal of the discussion facilitator is to maintain a high signal: noise ratio. This means ensuring that as much of the material as possible will be as relevant to as many of users as possible, regardless of the technology involved.

It's important to realize that there's no such thing as a noise-free channel, due to the nature of information itself. Data only becomes information when someone singles it out for attention from the flow of background noise. What's relevant to one person may not be relevant to another person, despite their similar interests. But it's possible to tip the balance in

It's important to realize that there's no such thing as a noise-free channel.

favour of greater relevance through the use of various aggregation and filtering methods.

One important activity in commonspace is that of devising filters to ensure the bulk of the content is relevant to users. There are various sorting mechanisms that can be used to help maintain a high signal: noise ratio. Here are the most effective ones:

FAQs

FAQs (Frequently Asked Questions) are usually available in both HTML and textfile versions and accessible from the front-page of a Web site or at the beginning of a discussion thread. Reading the FAQ before leaping into a discussion is the best way to avoid being flamed and bombarded with RTFM (Read the Fucking Manual) messages from other users.

Moderation/gated systems

The most powerful tool for ensuring high-quality content (but also the most expensive) is the moderator. This person (or persons) examines posts for messages that violate the community's rules, removes out-of-date postings, and watches for bugs and crashes. Moderators can be visible to varying degrees, from lurking demigods to participants on a first-name basis with users, and they can range from full-time paid employees to full-time unpaid volunteers.

It surprising, really, how long it's possible to run a very large system on largely unpaid moderators. AOL got away with paying over 14,000 volunteer 'community leaders' nothing more than the cost of their monthly account ($21.95 US) for most of its history. It wasn't until 1999 that the volunteers started to get testy about it and launched a class-action suit against AOL <www.wired.com/wired/archive/7.10/volunteers.html>. Moral of the story: if you treat your gatekeepers like dogs who'll be satisfied with the odd bone, they may well turn and bite you in the ass.

Observant readers of this book will have noted a certain lack of enthusiasm on our part regarding AOL's merits as commonspace. Why ignore the largest commonspace the world has ever seen? Six or seven years ago, it could be argued that along with Prodigy, CompuServe and like companies, AOL, was a laudable service, linking people together in commonspace at a time when Internet technology wasn't widely available and was difficult to use when you could get it at all. And some good things came out of AOL, including profitable commonspace businesses like the Motley Fool financial advice site <www.fool.com>, which began as a newsletter in 1994 and rode to fame on the strength of its AOL presence. But AOL was always the equivalent of a tidepool in a sea of information, shallow and walled off from the deep water where the big people swim. The perennial problem with AOL is that the people who run it would like their tidepool to replace the deep water.

Forum seeding

In order to start a good discussion, you need intelligent people who like to talk. Because there are so many venues for online discussion including good old-fashioned e-mail, there's no reason for people to use your forum rather than anyone else's — unless you give them one. Many fledgling discussion groups 'seed' their forum with authorities in the field in question, preferably voluble ones. If your moderators post to the groups, encourage them to ask questions of your seeded authorities to help fuel discussions. Seeding is an ongoing process; people inevitably get tired of posting and slow down or quit, and you have to keep adding new ones into the mix to ensure lively ongoing discussion.

Membership requirements

This strategy can cut either way. The rationale behind limiting membership (through invitations, user fees, or professional qualifications) is that you're more likely to attract users with a strong incentive to be there, and you'll eventually arrive at a more balanced mix of posters, lurkers, and moderators than you would with, say, a USENET newsgroup. However, membership requirements that are too stringent or involve cash usually fail to generate a healthy constituency. When faced with subscription costs or membership fees, many Internet users will simply go elsewhere. Often it's not possible to limit access to a forum at all unless there's an existing high demand for it. The WELL is one example of a service that's successfully managed to charge for membership, even after its migration to the Web. But it's the only reason they can do so is because — that's right — they have a good reputation.

Reward systems

Remember those gold foil stars that teachers used to put on your homework (or your forehead) if you got all your answers correct? Darren's Grade 3 teacher actually made a wall chart with every student's name in the class on it, and put a sticker beside their name for every completed assignment. The stickers varied in colour depending on how well you did on each test. The point was that every student knew how every other student was doing, and it was a remarkably effective motivation strategy for the most part. (This explains a lot about Darren, actually.)

This system is alive and well on many commonspace sites on the Internet today. It's the opposite of membership restriction and can be used either on its own or in combination with restrictions. For a reward system to work, frequent posting of high-signal material should produce be recognized in a way that's noticeable both by the person being rewarded and other users. Some sort of visual marker on the user's identification is frequently the only reward that sites give, but rewards for participation can also include extra service privileges, cash or exchange value on goods.

Instant karma: Respect as reward

Everyone wants to be liked, but it's most gratifying to be liked for making some positive contribution to a group rather than for your hairstyle, your clothes, or your collection of original Star Wars action figures. Many parts of commonspace have developed systems that provide user incentives for contributing to and improving commonspace.

The Slashdot karma system is a great example of egoboo in action. Karma points are a reflection of each Slashdot user's contribution to overall discussion onsite — *registered* users, that is: people who post without registering are identified by the epithet 'Anonymous Coward', a little bit of negative incentive that pushes some people into active membership more quickly. (Evidently, when the Internet powers-that-be grabbed the Grade 3 sticker-based motivational strategy, peer pressure and name-calling came along for the ride.)

Users receive karma points based on how their comments to news stories on Slashdot are received by the site's administrators, who review every submission before allowing it to be posted onsite. For each comment that users attach to a given news story, moderators select an adjective like 'Flamebait' (negative) or 'Informative' (positive) from a drop-down list that appears next to the comments in their special moderating windows. A negative rating reduces the comment's score by a single point, and a positive rating increases the comment's score by a single point. All comments are scored on an absolute scale from -1 to 5. Logged-in users start at 1 (although this can vary from 0 to 2 based on their karma) and anonymous users start at 0. Each user's Info page lists their current karma rating, and the number of comments they've posted in the past few weeks (including those that have been rejected).

When a user's comment is adjusted positively by a moderator, their karma will rise by one point. If it is moderated down, they lose a point. In addition, users can gain karma by submitting a news story that the moderators decide to post. Also, users can gain and lose karma through metamoderation, a system that allows any logged in Slashdot user to 'rate the rating' of ten randomly selected posts for fairness. Metamoderation encourages good moderating practices and helps to ensure that moderator access isn't granted to poor moderators on a repeated basis.

Slashdot has also developed checks and balances on moderators to ensure that they do not become all-powerful demigods who crush other users according to their whims. When users gain access to the moderator window, they are given a number of 'points of influence' to apply to comments. Each comment they moderate deducts a point from their total, and when they run out of points, they are done serving until their turn comes up again. Moreover, moderators cannot participate in discussions that they are moderating, and moderation points expire after three days if they are left unused.

So what do karma points do, really, other than make you look good? Answer: (this is the nifty part) karma points determine which users are selected to be moderators, so the maintenance of the system closes in on itself in a beautiful little loop. There are also other selection criteria in the Slashdot moderator selection system, including the following, which could well serve as guides for anyone choosing moderators:

- **User must be logged in to the system.**

- **User must be a regular reader.** The scripts which select moderators track the average number of accesses by each logged-in user, then choose from eligible users who read the site a set number of times. Simply accessing the homepage doesn't count; the user must be actively burrowing down through the site to follow particular stories. The scripts also pick users from the middle of the pack to avoid obsessive-compulsive people hitting the Reload button or people who've only read one article.

- **User must be a long-time reader.** The system throws out the newest few thousand accounts before beginning its moderator selection process. This prevents people from creating new accounts simply to gain moderator access. But more importantly, it ensures that new users understand the community before they gain access to the controls.

- **User must be willing to serve as a moderator.** Each user's preference page contains a button that allows them to designate themselves as 'Unwilling.' It's that simple.

- **User must be a positive contributor to the site.** A user with positive karma has posted more good comments than bad ones, and is therefore eligible to moderate. This weeds out spam accounts.

The end result is a pool of eligible users that represent average, positive Slashdot contributors. Every 30 minutes, the system checks the number of comments that have been posted, and gives a proportionate number of eligible users 'tokens.' When any user acquires a certain number of tokens, he or she becomes a moderator.

Slashdot is also a working example of a community where lurking actually makes sense. Most often when we're online, we're part of a community of readers more than we are a community of talkers. A quarter to a third of any forum's users are active in discussion at any given time; everybody else is lurking, watching for a moment when they're compelled to participate. Lurking allows users to learn how the site functions and helps ensure that when users decide to participate, their first efforts are smooth and successful. For the user, a lurking period also builds anticipation about participating more actively in the life of Slashdot — sort of like waiting for dessert.

If at first you don't succeed:
The value of persistence

Off the Net, most people have never heard of James 'Kibo' Parry. But among long-time Internet users, he's a minor legend. In his own words, Kibo is to the Internet what Charles Nelson Reilly was to Match Game '77. Kibo's realm is USENET, where for over a decade he's held forth on all manner of topics in all manner of groups (especially those named after him, such as alt.religion.kibology). Kibo's homepage on the Web <www.kibo.com> isn't much to look at; but as Kibo writes, 'This page has a philosophy. That makes it better than yours.' The Kibo philosophy is odd but interesting: that everything online should be legible (i.e. text-based), even if it's dadaesque nonsense. What the site does offer for the pragmatic surfer who's willing to sift through the sacred mountain of Kibological documents is some solid advice about how to configure a USENET newsreader for maximum efficiency. (If you're going to try to stay on top of even a fraction of the 35,000+ newsgroups currently in existence, some of which get thousands of posts a day, you'd better be pretty proficient at writing kill files and bozo filters.) For everyone else, Kibo's site is carries a powerful message: if you stick around for long enough and

We're part of a community of readers more than we are a community of talkers.

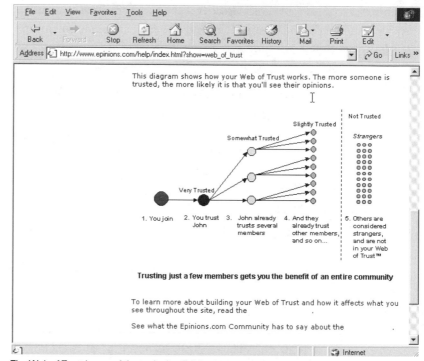

This diagram shows how your Web of Trust works. The more someone is trusted, the more likely it is that you'll see their opinions.

Not Trusted

Slightly Trusted

Strangers

Somewhat Trusted

Very Trusted

1. You join   2. You trust John   3. John already trusts several members   4. And they already trust other members, and so on...   5. Others are considered strangers, and are not in your Web of Trust™

Trusting just a few members gets you the benefit of an entire community

To learn more about building your Web of Trust and how it affects what you see throughout the site, read the

See what the Epinions.com Community has to say about the

The Web of Trust is one of the tools that Epinions.com uses to ensure that egoboo stays in check.

keep writing, people will eventually listen, even if they haven't the slightest idea what you're trying to tell them.

Kibo is on a grand scale what many users of the Internet's 'free advice' community aspire to be (whether they realize it or not). While most of the users of Epinions <www.epinions.com>, iVillage <www.ivillage.com>, AskMe <www.askme.com>, Abuzz <www.abuzz.com> and similar sites don't have religions or even newsgroups named after them, many of them display a Kibo-like determination to hold forth on, well, *whatever*. (Sometimes, the reviews are even produced in streaming video, which can produce unintentionally bizarre results. Check out Epinions user Jen's review video of an electric breast pump at < www.adcritic.com/content/epinions.com-breast-pump.html>. Watch the cat lick the leaky pump!

Watch the pizza guy's reaction! Reality TV has nothing on this stuff.) What's more, the free advice users long desperately for someone — anyone — to approve of their epistles.

On a free advice site, the Grade 3 sticker chart is hauled out once again, but this time with a vengeance. Any posting on Epinions can be rated by any user as as Highly Recommended, Recommended, Somewhat Recommended, or Not Recommended. In addition, on your Epinions home page, there's a sidebar listing other users that you trust — and those that you mistrust. In other words, on many free advice sites, it's possible to punish people as well as to reward them for their opinions, justly or unjustly.

The majority of advice site participants are well-meaning and sincere, striving to communicate with each other and solve problems for no more reward than the satisfaction of a thank-you. (Oh, and a 'Highly Recommended' rating while you're at it. Calculated altruism is the flip-side of mutual self-interest.) However, there are also always a percentage of 'trolls' — people who lurk in commonspace looking for easy targets for flaming. This exchange on iVillage — which allows users to post follow ups to expert answers — is instructive:

```
Cooking on the Grill

"Help! My husband just bought a gas grill. We love
cooking on it, but my kids are picky. They won't eat
anything but hot dogs and hamburgers. Any sugges-
tions? I'm desperate." —iVillager Chapmanville

What would you do?

EXPERT SAYS :

Maybe your kids would like these!
Grilled Parmesan Turkey Burgers
*       1 pound ground turkey
*       1/2 cup grated Parmesan cheese
*       1 tablespoon chopped fresh chives
*       1/4 teaspoon pepper
*       1/8 teaspoon salt
*       4 hamburger buns, split
```

On many free advice sites, it's possible to punish people as well as to reward them for their opinions, justly or unjustly.

Mix all ingredients except buns and onions. Shape mixture into 4 patties, about 1/2" thick. Cover and grill patties 4 to 6 inches from medium heat for 12 to 15 minutes, turning once, until no longer pink in the center. Add buns to grill, cut side down, for last 4 minutes of grilling. Serve on buns with grilled or raw onions.

—cl-cathy

How would you satisfy a picky child? Share your recipe suggestions with us.

Two waldorf salads with fries to go. I'm going down the sidewalk to the mall where I can buy some sneakers and pants.

10:47AM EDT 06/28/00

—-Posted by American twat

Can you help. Dooncan would love to meet your kids so long as they are over 16....

10:47AM EDT 06/28/00

—-Posted by Ivor Bigun

I would very much like to clarify the behaviour of my Uncle Thomas after his retirement from front bench politics. He was actually appointed Keeper of the King's Dew Flaps by George V a position entitling him to all the stout he could drink and an annual pension of four bob.

10:47AM EDT 06/28/00

—-Posted by Colonel Henry Ramsbottom

They could always eat my shorts.

10:45AM EDT 06/28/00

—-Posted by The Boxmaster

I am dismayed at the self indulgence rearing it's pathetic head on this page. Why don't you all think
about something that is more important than your pathetic little spoiled children who only eat burgers
or who can or can't drink alcohol. How about something more important like - paint drying

10:51AM EDT 06/28/00

—-Posted by Tony

Webmaster! Please do something! I can't find my
pants!

10:51AM EDT 06/28/00

—-Posted by Robert Pritchard

I AM STUPID AND HAVE NO FRIENDS! I LIVE ON SPAM!
MAYBE THIS WILL HELP ANSWER THE ORIGINAL QUESTION!
FEED YOUR KIDS SPAM! IT IS GOOD

10:51AM EDT 06/28/00

—-Posted by ROBERT PRITCHARD

Why dont you just feed them hagendaz and pancakes
with syrup. Kill the buggers off before they are 30
and we wont have to put up with them coming over here
wearing white socks and sandals, talking loudly and
having cameras that just ask to be mugged !!!!

10:48AM EDT 06/28/00

—-Posted by Ivor Bigun

```
This is so much fun! You have succeeded in driving
traffic to your site, now show the traffic stats to
you AD companies and tell them to pay more!

10:53AM EDT 06/28/00

--Posted by cricket
```

…and so on. This last post, from 'cricket' is the most interesting: it demonstrates a technical understanding of the business side of free advice sites that's far more sophisticated than the level of discourse itself. The bread and butter of free-advice commonspace is controversy, because controversy creates mountains of free content and does in fact drive traffic to the site, creating an attractive venue for advertisers. Clearly, beyond a certain bare minimum level of decorum, it's not in the best business interests of such a site's administrators to moderate too closely.

This exchange also demonstrates the type of obstacles faced by those who aspire to online fame. Many people simply don't have the filtering skills that allow Net-demigods like Kibo to tolerate the online torrents of crap and abuse. (The full extent of the iVillage flamefest cited above went on for over 65 pages of text when we found it, and may still be going on, for all we know.) But as we all get better at learning what we want and where to find it and stop tripping over each other in the process, the overall amount of noise in the channel will drop. And for the most part, we'll be a happier species as a result.

Your last 15 minutes

So what happens when the flames get too hot, or people find other corners of commonspace that they'd rather spend more time in than your site? Answer: your site dies.

All online communities, not just the business ones, are transaction-based, whether the transactions are of a restricted-economy nature (financial) or a gift-economy nature (egoboo, conversations, free advice). And communities last only as long as the transactions conducted by their members. Though it might take a long time, even the busiest communities will eventually cease to exist.

Online communities also have a finite size limit and a lifespan that's directly related to the exceeding of that size limit. What we used to call the 'I was a punk before you were a punk' syndrome is important in determining that limit. People want the feeling of having been there first and will often leave when they lose that feeling, or they will form new communities to regain that lost sense of control or innovation.

Even when the founders leave, many communities continue to live on and evolve. The WELL is a good example. It isn't the lively home of nethead impresarios that it once was. While some of the original community leaders still keep an affiliation, they don't spend the hours everyday sitting around the WELL's virtual coffee table that they once did. They have moved on, but the community still thrives. There are new members, new owners (Salon) and new energy. It is still The WELL.

On the other hand, some communities just fade away and die when the founders leave. The Internet is filled with the dusty skeletons of newsgroups, mailing lists, discussion forums and Web sites long since abandoned by the people who once inhabited them. But unlike ghost towns, these dead communities still provide value to commonspace. They serve as a collective memory. In writing this book, we often found the most useful information was in dusty old mailing list archives, information long forgotten by everyone but the search engines.

It's essential that we view this cycle of commonspace — with some communities growing, morphing and others fading away — as a healthy one. It helps us grow and learn. It helps us sort through what is still useful, and what is still not. It allows us to move in and out of leadership roles as we need to. And, unlike the firmly entrenched world of old media, this cycle allows new ideas and institutions to grow quickly as they are needed and old ones to fade away gracefully when they are not. Let's hope the cycle continues.

Dead newsgroups, mailing lists and discussion forums serve as a collective memory.

And the people who've used those communities to vault into the public view? Many of them, like Rheingold and Sterling, have gone on to even more impressive feats, and we probably haven't heard the last of them. Even Mahir is trying to do his bit for world hunger with his second homepage, 'I hug u then I kiss u anytime!!!' Like Smilin' Stan Lee, the author of *Spiderman*, used to write, with great power comes great responsibility.

The tools matter

Give me a lever long enough and a fulcrum on which to place it, and I shall move the world.

ARCHIMEDES

People make the Internet. People make community. People make commonspace. No question. This being said, the tools that people use to construct commonspace matter– a *lot*.

Why? Because the tools assemble the people, and the way they assemble them has a major impact on what we can do online and on how successful we are at doing it. USENET is different from the software that manages eBay. A Web discussion forum is different from an e-mail list. For that matter, Gnutella is different from Napster, and Netscape is different from Internet Explorer. Large or small, these differences matter. The interface, the features, the protocols — all have an impact on what you can do in commonspace.

Deep within the lines of code, all of these tools hold the potential to produce the online collective. This is precisely why they continue to thrive while others have failed.

Several companies have tried to create Internet tools that ignore the collective. Such attempts have always met with the massive indifference — and occasionally the wrath — of the online community. Microsoft, for one, has behaved like a hackneyed cartoon villain, launching scheme after

No one is selling modems or writing e-mail programs that only let you download. Not yet, at least.

hare-brained scheme to pacify Net users. First, they tried to replace HTML with their own proprietary programming language called Blackbird, which would have allowed people to write content solely for MSN. Bye bye Blackbird. Next, they bought WebTV, a technology which essentially lobotomized the computer, sucking the potential for interactivity out of the browser and replacing it with a remote control. [Evil baritone villain voice: 'Yes, my zombie minions…. Don't type. Don't say anything. Just surf and buy. Hahahahahahaha!']

In both of these cases, designers tried to do exactly what RCA did to radio in the 1930s. They tried to rip the transmitter out of the Internet. Luckily, they have failed miserably. [Evil baritone villain voice: 'And I would have gotten away with it too, if it weren't for you meddling kids and your dog!']

Many-to-many gadgets

In commonspace, the ability to create many-to-many connections matters a great deal. Internet tools need some kind of many-to-many capability, end stop. It is a basic precondition of their existence. They must allow anyone to send and many people to receive, if only to ask for another Web page or to order a pizza.

This rule runs to the very heart of the network itself — Internet protocol (TCP/IP) and Internet culture. As it routes traffic over the network, TCP/IP makes the technical assumption that every computer on the network is equally empowered to send and receive. Furthermore, most of the people building sites and software for the Internet regard it as inherently dedicated to various forms of many-to-many communication. For the most part, they design and implement tools that take advantage of TCP/IP, tools that encourage people to be creators as well as users. No one is selling modems or writing e-mail programs that only let you download (except WebTV). Not yet, at least.

How a tool provides many-to-many connections is much more interesting than the connections themselves. Some tools make it easy for everyone to be a sender and limit the amount of possible response. Other tools provide an equal flow of information between all senders and receivers. The features, the core technological design, the rules of use, the social mythology — all these factors determine what types of connections are possible with a given technology.

The different characteristics of the available tools determine the extent to which they lend themselves to commonspace applications:

- **The Web** provides people with a great deal of space to respond (i.e. Web-based forums) despite the fact that the underlying technology (HTTP) provides very limited abilities to the person on the 'client' side.

- **E-mail** has excellent potential for many-to-many applications but is usually used for one-on-one or small group communication.

- **Intranets** are built on many-to-many technologies but tend to place substantial social restrictions on who can be connected to them.

- **Napster** and other file-sharing tools are the closest thing we have to a pure many-to-many environment, connecting peers to peers. The interface and all the rules of use follow suit.

- **Newsgroups** also fall into the pure many-to-many category. They were designed by and feed into a culture founded on the premise that 'anyone can talk, and many will listen.'

Internet tools tend to float between the 'anyone can send' and 'many can receive' poles. In contrast, older forms of media have long since chosen sides. The telephone is squarely in the 'anyone can send' camp. Inversely, television works only in 'many can receive' mode.

How a tool provides many-to-many connections is much more interesting than the connections themselves.

Mapped out, the many-to-many commonspace tech spectrum might look like this:

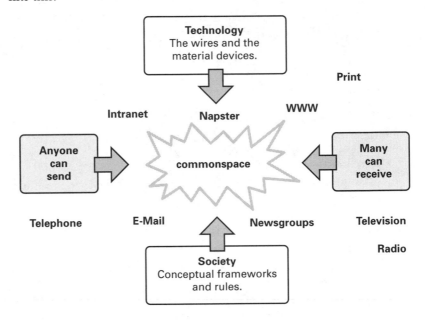

One of the biggest factors determining the nature of a given technology is *distributedness* — the degree to which it is centralized or decentralized. Is there a single access point, or are there many? Is the directory in one place, or is it spread across the Internet? Does the information reside in a single place, or is it replicated so that it exists in many places at once?

USENET is a good example of the impact of 'distributedness' on a tool's role. USENET is incredibly distributed, with its feed stored on thousands of different servers around the world. Each server provides a small group of users with the means to send and receive newsgroup messages. When there are new messages on one server, it sends these messages out to the rest of the network. At a technical level, this distributed approach lends redundancy and robustness to the system. It also protects against failure and data loss at any particular node in the network.

More importantly, the decentralization of USENET creates a culture of independence. Each access point in the network can choose which portions of USENET to include and which not to include. Just because someone creates alt.sex.fetish.rockclimbing.butt.naked doesn't mean that any other servers have to pick it up. If an ISP doesn't like (or doesn't want) to expose its users to naked people bumping uglies on mountaintops, it can drop this newsgroup from its feed. Administrators can also establish their own local or private newsgroups. As a result of the distributed design and culture, each small subset of USENET users can have a discussion forum system that responds to their local needs.

USENET's particular technological features and its approach to distributedness also define the limits of its usefulness:

- It's not a great place for selling the spare stuff in your garage (most people have abandoned the *.forsale* newsgroups for eBay);

- It's not a good tool for aggregating statistics about our mutual likes and dislikes (usage stats spread across thousands of servers are almost impossible to compile);

- And it's not a good tool for the collaborative development of a document (it doesn't include version control or a proper file archive).

But USENET isn't supposed to do these things. What it does it does well, and it does so by design. Other tools have evolved — and will continue to evolve — to meet these other needs.

Road warriors

Luckily for commonspace, people gravitate to tools that are designed for distributedness. They prefer tools that give anyone a voice and allow many to listen. This tendency became evident at the beginning of the last decade, during what we'll call the Battle of the Information Superhighways.

In the early 1990s, the media heralded the dawning of a new era. Video-on-demand. Online shopping and banking. Pick-your-own-camera-angle-

As people chose
Netscape and the
Web, talk of video-
on-demand and
proprietary
superhighways
faded away.

sports-and-porn. The five-hundred-channel universe. It was all just weeks away. And Time Warner, TCI and Microsoft were pouring hundreds of millions of dollars into creating 'set-top boxes' and proprietary networks that would make it all happen.

At the same time, the humble little Internet was chugging away quietly in the background. Nobody thought it would beat the proprietary info highway at its own game (not even people like Marc Andreessen[1]). It was more of a plaything and a test bed. But then the Web and Netscape happened. And then everything exploded. All of a sudden, people could create their own media, their own businesses, their own stores. More importantly, people could connect without paying homage to the corporate gatekeepers. The Internet was the little engine that could — and did — connect us to each other.

As people chose Netscape and the Web — and they chose it in droves — talk of video-on-demand and proprietary superhighways faded away. Time Warner shelved its much-heralded, multi-million dollar interactive TV tests in Florida. Microsoft dropped its Tiger video-on-demand server and its propriety Blackbird language for MSN content providers. Everyone, even those who had fought it tooth-and-nail, moved to the Web. It provided a platform to many who'd never had one before, and in doing so, it fed a revolution.

Tools matter.

Lingua franca

Another factor that determines the usefulness of tools is their ability to talk to each other. This is where open standards, the *lingua franca* of the Internet, come in.

Not too long ago, all e-mail programs had their own proprietary formats for moving messages. If you had e-mail on Compuserve, or through cc:Mail at the office, your mail system wasn't compatible with your friend's mail system on AOL or with a neighbouring office's Novell system. If you were lucky, you might have been able to send e-mail to your friend via a 'gateway' (which you had to specify and know how to use). If you were unlucky, you simply couldn't send mail to people outside of your own system.

In the world of proprietary protocols, e-mail looked like this:

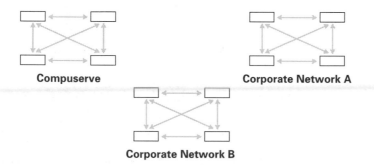

Compuserve   **Corporate Network A**

Corporate Network B

Figure 7: E-mail before open standards

But in the background, the Unix hackers who created the building blocks of the Internet were changing things. They wanted to talk to each other and were making it possible by using an open standard mail system that they shared amongst themselves — the Simple Mail Transport Protocol (SMTP). SMTP suddenly enabled users to send e-mail between technologically different organizations. The e-mail tsunami began.

By the mid-1990s, SMTP had replaced proprietary mail protocols almost everywhere. And even where proprietary tools continued to exist, they talked via SMTP to the outside world. E-mail started to look like this:

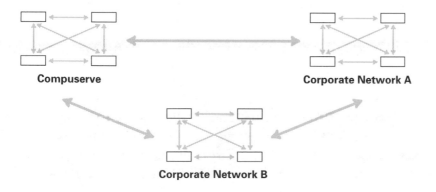

Compuserve   **Corporate Network A**

Corporate Network B

Figure 8: E-mail after the wide acceptance of open standards

The result was the e-mail system we have today. While we may take it for granted, it's actually quite a feat that e-mail can leap organizational boundaries in a single bound. Even as recently in the early 1990s, proprietary e-mail seemed like a sensible idea. Why make your system work with other systems? It would erode market share or pollute the content of the network. But the leap happened all the same. And it has changed our preceptions of the technology to the point where proprietary e-mail now sounds like a crazy joke made at the end of a drunken evening.

Commonspace and collective work thrive when data becomes free of boundaries. Data needs to flow between people and between organizations. This is not possible in a world of proprietary tools. Open standards are necessary to liberate data and help us connect.

Luckily, there are a lot of smart people out there who understand the importance of standards and data exchange to the development of commonspace. New protocols and standards are constantly under development. From B2B process automation to information about international aid and disaster relief, someone out there is developing a standard that will make it easier for information to flow between diverse systems.

XML — everything, everywhere

One of the most exciting technical developments in commonspace in years is eXtensible Markup Language, or XML. Intended as a replacement for HTML, XML deals not only with presentation elements of a page (i.e. bold text, picture placement, columns) but also with the data elements (i.e. title, body content, contact information).

So what, you say? Why get so excited about a three letter acronym replacing a four letter acronym? Isn't it all just the Web?

With XML, Web pages will come alive. One computer will be able to talk to another, sharing information about the content that's available on the Web pages it hosts. Computers will be able to interact, exchange information, and update each other — to work together as if they were one. The entire Web will begin to work as if everything were all on the same computer and stored in the same database. The resulting fluidity will also create new opportunities for collaboration and collective work. Moreover, it will fuel the fire of commonspace phenomena such as Web constellations, aggregated data pools and distributed computing.

XML is still in its infancy. Nonetheless, it's already being used in some simple but powerful applications. Take the swapping of news content in the open source tech community. This swirl of collective content uses an XML document template called Rich Site Summary (RSS). With RSS, sites like SlashDot constantly send out summary info about the content they want to share. Other sites pick up this summary information and list the stories on their own sites. Likewise, Slashdot publishes RSS summaries from other sites. Voilà: a collective news network of 'smart' content, all of it automated. Machines talking to machines, taking the best of what is fed to them from trustworthy humans.

Because XML is 'extensible,' anyone can dream up a new use for it.

Because XML is 'extensible,' anyone can dream up a new use for it. Doctors are working on an XML-based system that lets medical systems talk to each other. Aid workers are building tools to find and connect international development data, no matter where it exists. Whatever the application, people are using XML to break down barriers and connect things. They are running towards commonspace with open arms.

KISS

The essence of commonspace design philosophy is simple: choose the Laguiole Knife over the Swiss Army Knife.

We've all seen Swiss Army Knives, and many of us have one (they make great stocking stuffers). But how many people ever use anything other than the main blade? What could you possibly do with those other little tiny blades? Or the stupid saw thing?

In contrast, the Laguiole Knife, which has been around since 1829, is an uncomplicated, elegant tool, featuring just one large, sharp blade of high-quality steel, and (optionally) a corkscrew and a sharp metal spur for

Successful
technologies
always
complement each
other and allow
for overlap.

letting the gas out of the stomach and intestines of freshly killed animals. The analogy to software is clear: massive 'all-in-one' solutions (bloatware) are popular, but smaller specialty tools accomplish the same tasks just as well, or better, and for less capital investment. They're also easier to debug if something goes wrong. (And let's face it: when there are computers involved, there are always problems.)

But the tools you choose to build commonspace don't require you to sacrifice other tools. Successful technologies always complement each other and allow for overlap without needless duplication or interference. It's also important that tools use open standards for communicating with other specialized tools to balance focus and versatility.

GameSpy is a tool with one purpose: combining access points to various online games into one elegant interface. Its simplicity allows a level of interactivity between gamers that many commercial software packages can't match. For the most part, GameSpy does a better job of pinging the servers of many game networks than the crude interfaces bundled in with the game software itself. GameSpy allows users to filter server lists using their own parameters (such as ping time), to create sub-lists based on game types, to perform quick refreshes of server lists, to compile sophisticated stats on particular games in play (up to and including lists of participat-

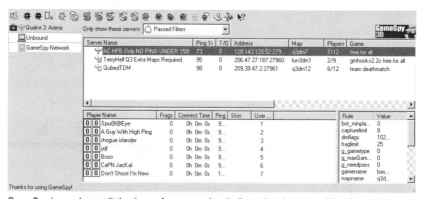

GameSpy is an elegant little piece of programming dedicated to the proposition that software should do one thing, and do it well.

ing players and the 'skins' or character types they happen to be using), to locate buddies who happen to be online, and to chat. Moreover, it consolidates the operation of a large number of games under a single interface.

Gnutella is an even more extreme example of simplicity in action. In the Gnutella interface, there is no provision for chat of any kind, or even for sophisticated searching or monitoring. There's just a simple form with a search box and a results box, and a tab to a window which scrolls current search strings. The only internal clues about how to operate the program come from the watching search strings as they zip past. The reason for Gnutella's minimal interface is that the project was killed before its interface had been developed further. Nevertheless, it does the job. Some users have cloned and modified the program to solve problems such as bugs and spamming; others have improved on the aesthetics of the original interface, and still others are working on improving the program's scalability to alleviate traffic jams caused by apprehensive Napster users migrating to Gnutella. However, the majority of users continue to use the original release despite its Spartan design.

Application Service Providers (ASPs) are another result of the drive for simplicity. ASP companies provide software 'for rent' over the Internet. They do all the configuration and maintenance and tailor their product to the needs of their users. All the user needs to do is fire up a Web browser. ASPs with a focus on commonspace are growing. Take eGroups, for example. When you set up your community with eGroups, they do all the gruntwork. Other organizations, such as b2bScene.com, are taking complex and expensive intranet software and delivering it as an ASP-style service. Click a few buttons, enter your credit card, and you have a trading community or project intranet.

Amidst all of this, there is only one thing to remember — KISS. Keep It Simple, Stupid.

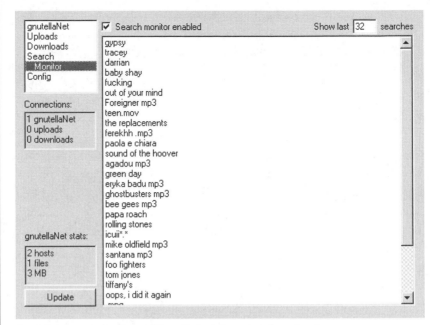

Spreading the nutty goodness of Gnutella doesn't require a fancy interface.

Tools people want

If tools are going to be successful, people have to like using them. Simple, convenient tools put power in the hands of their users. In principle, it's not hard to design such tools. If you can:

- balance simplicity, access and power;

- fit in with the normal daily routine of users;

- empower users, not service providers;

- make it free or cheap;

- listen constantly to what users are saying;

you'll do fine in the 'give people what they want' department. Of course, 'just' doing these things isn't always easy. We all get caught up in our own rigid, obstinate ways of doing things. It takes practice to fit into the groove of giving people what they want.

Take mail lists, for example. Mail lists are by far the most popular many-to-many discussion tools on the Net. eGroups alone hosts over 18 million members who participate in thousands of mail lists.[2] As of August 2000, CataList, the catalogue of LISTSERV lists estimates that there are 30,792 public listserv mail lists out of a total of 166,665 mail lists on the Internet today.[3]

But mail lists are a frumpy old technology — aren't they? Why doesn't everyone just switch over to Web-based forums? Simple: Web forums are closed systems that take people out of their way and inconvenience users. In other words, they are a pain in the ass to use.

Look at the evidence. On most of the 'give people what they want' fronts, mail lists put the smack on Web forums:

	Mail Lists	**Web-Based Discussions**
Simplicity and power	Yes. What's more simple and direct than an e-mail message?	No. Usually the interfaces are cluttered and confusing.
Daily routine	Yes. Users check their e-mail anyway.	No. Users have to take the initiative to visit the forum site.
Empower users	Yes. Users can set up and configure mail lists with ease.	No. Space is controlled by the service provider.
Free or cheap	Yes. Mail lists are available for free from many sources. Even where you pay, they are cheap.	No. Web-based discussions usually require the purchase and configuration of expensive server software.

These differences have contributed to the continued success of the mailing list as a collaboration and community building tool and to the almost complete failure of Web-based discussion.

Wallowing in complexity

Of course, complexity has its attractions. Grand technological dreams are often built on the field of complexity. Consider Ted Nelson and Xanadu.

Hypertext didn't start with the World Wide Web in 1992, or even with Apple's HyperCard in the 1980s. It started with Ted Nelson and the Xanadu project back in 1960 <www.xanadu.net>. Named after the mythical locale in Coleridge's 'Kubla Khan', Nelson's Xanadu project outlined a grand dream for the world's first workable hypertext system. It was a system that

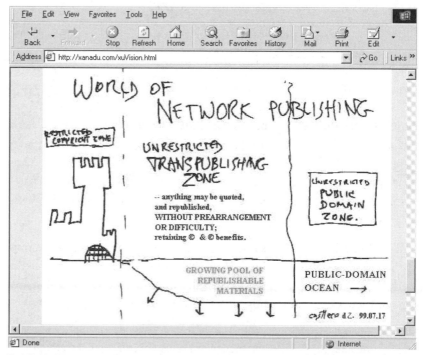

Ted 'Kubla Khan' Nelson drops some science on the subject of hypertext and copyright.

would link not only one document to another, but also one section of one document to another. It was going to create parallel documents, monitor versions and provide for two-way links. In other words, it was going to create an interwoven, self-aware knowledge network.

Even from today's perspective, Nelson's ideas from the 60s and 70s are brilliant. He proposed a technical system based on connection and collaboration — data knowing about other data, people creating collaborative documents (easily linking individual chunks of data), and aggregating data simply and powerfully. Both the technical and social aspects of Xanadu embodied the very essence of commonspace.

Unfortunately, plans went awry as Nelson tried to turn the grand dream into a reality. Working with a number of collaborators, Nelson strove to create a workable Xanadu system throughout the 70s and early 80s. Little pieces of code came together, but nothing complete ever emerged to be 'productized' (Nelson's own word).[4] In 1988, software giant AutoDesk came along with investment money to make Xanadu real. But with little to show for its money by 1992, it abandoned the project.

Meanwhile, the Internet was growing in the background. The first examples of hypertext were appearing. Lotus Notes came out as an interconnected, self-replicating database environment. Millions of Mac users were futzing around with Hypercard. Then World Wide Web burst onto the scene. While all of these technologies owe a debt of gratitude to Xanadu (as their developers will freely admit), they are distinct from the Xanadu project in one crucial respect: they are simpler. And, as simple, powerful tools, they have fueled a revolution.

The sad thing in all of this is not that Xanadu's complexity got in the way of the grand dream becoming a reality. No, the sad thing is that Nelson seems bitter about the success of simpler hypertext systems. The front page of www.xanadu.net reads:

Since 1960, we have fought for a world of deep electronic documents— with side-by-side intercomparison and frictionless re-use of copyrighted material.

Successful Internet tools are distinct from the Xanadu project in one crucial respect: they are simpler.

We have an exact and simple structure. Our model handles automatic version management and rights management through deep connection.

Today's popular software simulates paper. The World Wide Web (another imitation of paper) trivializes our original hypertext model with one-way ever-breaking links and no management of version or contents.

WE FIGHT ON.

Nelson sees the World Wide Web as a massively nerfed version of his original dream. Maybe it is. But the Web is effective in its simplicity, because it is creating commonspace and changing the world.

Welcome to the pleasure dome

The simplicity of Internet technology is vital because the Internet and commonspace are complex to start with. But their complexity is more like that of an ecosystem than a technological masterplan. It's not a rigidly planned whole; it is an interwoven mesh of ideas and systems. Like an ecosystem, it grows organically. Simple new ideas enter the system. The good ones survive and propagate, the bad ones are reabsorbed and fuel other new growth. The system evolves.

As with an ecosystem, online diversity is everything. The system isn't about one grand vision, but about a multiplicity of visions combining together synergistically. These visions are different, sometimes even conflicting; but in a massive conceptual pool where the simple ideas survive, this kind of diversity is good. In fact, it is to be celebrated. It feeds change. It allows for options. It creates unexpected synergies that feed into astounding watersheds.

All of this is what makes commonspace so exciting.It is based on a system of communication that isn't monolithic. We can all contribute a piece to the pie and see if it weaves into the overall fabric. We can all benefit from each other's contributions. And as this happens, we move slowly towards Ted Nelson's grand dream.

9

The unexpected is the best source for inspiration.

PETER DRUCKER

Despite the commercial veneer and increasing degree of regulation it's acquired in recent years, the Internet is still the best large-scale example of functional anarchy to come down the pipe in a long time. What's more, it's an anarchy that's been built entirely on someone else's property. Computers belonging to universities, big business and even the military have been hosting the digital equivalent of a squatter's tent city for decades now. And, like absentee landlords, the institutions that own the machines have been largely indifferent to the activities of their tenants.

Those tenants have been busy redecorating and renovating, too. The last two decades of radically different technologies have been created by people with unapologetically unorthodox mindsets and belief systems, not corporate boffins 'thinking outside the box.' While they were adapting the Internet's infrastructure to their own ends by creating everything from Coke machines connected to the Net (so that you could check if the machine downstairs had cold drinks in it without leaving your desk or going offline; the fact that a guy in Finland could also check the same machine was an amusing side-effect) to military-strength encryption software, these people also spent a large amount of time and energy writing vast amounts of material describing *why* they were bothering to do so. The result has

The fringes of
online culture
are tomorrow's
mainstream
Internet.

been the widespread online circulation and adoption of ideas ranging from the revolutionary to the ridiculous.

If you *really* want to know what the next big thing will be, the next 'killer app' or billion-dollar company, you're going to have to start paying closer attention to these ideas. The fringes of online culture are tomorrow's mainstream Internet. Even when new ideas don't originate in the fringe, there will probably be passionate discussion of them in fringe forums long before they reach the pages of any self-proclaimed 'cutting edge' print media. As Bruce Sterling writes of his *Mirrorshades* group on The WELL, 'If it's in Mirrorshades, it'll be science fiction in a year. In two years it will be in *Wired* magazine. In three years teenage girls will be wearing it. In four years it'll be mentioned on CNN. In five years it'll be "discovered."'[1] The question is, do you want to wait five years, or do you want to know *now*?

The TAZ

'TAZ' stands for 'Temporary Autonomous Zone.' The phrase was coined by gay Islamic philosopher Hakim Bey (aka Peter Lamborn Wilson) in his book of the same name, published by Autonomedia in 1991. In brief, *TAZ* outlines a theory that anarchistic temporary communities are a means of reclaiming a more intense, fulfilling, 'immediate' existence, not just online, but everywhere.

Though it sounds as if it had been custom-tailored for the Internet era, the theory of the TAZ isn't just something that Bey pulled out of the ether. It's based on the existence of actual 'pirate utopias' in the 18th century:

The sea-rovers and corsairs of the 18th century created an 'Information Network' that spanned the globe: primitive and devoted primarily to grim business, the Net nevertheless functioned admirably. Scattered throughout the Net were islands, remote hideouts where ships could be watered and provisioned, booty traded for luxuries and necessities. Some of these islands supported 'intentional communities,' whole mini-societies living consciously outside the law and determined to keep it up, even if only for a short but merry life.[2]

While plenty of French philosophy advances similar ideas (such as Deleuze & Guattari's notion of nomadology), geeks and hackers by-and-large don't read French philosophy. They do read science fiction and fringe literature, though. Themes similar to the TAZ (because they were based on the same subject matter) also appear in the work of geek icons Bruce Sterling (*Islands in the Net*), Neal Stephenson, (*Cryptonomicon*), William. S. Burroughs (*Cities of the Red Night; The Place of Dead Roads*), and Kathy Acker (*Pussy, King of the Pirates*).Consequently, Bey's notion of the TAZ (or ideas close enough to it that there's no essential difference) were and remain inspirational to a whole generation of hackers. The text of the *TAZ* book itself is available in many places online, including <www.hermetic.com/bey>. Because it is explicitly anticopyright, it has become one of those texts that circulate in ascii format as part of the secret and revered literature of the Net.

As Bey describes them, Temporary Autonomous Zones have the following salient features:

- They're **small** in size, typically consisting of only a handful of people at any given time, though the constituency may change frequently.

- Members tend to be **anonymous**, or at least pseudonymous.

- They're **mobile**, not tied to a specific physical location.

- They're **exclusive**, existing beyond the pale of social norms and well-frequented locales.

- As the first word in the name says, they're **temporary**, because a long-term existence would eventually result in the development of unwanted rules and regulations.

- Likewise, they tend to be focussed around the accomplishment of **short-term goals**. The TAZ follows that general axiom of hipness: by the time you know about it, it's probably over.

- These short-term goals **frequently involve illegal activity**.[3]

The TAZ is the best model we've come across for describing what's driving the action in peer-to-peer networks like Gnutella, Napster, and Hotline.

Starting to sound familiar, isn't it? The TAZ is the best model we've come across for describing what's driving the action in peer-to-peer networks like Gnutella, Napster, and Hotline. The spirit of these networks lies at the very core of Internet culture and commonspace.

But the TAZ isn't a run-of-the-mill Internet experience; it exhibits behaviour that runs counter to perceived wisdom about networking in general. Robert Metcalfe, the founder of 3Com and designer of the Ethernet protocol — in anyone's books, a very smart guy — once observed that *the usefulness, or utility, of a Network equals the square of the number of users.*[4]

This observation, known as Metcalfe's Law, generally holds true in commonspace: the more people who use a service, the more valuable that service becomes. However, over a certain size, the TAZ fails. The size limit varies according to the TAZ in question; some raves can hold thousands of

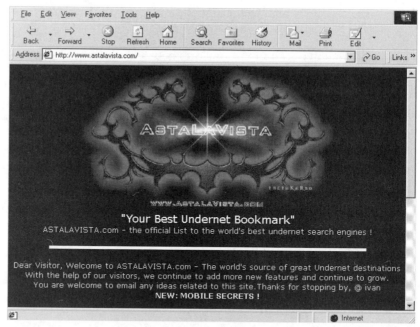

Astalavista, Baby: your personal gateway into the 'Undernet' of hackers, crackers and warez (oh my).

attendees, and Napster currently has millions of users. But once such festivities get big enough, they start to attract the attention of the authorities, and the whip comes down: the cops move in and break up the raves; Napster gets sued. And then what? Well, that's the interesting part. Another TAZ appears, somewhere else, and the cycle begins again.

NetHistory 101: Birth of an invisible nation

In a very real sense, the online TAZ existed before the Internet and migrated online once cheap modems and public net connections became widely available. But until that point, the same kind of behaviour that occurs now in the clandestine corners of the Internet occurred in clandestine corners of FidoNet, a loose networking system that sent packets of e-mail and newsgroup data between BBSes (bulletin board services usually hosted on local PCs) late at night, when long-distance calls were cheap. Pirate BBSes were very much like every other kind of BBS, save for their content — the usual assortment of cracked and pirated software, specialized cracking software, instructions for making 'blue boxes' and other phone-phreaking tools, porn, anarchists' cookbooks, etc. Many 'legitimate' BBSes also had secret 'Elite' zones for crackers accessible only with the use of special passwords.

With the growing availability of Internet access through universities and mega-BBS services like The WELL, anonymous FTP (File Transfer Protocol) sites on Unix systems scattered across the Internet began to supplant the archival functions of the pirate BBSes. Unix-based university computer networks are vast, complex entities, and it's entirely possible to tuck something away in a remote corner and not have it discovered for years (or to use an unauthorized account for years). The relative anonymity of USENET (and later, IRC) was enough to put the minds of most crackers, phone phreaks and other habitués of the TAZ at ease, and discussions about every subject imaginable flowed freely.

(There were also more than a few *un*imaginable discussions, such as alt.pave.the.earth, whose members continue to insist to this day that their

Plan™ for the complete coverage of the planet's surface in asphalt is not only a necessary but desirable goal. Within alt.pave.the.earth is an even *more* hermetic group, the 'chrome the moon' subfaction, who sometimes go so far as encrypting their heretical messages to each other with the use of PGP.)

Things heated up again when Netscape made widespread Web use a reality in 1995. Now there's nothing stopping anyone from putting up any kind of content on a Web page. Unless an ISP receives a sufficient number of complaints, sites featuring even the dodgiest content can continue to exist for a very long time.

Warez Web sites (repositories of cracked software) were fairly common in the early days of the Web, and it's still very easy to find pages stuffed with stolen serial numbers for commercial software. In fact, the digital rabbit-hole leading to this portion of the TAZ is in plain sight. Go to any search engine and type the phrase 'serial numbers.' You'll get an extensive listing of Web pages that baldly list serial numbers for all manner of software types and purport to connect to real 'Warez' sites.

Warez Web sites are all about greed and rites of initiation. Almost all of them make a little money on the side by placing interminable clickthrough ads for porn sites on their pages. In order to gain access to the warez, you are directed to click on a certain number of these ads, which open a bewildering number of browser windows, many of which will refuse to close. Often, the only way out is to close your browser entirely. In theory, by following the links, you will eventually arrive at the 'real' warez, or at a secret password from one of the porn pages which will allow you to connect to a real warez site. But the hassle is rarely worth the effort.

Is that *really* what being an 'elite' cracker is about? Though the iconography of heavy metal and punk is everywhere on cracker sites — skulls, dripping blood, swords — crackers (a.k.a. 'warez d00dz') are not really as subversive as they like to think they are. Usually, they're just teenagers blowing off steam. The motivation for cracking is the same thing that drives even the normative parts of teen culture (and much of commonspace, for that matter) a craving for reputation. This is a long way from saying that crackers are either incompetent or stupid: the 'I Love You' virus and the tales in Sterling's *The Hacker Crackdown* are testament to their intelligence. If provoked, they'll prove that they're more skilled than you are and probably more dangerous. But left to their own devices, they rarely intersect with the straight world that sits on the surface of the Internet.

Eric Raymond argues that behaviour in the portion of commonspace occupied by crackers differs from the open source/hacker portion in significant ways.[5] Both types of commonspace operate according to gift economies. But crackers have stronger group identification and are more exclusive than hackers. Furthermore, crackers hoard secrets rather than sharing them. While it's true that they share cracked software, serial numbers, and key generators, information on how to duplicate their feats is difficult to obtain. Because of the secrecy and status-seeking behaviour, the knowledge base of the cracker community, and therefore the community itself, grows much more slowly than portions of commonspace where information is shared freely.

Now that the Web has been largely domesticated, the energy of the TAZ has transferred to client-server and peer-to-peer systems such as Hotline, Napster and Gnutella. Peer-to-peer systems, the 'killer app' of the late nineties, could change the overall shape of Internet life and use as dramatically as the Web did when it became graphical.

And if you're thinking right now, 'Wait a minute. Is there more to the Internet than the Web?' then thank you. You just proved our point.

Fun with pantyhose

Internet culture is built of bits, literally and metaphorically. Everything that's new online is the result of assembling fragments of something else. It's not surprising, then, that the overall net aesthetics is one of *bricolage*, or, as William Gibson says in his paradigm-shifting short story 'Burning Chrome,' 'the street finds is own uses for things.'[6]

Now that the Web has been largely domesticated, the energy of the TAZ has transferred to client-server and peer-to-peer systems such as Hotline, Napster and Gnutella.

Internet bricolage takes many forms: open source software development, where hackers build on each others' code; the use of public domain CGI scripts, Java applets and so on to build Web pages; and the gradual mutation of bits of Net folklore and literature into new permutations.

Of particular interest to the TAZ theory is the adaptation or swarming of corporate software platforms, or the use of orthodox tools for unorthodox ends — including the construction of unorthodox tools. 'Swarming' is the old Internet practice of invading some unsuspecting USENET group, Web forum or other service, by a group of people other than the intended users who are bent on having the space for their own. In the halcyon days of USENET, many newsgroups maintained friendly rivalries with other groups as a method of boosting member loyalty and increasing posts. For instance, the Pavers of alt.pave.the.earth maintained a 'bitter' opposition to their sworn enemies, the members of the alt.destroy.the.earth newsgroup. All the names of interlopers from alt.destroy invariably ended up on the Pavers' The List™, an index of those who will become PitSlaves when PaveDay finally arrives. Go figure.

There are also non-malicious forms of swarming. These types of swarming are the results of a product or service that appeals to a demographic group other than the expected one. A semi-reliable corporate wonk of our acquaintance relayed to us the story of a pantyhose company that built a Web forum for its users. This was in the early, naive period of post-*net gain* hysteria, when many corporations assumed that all they had to do to incorporate 'community' into their sales mix was build a space for one. What the company didn't take into account was that a community usually requires people with something other than the use of a product in order to make it coalesce. In any event, the pantyhose forum was swarmed by transvestites, offering each other advice on how to match pantyhose with skintones, which ones covered up stubble the most successfully, etc. In other words, a perfect commonspace in action — the real customers talking to each other about their real uses of the product. But both the pantyhose company and the corporate wonk who relayed the story to us were horrified, overcome by their prejudices and the loss of all-important control over a brand. The lesson here is not simply one of tolerance: it's also about how to conduct online business in the new millennium. Devoted and active online communities don't just fall out of the sky. When the pantyhose company closed the forum down, they blew an excellent attempt to connect to and build the trust of the people who keep them in business.

Hotline has no such qualms. Of the 'big three' file-sharing networks, Hotline, founded in 1996, is the oldest and the farthest from being a true peer-to-peer system. The Hotline client, an arcane piece of software that distributes chunks of its interface into a number of confusing little windows, inserts the user into a private extranet where hotline 'Trackers' list individual Hotline sites. In theory, a user can connect to any of these sites, though many are password-protected. (Instructions for obtaining the password, called 'banners' by Hotline regulars, are remarkably similar to those found on warez Web pages: "Go to page X, do Y, and use the Xth word from the bottom of the page.') The basic hotline tools, which offer chat, whiteboard and file-sharing options, were originally designed for business applications such as online meetings and file-sharing. But they have been largely hijacked by pirates trading software, MP3s, and full-length movies still in the theatres. (This is a spectacular example of what can result from bad interface design. We know from experience that most people have little tolerance for anything more complex than their e-mail program).

Oddly enough, Hotline seems to have been overlooked in the current wave of copyright-infringement lawsuits sweeping the Net. In the meantime, the eyeballs of their three million-odd users constitute an attractive audience for potential advertisers. (Banner ads are built into the Hotline client software itself, removing the possibility that users can block them without hacking the client software.) Individual Hotline site administrators have also adopted the old warez Web site trick of making users click through banner ads or join mailing lists in order to obtain passwords — a small inconvenience for the user (who will likely comply on the chance of getting some free illicit goodies), but one that generates a modest revenue stream for the admin.

Devoted and active online communities don't just fall out of the sky.

With no central
server, it's
impossible to shut
down the Gnutella
network short of
some very extreme
measure.

When Napster was released in 1999, it provided a simpler user interface and a greater autonomy than Hotline. However, Napster still has a number of shortcomings. First, all Napster clients must go through the central Napster server before they can connect with other users. Its centralized or 'arboreal' structure means that all data flows through one trunk. In order to shut down the system, all someone has to do is collapse the central Napster server. Second, MP3s are the only type of file that can be shared on Napster. (However, this is not an inherent limitation, and the software can and has been easily adapted to other file types.) If Napster survives its lawsuits, it's likely the new business model will require users to pay a monthly fee for the use of its services, and a portion of the monies from the user fees will go toward paying royalties for artists. But the big assumption here is that the Napster user base won't migrate elsewhere for free music — 'elsewhere' being Gnutella and other nascent peer-to-peer networks.

Gnutella, on the other hand, is a true 'rhizomatic' peer-to-peer system. With no central server, it's impossible to shut down the network short of some very extreme measure, such as firewalling Gnutella traffic at the level of every ISP and other servers on the Internet (something that Sony claims they're ready to try if necessary). It's possible to share any type of file on Gnutella. This may spell success for Gnutella in the short term, but may ultimately be its downfall, unless its primitive interface evolves some filtering capabilities to deal with the massive glut of available data. Despite its radically decentralized nature, there are nonetheless business models possible for Gnutella (search engines and ad spamming, to name two).

While the above examples of functioning online TAZs are software-specific, it's important to realize that the community is not the software. Though groups of users, or even patterns of use that transcend specific users, may coalesce on one platform, they often overlap onto other services or even migrate to new platforms. ICQ users can often be found in specific watering holes on GameSpy, Battle.Net, Kali, and IRC. Napster users who are getting cold feet as the court cases press on may switch to Gnutella. It may even be possible to inspire a migration of users from one TAZ to another by presenting a superior alternative in the right forums. However, much depends on the perception of the new service in the eyes of the user group AOL's Instant Messenger didn't stand a chance of impressing any long-term ICQ users, despite the ubiquity of its distribution methods.

Virtual reality check

So now that you know what the TAZ is and a little bit about how it operates in theory and in practice, it's time for a little skepticism. As Hakim Bey points out in his original essay on the subject, the reality of the TAZ is much more banal than its promise.

You offer me secret information? Well … perhaps I'm tempted — but still I demand *marvelous* secrets, not just unlisted telephone numbers or the trivia of cops and politicians. Most of all I want computers to provide me with information linked to real goods …. In short, assume that I'm fed up with mere information. According to you [hackers and BBSers], computers should already be quite capable of facilitating my desires for food, drugs, sex, tax evasion. So what's the matter? Why isn't it happening?[7]

Despite the radical potential of the TAZ, most of its online manifestations turn out to be populated by intelligent, antisocial teenagers (who, despite recent government hysteria over denial-of-service attacks or the Columbine High shootings, are not 'cyberterrorists'). And really, the clandestine goods they circulate are fairly tame, despite the concerns of overanxious vice-principals, religious fundamentalists and other guardians of public morality. Certainly an adult with a little pocket change can come by most of the commodities being traded online far more easily, without really missing the money. So much for the revolution. Or is there more?

HavenCo: A real-world TAZ

In his epic novel *Cryptonomicon*, Neal Stephenson spins the tale of a group of enterprising geeks who set out to build themselves a data haven — the computer-storage equivalent of the Cayman Islands banking system, where data could be stored by any paying customer without fear of that data

Certainly an adult with a little pocket change can come by most of the commodities being traded online far more easily.

being accessible to any person, business, or government on the planet.[8] Right now, in the North Sea, a group of enterprising geeks is in the process of doing just that.

A startup called HavenCo Ltd. <www.havenco.com> is betting its existence on the belief that Roughs Tower, an abandoned World War II anti-aircraft gunning platform six miles off the shores of Britain, is actually what its owner says it is: the sovereign principality of Sealand <www.sealandgov.com>. The company's home page claims that 'The independence of Sealand was upheld in a 1968 British court decision where the judge held that Roughs Tower stood in international waters and did not fall under the legal jurisdiction of the United Kingdom,' though neither the British or U.S. governments officially recognize Sealand's existence.

If Sealand really *is* its own country, all 6000 square feet of it may well become the realization of Stephenson's fiction: millions of dollars of networking gear communicating with the rest of the Net via satellite, undersea fiber-optic cables, and microwave, busily archiving data that nothing short of a small armed invasion will be able to access. In other words, a 24/7,

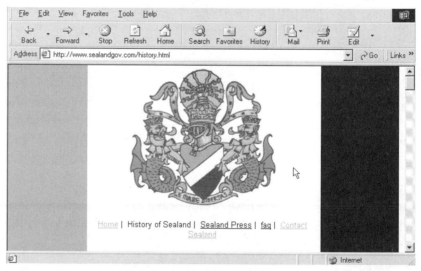

In Sealand We Trust: the official Web site of a real-world TAZ.

Permanent Autonomous Zone. The HavenCo FAQ claims that they won't allow spam, corporate sabotage, child pornography or money laundering to occur on their system; but subpoena-proof e-mail, pyramid schemes, gambling, adult pornography, and untraceable bank accounts all get the green light. You may not find such practices ethical, but they'll be legal, at least in Sealand. And there are many, many businesses in the world without any ethics.

Not that HavenCo lacks a cuddly, humanist side. The company is already donating free server space to NGOs (Non-Governmental Organizations) that promote free speech, human rights or give a voice to minority and oppressed groups. They've already signed up Tibet Online <www.tibet.org> and the CryptoRights Foundation <www.cryptorights.org>.

If HavenCo becomes fully operational and manages to avoid the ire of the British government for even a few years (and that's a *big* if), a precedent will have been set, and the repercussions for the Internet and for business culture could be substantial. But even if HavenCo doesn't succeed in building a data haven/TAZ, someone else will. As media theorist Avital Ronell has noted, technology has no 'off switch.'[9]

Dispatches from the edge

So: what lessons does the TAZ hold for the larger Internet, and specifically, for those interested in how commonspace connects to their online lives?

- The power of commonspace exist in potential; all it requires is a vehicle.

Look around you. The world is full of associations, clubs, networks, and other groups. Some of them have already begun to extend themselves online and into commonspace. Many others haven't, but could, given the opportunity and an attractive enough platform (in the sense that it offers them something tangible). If that tangible good is made of bits, it's

Commonspace
works much
better when the
collective
community goal
is explicit.

duplicable and shareable and will in turn becomes a reason to interact with other users.

Alternatively, there may be ways to 'slice' the constituency of the Internet that no one else has dreamed up yet. If you create the slice, i.e. develop a platform for people who are just in the process of realizing that they have a reason to interact, you're off to the races.

- Commonspace is goal-driven, even if the goals are obscure or highly specialized.

People come together for a reason. Whether playing a game, trading stock tips, swapping illegal copies of current-release feature films, or arguing about the intricacies of how to cover the moon in chrome, there has to be some sort of motivation for people to gather. Commonspace works much better when the collective community goal is explicit.

There's nothing wrong with short-term goals, either. A commonspace can last for as long as it takes to download a file, or for the entire life of a software operating system. Don't be afraid to close one down when the job is done. Others will appear.

- Infamy is good P.R.

Before the lawsuits started, Napster was a well-kept secret, something that most adults were vaguely aware of but wouldn't ever have used themselves. Now it's a household word. You can't buy P.R. like that.

There's also the fact that while Napster has no clear business model and is up to its armpits in lawsuits, venture capital firms are still pumping millions of dollars into the company. If millions of people use it daily, there has to be a way to make money off of it. Which leads to our next point:

- No matter how weird the constituents of commonspace appear, a large user base = a highly specific target market.

Before you turn up your nose at the people who've found their way into your brand-new Web site, relax a little. Once you've figured out who your audience is and what their interests are, there are plenty of ways to market to them: banner ads, e-mails, chat groups, sales incentives and so on. Don't have a clue what their interests are, or why they're here? You could always ask. You may get the odd flame, but eventually a picture will begin to emerge.

- **Don't Panic.**

Douglas Adams was right: the first thing that people should see when they turn on a computer is 'Don't Panic.'[10] This is doubly true of common-space, because there's so much propensity for unexpected, emergent behaviour. One day you're designing a spiffy new digital whiteboard app for your online groupware, the next day all of your virtual boardrooms are full of sarcastic, foul-mouthed kids trading hot files. You can shut down your server, or you can try to figure out a way to spin the situation. (Ever think about *hiring* some of those kids?)

- **Commonspace is not the software.**

Sooner or later, communities will either outgrow and overlap their initial vehicle or shrivel up and die. If you want to stay ahead of the game, you have to keep upgrading your platform. Try open-sourcing it and putting it in the hands of the people who use it. It may just evolve on its own.

- **The Soap Bubble Principle.**

Some aspects of commonspace are incredibly fragile. Your interference, or even public awareness, may kill the community altogether. Sometimes it's better to leave a situation until it stabilizes: you never know what positive things might emerge.

The end of property

Monitor the bleeding edge of commonspace, and you'll stay aware of the wildfire trends that the people in marketing discover years after they're everywhere.

Think of the process of monitoring the TAZ as the Internet equivalent of the DEW Line — a string of radar stations that will show you what's just about to come over the horizon. And you already know that all software has a definite life-cycle. First, hackers invent software, which they can either open source or release commercially. Then, whether the product is commercial or open source, it's adopted by mainstream users. More or less simultaneously, it's adapted or appropriated by hackers, crackers and geeks, who in turn find new uses for the software, which creates new products…and so on. So why not catch a new wave at its beginning?

Unless you spend a lot of time on sites like Blue's News (or its content syndicates, such as Slashdot), you've probably never heard of Machinima <www.machinima.com>. Too bad. That means you probably also don't know about their ultra-low-budget computer-generated film-making that utilizes technology originally designed for computer games. In other words, the Machinimaniacs use the Quake II engine to make movies. Think about it: you spend hundreds of thousands of dollars on expensive 3-D rendering and animation software and hardware; they use a customizable out-of-the-box solution like Quake or Half-Life on their PC for a total cost of about $1200, and then draw on the free expertise of the community for technical advice.

The Machinima people do what they're doing for love, not money. Some of them are amateurs, other are people who've spent time studying filmmaking, acting and vocal improvisation. There's a thriving commonspace at work there, with opportunity for both serious amateurs and real commercial filmmaking ventures.

Good ideas come from the fringe. Machinima is one example, but there are many, many others. You no longer have to wait for those ideas to come to you. You can go looking for them where they're busy being born.

PART 3

Virtual business for real people

Applications of commonspace

10

(Not) strictly commercial

It takes a village to make a mall.
KEVIN KELLY

The Internet changes the dynamics of business by relocating the market-place squarely back in the middle of the town commons. Conversations flow from customer to customer and from vendor to customer. Some are about the weather, others are about the businesses hawking their wares in the surrounding stalls. Conversations also happen between the stalls, with competing vendors sharing stories, shooting the shit and sometimes offering a hand. It's this buzz of discussion and laughter that feeds the marketplace. It's about social flux and people connecting, and as such, it makes the commons a pleasant place to do business.

The commons is a microcosm of the village, the setting for all the connections that make daily life bearable as well as possible. It takes a village to create The WELL, Red Hat, eBay, Salon or any kind of business where people linked to each other. As we've said throughout this book, building a business in commonspace requires connections between people and information. But it also requires the collective spirit that the village commons represents. And hopefully, it requires a business vision that looks more like the marketplace in the town commons than the food court in the mall.

The question is, what do businesses in commonspace look like? Can you actually make a living and pay the bills with the work you are doing in commonspace?

Yes, Virginia, there are real business models in commonspace.

Of course you can. You can make a good living in commonspace. Making money online doesn't just have to be about fantasy-IPO-overheated-stock-market money. There is money to be made running small online businesses from basements. There is money to be made through online advertising, from marketing products built of bits or atoms, and from offering services ranging from file downloads to grocery delivery. This doesn't change the fact that entirely too many companies are gleefully burning their way through hayracks of VC money, or that not every Internet CEO will one day be a billionaire. But some commonspace businesses are succeeding on their own terms and are doing so because they speak the language of the village.

As it is with the village, not everyone makes their living in the same way. There are some businesses that make their living solely from commonspace — connecting, aggregating, collaborating and collectivizing. But there are also businesses that draw on the collective power of the virtual village to support their real-world work. By drawing on the group mind, they improve the ways they produce goods and offer services to individuals. Whatever the case, solid business opportunities exist for those who understand the importance of the village, and those who are willing to engage in the conversation of the marketplace on its own terms.

Yes, Virginia, there are real business models in commonspace. Just look ...

Pay at the door

How did the first online communities pay the bills? By charging admission.

Throughout the 1980s, online communities were popping up all over the place. The megasized commercial online services — CompuServe, The Source, Prodigy, AOL — were thriving. Every North American city had dozens of homegrown Bulletin Board Systems (BBSs). The WELL was in

From today's perspective, the idea of charging for access to an online community seems ludicrous — especially at almost $12/hour.

its heyday. Smaller, niche-focused online communities like Web Networks in Canada and IGC in the U.S. were thriving. While they were tiny by the standards of today's Internet, these early online communities were the digital boomtowns of their time.

Almost without exception, these pioneering communities paid the bills by charging users a monthly membership fee. Yes, there were volunteer-run BBSs and city-wide 'Freenets.' People with Internet accounts at universities could access USENET and mailing lists as part of their tuition package. But all of the communities that had to find money to support themselves 'charged at the door.' Users paid for connection time, e-mail and access to community forums. In exchange, the online services provided the tools and spaces that people needed to connect with each other.

The user fees weren't peanuts either. In the late 80s/early 90s, our old alma mater Web Networks was charging about $30.00 per month. This included two hours of connect time. Additional connect time was $6.00/hour. In addition, e-mail to some external systems was charged on a per-kilobyte basis. Around the same time, The WELL was charging $8 per month plus $2/hour. In 1988, Compuserve — the biggest online service in the U.S. at the time with 250,000 subscribers and 500 forum — was charging $11.75/hour.[1]

From today's perspective, the idea of charging for access to an online community seems ludicrous, especially at almost $12/hour. But from the perspective of the time, it was the perfect business model. Services were scarce, and people were willing to pay for the privilege of connecting to their peers. It was also a 'fair' business model: the people who used the system and benefited from it also paid for it. It was a very simple economic equation.

The paid membership model was also supported by the technological limitations of the day. With almost all of the early online services, you had to dial in directly to that service to access the community. If you wanted to connect to the AOL community, you dialed into AOL's modems. If you wanted to access your friends using Web Networks discussion groups, you dialed into Web Networks' modems. (Although, if you were one of the lucky few with a university account, you could Telnet into The WELL, and avoid long distance charges.) There was a direct, almost physical link between connectivity and community. As a result, it was easy to create 'gated communities' where only the people who paid for connect time had access. This was not an elitist gesture; at the time it seemed like the most sensible option. Running modem banks all over the country and providing technical support was an expensive business. In that context, it was hard to imagine a world of online communities without high monthly user fees.

Bum-rush the show

So why is it now common wisdom that access to online communities needs to be free in all but the most exceptional of circumstances? What happened?

The Internet happened.

The Internet explosion and the emergence of the Web severed the link between connectivity and community that had seemed so necessary until about 1993. Throughout the 1980s, the Internet was one of the best-kept secrets of the hallowed halls of academia. But in the early 1990s, small commercial ISPs started appearing. All of a sudden, you could get an Internet connection and e-mail account from any mom, pop, Tom, Dick, Harry or teenage hacker on the block. It became easy and cheap to get a *generic* connection to the online world, one that would take you anywhere. The necessity of dialing in directly to locate online community or content was gone forever.

For traditional online services, this turn of events presented several new problems. Many users started dumping their expensive Compuserve and AOL accounts for service with a local ISP. At the same time, the users started demanding access to their old gated-community homes via the public Internet. This came with the expectation that monthly fees would drop dramatically or even disappear. Users weren't connecting through these communities any more, so why should they keep paying for the privilege?

Pioneers survived
by morphing and
adapting with the
times.

At the same time, new types of free communities and content sources were appearing on the Web. Generic Internet connections were providing a whole new wave of users with access to USENET and public mailing lists. For users of traditional online services, the community horizons expanded massively, and the price of membership plummeted.

By the late 1990s, traditional online services had stopped bucking the trend, and large-scale examples of the 'pay at the door' business model had pretty much disappeared. A lot of large, formerly profitable companies disappeared too. The Source is dead. Delphi is dead too, although there is now an online forum company called Delphi. CompuServe was rolled into AOL. Many of the older niche communities have also died or been eaten alive by large conglomerates. For example, Web Network's sister networks, Alternex in Brazil and Pegasus in Australia, were bought up by private competitors looking for already-established pools of ISP customers. In the process, the online communities run by these organizations were demolished.

Some of the pioneers survived by morphing and adapting with the times. For example, AOL was once a two-way gated community where users could neither come in from other providers nor go out to the Internet. Just in the nick of time, AOL switched gears and became the world's largest ISP. Sure, you can still get AOL-only content, but for most people AOL is the only way they know to get onto the Internet. It's a cheap, easy, ubiquitous and (mostly) reliable ISP.

Other survivors radically switched business models, opening up their content for free or turning to the provision of alternate services. For example, the Motley Fool moved outside the walls of the AOL forum where it had been founded and built a huge business providing investment advice on the Web, all paid for by advertising. Web Networks has tried to switch-hit by becoming an Application Service Provider (ASP) and content aggregator.

And then there were a few cases, such as The WELL, where communities were able to survive on a scaled-back, paid-membership model. The WELL's fame as *the* mother of all online communities allows it to continue as a paid service. But its rates haven't changed all that much, ($10/month), and it no longer offers any kind of direct dial-in service. As to profitability, it's hard to tell whether the community is sustaining itself or living off of stock-market money from Salon (which exists on a shoestring itself). Whatever the case, The WELL's continued success as a paid online community probably has more to do with the mythology that's accrued around it than anything else.

Collective eyeballs — advertising in commonspace

With paid membership in its death throes, the majority of existing online communities began frantically looking around for a new way to make a living. Meanwhile, the expansion of the Web was also feeding a related explosion in new online communities and other types of commonspace content services, and all of them were free to their users. The most obvious business model for such services was advertising. For better or for worse, advertising replaced paid membership as the way most community and content sites pay the bills.

The attraction of advertising is obvious. Not only is advertising a proven way of paying for content, but commonspace delivers something that advertisers have been searching for since the first adman hung the first red light over the first brothel door — niche, focus and targeting. New online communities and content services were so specialized that they lent themselves perfectly to the advertiser's desire to deliver a message to exactly the right demographic. Many structural features of the Internet, especially the aggregating effects of commonspace, make it ridiculously easy to target not only broad audiences, but also individual users, based on their past preferences. Advances in user tracking technology soon made it possible to evaluate whether or not an ad actually caught the users' attention (i.e. did they click on it?).

The promise of quantifiable success fuelled a tsunami of online advertising. In 1999, global spending on Internet banner ads was over $4.2 bil-

Commonspace delivers something that advertisers have been searching for since the first adman hung the first red light over the first brothel door — niche, focus and targeting.

The advertising-
driven online
communities that
exist today are
certainly a
different beast from
their ancestors.

lion, with an expected growth to $7 billion in 2000. Depending on whose figures you believe, online ad sales will reach between $22 billion (Jupiter Communications)[2] and $33 billion (Forrester Research)[3] by 2004. At that point, online advertising will have far surpassed magazine advertising in market size.

The advertising-driven online communities that exist today are certainly a different beast from their ancestors. The services they offer are much more diverse, going beyond discussion forums to include expert opinions, original content, aggregated user data and other nifty stuff. And of course there are also all kinds of 'commonspace sites' that aren't communities at all, at least in the traditional sense: consumer rating sites like Deja.com and ePinions.com, and 'consumer ASPs' like eGroups and Blogger. File-sharing networks like Hotline include banner ads in the client software itself (a model that the venerable e-mail program Eudora has also adopted).

Many of these changes stem from the emergence of the Web itself. But some changes are driven by the introduction of advertising, or at least by the traditional media culture of which advertising is a part. Many commercial online 'communities' place a stronger emphasis on one-way, broadcast-style content than on people-to-people connections. This may be because it's what 'we,' the passive Web-surfing audience, really want from Web sites. But it's more likely that this shift is driven by the need to sell ads. Ad buyers understand one-way media and feel comfortable with it because the site owners are in full control of the content. There is virtually no chance of their ad appearing next to some unmoderated yob ranting about how the world is flat and controlled by the Masons, or next to some activist's claim that the advertiser at the top of the page is an unethical slavedriver who employs child labourers in India.

Take iVillage.com for example. The site is the digital equivalent of a supermarket check-out magazine. Most of the content is from columnists and experts writing about astrology, beauty tips and fad diets. And as we saw in a previous chapters, iVillage's discussion forums are just as open to abuse and hacker humour as they are to constructive community building. The ads on the site (which provide 75% of iVillage's revenue[4]) definitely fit the traditional media bill as well. The last time we visited the site, the first thing we saw looked like a banner version of a weight-loss fantasy ad from the *National Enquirer* — 'I dropped 27 pounds! I feel great! Lose 27 pounds in by September 17! Click here!' And then there was the Clinique 'Zits Happen! But they don't have to happen to you!' ad. Jesus wept.

There is no question that this kind of one-way niche content with a little bit of commonspace sprinkled on top brings in traditional advertisers. The revenue is there. But is it an online media model that will last?

The revenue is thoro. But io it on online media model that will last?

One-way media isn't going to disappear. In fact, we will always need professional journalism and entertainment as a part of our overall media mix. But the space available to one-way media is already shrinking. Statistics show that people are spending more time communicating with each other online than they are sitting in front of the TV. So online companies that want to survive as leaders in the one-way space will also need to strengthen their many-to-many components — and to do a better job of it than iVillage.

Death of a salesman

The perils of setting up shop with a smug 'I-don't-need-no-stinkin'-commonspace' attitude are well demonstrated by the story of Time Warner's Pathfinder site. Pathfinder was supposed to be a one-stop umbrella brand for Time Warner's magazines, and a source of new subscription revenues. But the site fell prey to the usual problems encountered by sites that don't take the Web's strengths and weaknesses into consideration. As a gateway, it failed miserably: 98% of the people who used the site at all went directly to the individual magazines instead of passing through the home page.[5] Pathfinder was also criticized for presenting content recycled from its print magazines rather than new or simultaneous content. From its creation in 1994 until its demise in the spring of 1999, Time Warner spent over $15 million annually on the poorly designed, bug-ridden site, but has been too embarrassed to divulge its final losses.[6] From the beginning, many of the people immersed in Internet culture had predicted this turn of events. 'What you are doing is expensive and doesn't work online,' they had insisted. Time didn't listen and failed.

Increasingly, it's become obvious that companies focussed on one-way media with a little bit of community jerry-rigged on the side are struggling to stay afloat. In June 2000, Salon laid off 13 employees and cut editorial costs by 20%,[7] and its stock has been hovering around a miserable $2 for months. Similar stories fill dot-com death watch sections of sites like Fucked Company <www.fuckedcompany.com> and The Industry Standard <www.thestandard.com>.

Our bet is that the smart advertisers (and investors) will move to sites more deeply immersed in commonspace. In other words, they will move to places like Slashdot that connect users to each other around a core of serious, rich, focussed content, and connect advertisers with a smart, loyal, gadget-buying audience. Such sites are incredibly sticky: users stay loyal to them for a long time, and they come back regularly. More importantly, these sites have the respect of their users. When you visit a site like Slashdot or Blue's News or Ultima Online, you aren't just supporting a company that provides media; you are also supporting a community about which people feel collective ownership and involvement. A company that chooses to advertise on such a site may find themselves on the receiving end of some of this respect as well.

There is no question that advertising is one of the major revenue streams for online media. The hanging question really is, which sites will get the lion's share of the considerable — but still finite — supply of ad dollars? Jupiter Communications predicts that people will receive in excess of 950 Internet-based marketing messages per *day* by 2004.[8] In this environment, what will we pay attention to — well-conceived messages from people who are a part of the communities we build and believe in, or vapid banners sitting next to the weather report and the horoscope?

Become a tool merchant

eBay is providing
the social glue that
holds the bazaar
together.

If membership and advertising are the models supporting the majority of online communities, selling tools and services are the driving energy behind much of the rest of commonspace. There is huge money in simply being *the* platform of choice for a given sector.

The obvious example is eBay. eBay doesn't sell anything. In fact, eBay doesn't even provide transaction-processing services. Users have to find these themselves (which explains the rise of PayPal, rapidly emerging as *the* platform for small financial transactions). Rather, eBay is the infrastructure for the Internet bazaar that brings buyers and sellers together. The spaces it creates for tens of thousands of other people to sell are much more than sterile slots in a mall. eBay is providing the social glue that holds the bazaar together — ratings systems, discussion forums, and a loose police force. It is this social connection that pulls both buyers and sellers to eBay, as it is the most important component of the bazaar.

Providing the platform and the social glue for commonspace commerce is incredibly lucrative. For every auction, eBay takes between 1.25 and 5 percent of the sale price. Almost $3 billion in goods were sold in eBay auctions in 1999, with eBay taking a cut of every dollar.[9]

It's exactly this kind of opportunity that spurred the recent huge expansion of vertical B2B marketplaces. Companies like VerticalNet are essentially eBays for industry. They provide the social and technological infrastructure that enables the bazaar, and that has the potential to turn markets back into conversations. The expected market of B2B is expected to be $6.3 trillion by 2004.[10] However, a lot of players have their eyes on this very, very tall pile of money. As the rise of industry-backed exchanges has demonstrated, everyone suddenly wants to be a B2B marketplace. Only some will survive.

No ASP is an island

The market for commonspace tools and services goes well beyond the world of trading and transactions. People need intranets, discussion forums, databases and other kinds of other applications to support their online activities. These tools are the raw material of commonspace infrastructure: everyone has to have them in some fashion or other.

Increasingly, these services are being provided by Application Service Providers (ASPs), companies that 'rent' software, doing all of the hosting and technical work for you. The problem with early ASPs was that most of their solutions were completely siloed. For example, if you set up a team workspace on a site like HotOffice, Lotus Instant Teamroom or Instinctive eRoom, you were limited to working within that space. These tools were useful if everyone in the team was working only on one project and didn't already have their own intranet. But for people working across projects and companies, these services are a real nightmare. They don't talk to other tools very easily, which means that individuals need to be working within a variety of different spaces at once. This goes against the diversity and interoperability principles of commonspace: people want their information flexible, and they want it in the environments they use every day.

Thankfully, companies such as b2bScene <www.b2bscene.com> are starting to realize that 'no ASP is an island,' and are creating more flexible tools and infrastructures in response. At one level, b2bScene is just a rentable intranet company providing project management and workflow tools. But b2bScene also recognizes that the two-way flow of information between diverse systems is essential if you want to keep the attention of your users. People with b2bScene accounts can not only collaborate across multiple projects, but they can also pull in information from external intranets and the Internet using XML. Likewise, people with their own existing Live Link intranets can join b2bscene projects using an XML bridge.

This approach provides people in collaborative projects with flexibility to spare. One person on a project might have a b2bScene account. Their b2bScene login screen could include the tasks and progress reports for the project in question, as well as the weather, a Slashdot news summary, and information on five other projects. Other people on the same project may never even log in to b2bScene, but the tasks for the project will show up in their existing intranet accounts all the same. The result is a degree of fluidity that people need as they work with increasingly diverse and complex information, often across the boundaries of companies.

The revenue models for ASP services are often similar to those used by online communities — advertising or monthly fees. On the advertising-driven side, 'consumer ASPs' like eGroups.com tack ads not only onto the onsite collaboration tools, but also onto the top of every piece of e-mail that

The revenue models for ASP services are often similar to those used by online communities.

Rentable intranets, like b2bScene's version of Live Link have many applications, including the writing of books like this one.

list members post (unless you pay them to stop the ads, a process that seems to be deliberately difficult). This model is likely to endure for the same reasons that advertising works on sites like Slashdot: the users are ultra-loyal, and the spaces ultra-targeted.

Free ASPs tend to appeal more to community groups and very small businesses than to larger groups of business users. Most people don't want to be bombarded with advertising in their private workplaces. In addition, people often worry about the security of semi-public sites like eGroups, because collaboration in commonspace often deals with subjects you don't want circulating in the broader world.

As a result, the monthly membership fee is alive and well in the ASP market. People will pay for their tools if they are efficient and trustworthy. Of course, interoperability is key, since people want the convenience of a single solution, and they do not want the hassle of paying a different fee to a different provider every month. Opening applications to the outside world using technologies like XML is the best strategy for businesses trying to meet this need.

Pull it together: Emerging models for content aggregators

Another spin on the ASP model is the connection of online tools to some sort of data or traffic aggregation service: ad servers plus market knowledge; Web publishing tools plus online marketing; development tools plus a community of developers. This kind of connection between tools and people can be an amazing way to build your business in commonspace.

Consider DoubleClick. DoubleClick is an ASP for ad delivery, providing ad servers that spit out banners onto hundred of sites. It's also an ad space broker, marketing these sites in its network to a pool of over 3000 advertisers.[11] At one level, it's just a way for advertisers to get their banners on a large number of sites quickly, and for sites to avoid dealing with advertisers directly.

But DoubleClick is also a user data and traffic aggregator. For every site in its network, DoubleClick tracks user information such as time of day, geographic location, and repeat visits to a site. It then pools this information together and uses it to target ads not only by site, but by user, on all 11,500+ sites in the network.[12] For example, if a person who has recently visited two gardening sites in the DoubleClick network shows up at the *New York Times* site, the ad server would send a gardening-related banner. From an advertiser's perspective, this aggregation-based targeting is a wet dream come true. It means ad dollars are spent much efficiently on pre-qualified consumers. In DoubleClick speak, they're 'getting the right ad to the right person.'

What turns on advertisers scares the shit out of privacy advocates and plain old Internet users.

Not surprisingly, what turns on advertisers scares the shit out of privacy advocates and plain old Internet users. In July 2000, DoubleClick purchased Abacus Direct Corporation, a direct-marketing company that maintains a database of the names, addresses, and shopping habits of 90% of American households. With this merger, it was suddenly possible for DoubleClick (in cooperation with partner sites which can positively identify users' names from their e-mail addresses) to correlate real-world names with the habits of heretofore 'anonymous' surfers.[13] This practice, called 'profiling', incensed all manner of privacy advocates, from Junkbusters to the Federal Trade Commission. The result was an intense P.R. nightmare. There was a lawsuit from California and another from Michigan. AltaVista and other partners publicly pulled out of their agreements to help DoubleClick positively identify users. Dizzy from the public uproar, the company reversed tracks and announced it will wait for the government and industry to establish privacy standards before proceeding further with profiling attempts.

Assuming that DoubleClick can make good on their promise to protect people's privacy and gain their trust, they have a commonspace business model that is destined to succeed. Used well and used honestly, DoubleClick's services might actually contribute to the conversation that makes up markets. They have the potential to give us ad information about things we want to know about, or at least about things that are mildly

While it may be an
exaggeration to
claim that a
consortium of
community
newspapers could
create a 'meta-
community
newspaper' that
could compete
with the New York
Times, it's not that
far off.

more interesting than the run of the mill banner schlock. But if DoubleClick uses its position poorly, they'll be doomed. Another huge backlash like the one early in 2000 could alienate Internet users and scare away advertisers for good.

Gimme one constellation to go

The 'constellation provider' is another possible tools-plus-aggregation model. As we said earlier, aggregation of information across a constellation can give a big advantage to small online players by allowing them to scale up to compete with much bigger competitors. While it may be an exaggeration to claim that a consortium of community newspapers could create a 'meta-community newspaper' constellation that could compete with the *New York Times*, it's not that far off from the truth.

As this kind of collaboration among sites grows, companies that provide the publishing tools and people connections will have a real opportunity. At Web Networks, we had to teach ourselves to see the opportunities when the old-style community membership model had started to decline. With the Action Applications, we began providing people with the Web publishing tools they wanted to maintain their sites. At the same time, we equipped them with the means to gather their information together into constellations. This made it possible for local unions to swap information with the national federation, and for employment training groups to swap course and events listings across town — all through automated constellation channels. Of course, much of this information also fed back into the main Web Networks portal site. Thus both the main site and the constellations were able to act as traffic aggregators.

Combining tools with aggregated content and traffic seems to be working at Web Networks. In the first two quarters of 2000, revenues shifted dramatically from ISP services to ASP-style hosting packages that include Action Applications bundled into the mix.

Aggregated people power

It's aggregated people power that makes companies like DoubleClick and Web Networks different from their competitors. There are plenty of companies that offer ad banner servers and Web-publishing tools. While the competition in these markets is fierce, most of the companies in the game focus primarily on technical services. But this isn't where the action is. Sure, everyone needs technical services. But the real purpose of these technical services is to connect people. If you can aggregate people-power up front, your tools are instantly more valuable than run-of-the-mill technical service. In DoubleClick's case, ad servers and aggregated people information are being offered to make ad targeting easier. In Web Networks' case, a basic publishing tool is being offered and to people who are willing to share content combined with an existing pool of traffic. In both cases, the companies are both selling technical services *and* people connections bundled together. This kind of bundling will be essential for successful ASPs.

Seamless integration is an essential ingredient in this market. Successful ASP services will need to blend themselves into the look, feel and structure of existing customer Web sites. Blogger <www.blogger.com>, a free weblogging service that plugs into existing Web sites, does this well. With Blogger added to your site, anyone can interact and comment on your site (à la Slashdot). The logs look like a part of the local site, but they are actually generated from Blogger's central servers. Blogger takes advantage of the 'self-interest plus common good' principle of commonspace by building content from local Blogs fed into its central 'Blog' portal and gaining a huge number of advertising channels (on user sites) in return. On the other side, users gain a high-quality weblog that appears as a tightly integrated part of their site. There is no conflict between the information appearing in two places at once. In fact, it's essential to the success of the product.

> If you can aggregate people-power up front, your tools are instantly more valuable than run-of-the-mill technical service.

It's these two factors
— aggregated
people power and
seamless
integration — that
will make the
biggest difference in
the ASP market.

No, it's not a British swear word. 'Blogger' (short for 'weblogger') is an ASP that lets you build your own weblog, no fuss, no muss.

In the end, it's these two factors — aggregated people power and seamless integration — that will make the biggest difference in the ASP market in the coming years. Surviving in commonspace will be about more than just providing technical services (even if these services are the platform for commonspace). It will be about people and the common good.

Join the collective — the business of open source

And then there is open source.

Open source sits at the center of many debates about commonspace and business. Even though it's undeniable that the open source movement can produce mind-blowing software, many people are still skeptical of the business opportunities that the model offers. How can you build a hugely successful business out of something that, in effect, you give away for free? Where's the money when the software is free? Sure, there's the gift economy and all that nice theory, but where is it happening in reality? What concrete steps are people taking to generate revenue from open source?

Where's the money when the software is free?

In *The Magic Cauldron,* Eric Raymond outlines a number of concrete business models being used to support open source development.[14] He divides these models into two basic categories:

- **Use Value** - This category covers instances where the software isn't being created for sale, but rather to meet some sort of internal need for the creator;

and

- **Indirect Sale Value** - This category covers instances where you make money selling something related to the software.

We could also add open source-based ASPs to make a third category, since some enterprising businesses have found a way to make a profit from them as well.

Use value

With use value applications, revenue isn't the issue because the people making the software aren't in the software business. They are in the hardware business, the car business, the gardening business, or any other kind of business. They just happen to be writing or contributing to software because they need it to run the business that generates their income. In this scenario, there is no money to be lost from software sales and everything to be gained from a broader community of users.

The example Raymond provides is the Apache Web server. If you want a Web server, he argues, you have three choices:

- Buy one and accept the features and programming hooks provided by the vendor (closed source);

- Write your own from scratch (your source);

- Join the Apache group (open source)[15].

By joining the Apache group, you instantly gain all the advantages of 'rolling your own server' as well as the advantages of a huge development community. For people on the techie side of the Internet, this double advantage is essential. You need a solid server as well as access to the source code to modify the Web applications that will run your business. With Netscape or Microsoft IIS, this access is limited. With Apache, you just open the hood and get greasy.

The popularity of Apache is a testament to its value. It is the number one Web server on the Internet, with a 61% (and growing) market share.[16] This is over three times Microsoft's market share and almost 10 times bigger than the share of the market held by Netscape. More importantly, the people who maintain and grow the software are the people who use it. They do this because it helps them in their day-to-day work, which in turn helps them make money.

But Apache is by no means the only example. In fact, a great deal of open source software falls into this use-value category: tools written for webmasters; drivers and other software that people are unlikely to pay for separately; loss-leaders for other products; and accessories for bigger offerings.

'Aha!' you might say, 'then there really isn't any business value in open source.' Wrong. Useful and solid open source software is incredibly valuable to the businesses that create it and use it. In some cases, this value comes in the form of tools that drive the important business processes that make a company money. For example, Yahoo — and even Microsoft's HotMail service — run their businesses servers on open source tools. These tools are the foundation of their business. As a result, programmers in companies like these contribute back to the pool of open source software they have drawn from. In other cases, open source tools add value to a company's core offerings, which drives up sales.

Indiroot oalo valuo

There are also businesses that tie all of their revenue directly to their work in open source. This category includes companies like Red Hat, Caldera, Corel, VALinux, and Penguin Computing. None of them sell the open source software itself — this doesn't work well in open source culture. But they do sell a lot of hardware and expertise right around the edges of the software, which is why Raymond put these businesses in the 'indirect sale value' category.[17]

Burning Linux onto a CD, putting it in a box, and offering support is the most obvious example. This is what Red Hat, Caldera and Corel do. Each of these companies has developed their own distribution or 'flavour' of Linux, which both draws on and feeds back into other people's releases. This source diversity helps keep the software clean and bug-free (remember Linus' Law).

On the flip side, these companies provide users with services that help them 'trust' Linux — quality assurance and technical support. The price of this helpfulness ranges widely. A boxed copy of Linux with a couple of weeks of install support costs about $20. Twenty calls to the Caldera support desk costs around $1500.[18] And Red Hat's Enterprise Edition with a year of incredibly specialized support and special hooks for Oracle8i runs around $2500.[19] Support is where the gravy starts to flow.

In the end, what you are buying with your support dollar is software expertise. But this expertise doesn't drop out of the blue. More often than not, it comes from being at the core of developing and sharing a piece of open source software. Such involvement is what makes businesses like Red Hat possible.

The example that Raymond provides to illustrate this is a Web development house called Digital Creations <www.digicool.com>. In order to get venture capital, Digital Creations started peddling an object publishing tool it had developed and called Zope. The VC they ended up getting took one look at Zope and recommended that it be released as open source. Raymond writes:

By traditional software-industry standards, this looks like an absolutely crazy move. Conventional business-school wisdom has it that core intellectual property like Zope is a company's crown jewels, never under any circumstances to be given away. But the VC had two related insights. One is that Zope's true core asset is actually the brains and skills of its people. The second is that Zope is likely to generate more value as a market-builder than as a secret tool.[20]

Releasing Zope as open source has transformed it from an interesting piece of code in a private Web shop to software that hundreds of companies around the world are using to run their online business. In turn, Digital Creations has become a world expert in a good-sized consulting niche. The whole process took place in less than 18 months. Creating a consulting business of this size using a traditional marketing approach would have taken much, much longer.

Open source ASPs

Open source is the perfect match for ASPs, as they are not selling software: they are renting it. More precisely, they are selling the hosting, maintenance and support services for a specific set of applications. Whether or not the software is open source doesn't really make a difference to the service provided, since signing up with an ASP is more like buying a service than purchasing a software license. If the service works well, that's what matters.

Hence the Association for Progressive Communications' open source release of the Action Application platform. Like Web Networks, all of the APC's members are essentially ASPs providing services to non-profits and charities. To help its Internet provider members develop new offerings, the APC asked Web Networks if it would be possible to redevelop its applications as open source. There are a number of advantages to this approach. APC members can offer useful ASP services to their non-profit customers while at the same time giving back to the open source community. In addition, open source developers may pick up the code and add to it. If this happens, APC members benefit not only from improved code, but also from a bigger installed base of organizations to swap content with.

Open source success

The benefits of giving your software away for free — and being part of a larger community sharing this software — are clear: increased reliability, faster response time, and better customer service. But where is the business in it? Microsoft charges hundreds or even thousands of dollars for its products. Red Hat charges zilch if you want to download their version of Linux from their Web site. How can an open source company survive, no matter how low the overhead it is?

The answer: Don't charge for what you're hoarding (actually, don't hoard at all). Charge for what you know, and for the ways that you can use that knowledge to help others.

It may seem like a contradiction to sell software and give it away at the same time. But the Linux community has no problem with such unorthodox notions, especially while they're making profits. Analyst Prakesh Patel of WR Hambrecht predicts the Linux market will grow to $4.3 billion by 2003.[21] At the time we wrote this book, Red Hat, a company which tripled its value during its IPO, experienced a 292% sales growth over the last year, with $42.4 million in sales for the year.[22] VA Linux did $17 million in business last year, experienced 218% growth, *and* made the *Fortune* list of 'cool' companies[23] (Microsoft was notable in its absence). Scores of small companies are appearing around the world to sell open source consulting wisdom and set up open source-based systems.

But more important than the numbers is the success of open source in creating incredibly valuable, innovative and (admit it) downright cool applications. You can use Linux on your PalmPilot and other handheld computers. IBM is developing a Linux wristwatch. You can even use it to power little robots built out of Lego MindStorms. Much of this coding comes from tiny companies or 'amateurs' bitten by the open source bug. Even the projects that seem worthless or of little commercial value (such as Linux-based textmode Quake <webpages.mr.net/bobz/ttyquake/>, which

Don't charge for what you're hoarding (actually, don't hoard at all). Charge for what you know.

The path to the
best business
model of all may
be to follow
your heart — or
your fetish.

wins hands-down in the 'too much spare time' category) can act as a sort of apprenticeship, training their coders.

It can't be stressed enough that the collective model is a dramatic change from the previous norm. In many areas, collective work is producing tools better, faster and more enjoyably than closed corporate campuses. Furthermore, open source is attracting the loyalty of the brightest technical minds we have. Looking at open source, it is hard to imagine anything stopping the collective juggernaut.

Success comes from the strangest places

The fundamental elements of commonspace business are the same as those of any other business: clear, reliable revenue; vision and leadership (which may well be distributed leadership); and good customer relationships. You need all these fundamentals to create a product or service that people will want and pay for.

But commonspace businesses are different because relationships and value follow different rules. The result is that it's not always easy to see where the revenue is going to come from. The best business opportunities don't always fit our traditional frameworks. In fact, they often sneak up and sideswipe us. Financial success in commonspace can just as easily come from a hobby, or an interest, or a passion that you are driven by as it can from a 'big business idea'. The path to the best business model of all may be to follow your heart — or your fetish.

The story of Yahoo! and Netscape is now a classic fable illustrating this point. Once upon a time, two Stanford University students started Yahoo! as a part-time hobby. They posted links and aggregated content as a friendly way to help others get around the Web. There was no real business plan, no real idea of how to make money.

At about the same time, Jim Clark was founding Netscape as part of his obsessive quest to build The Next Big Thing in the computer business. To be fair, Clark and his technical compadre Marc Andressen did make The

Next Big Thing. In spades. And once they built it, they moved quickly onto the traditional path for generating revenue in the computer world: selling software (servers) and consulting services.

In the early days, Netscape looked like the 'real business' and Yahoo! looked like Amateur Hour. Netscape had significant revenue flowing in from the sale of its products and from big custom jobs with the likes of MCI. Yahoo!, on the other hand, had a measly trickle of advertising revenue. Netscape had the chance to buy Yahoo! a number of times. They could have easily plugged Yahoo! in as the default home page for millions of Netscape users. As Andressen tells it, 'We could have been Yahoo! If Netscape was to become a $100 billion company, that would have been how to do it. There was a point in time when that could have been done.'[24] But Netscape didn't regard the revenue streams from Yahoo as worth the effort. 'Stick to what you know: sell software,' Netscape's logic went.

As Homer Simpson would say, 'Doh!'

Today, Yahoo is the real commonspace success story. It aggregates information about millions of Web sites and attracting the traffic of millions of people trying to find these sites. In August 2000, it had a market capitalization of over $70 billion.[25] Netscape, on the other hand, has virtually disappeared. After being sucked into the AOL monolith, its ability to innovate (and hold the interest of the innovators) virtually came to a halt. It has since been relegated to the roles of in-house software developer (at AOL) and minor player in the Web server market (iPlanet).

Given the fact that success comes from the strangest places in commonspace, one should not discount the emergence of new, unpredicted business models. Sure, hugely successful phenomena like Napster are spinning around out in cyberspace with no clear revenue streams. But you can count on the fact that those revenues will emerge eventually, and probably in ways we don't expect. Who knows, maybe The Next Big Thing is lurking in the TAZ with the anarchists and the weirdos, in some musty basement full of gamers or, as is often the case, in some existing business just turning itself on to the power of the collective.

In the early days, Netscape looked like the 'real business' and Yahoo looked like Amateur Hour.

11 Back to the bazaar

A world where everybody is doing business with everybody else appears to be quite viable, if not always hugely inspired.
DERRICK DE KERCKHOVE, *THE SKIN OF CULTURE*

In the middle of the first year of the new millennium, the fact that more traditional businesses are making big online plays is a huge media story. Why? Because the business press seems to think it's time for a fight — a battle between 'bricks-and-mortar' businesses and 'pure-play' dot-coms. Will Sears beat Amazon? Which e-commerce site is laying staff members off today? Will 'meatspace' (the physical world) win? Or will the cybernauts from beyond the planet-of-the-bits be victorious? The continuing saga of old economy vs. new economy is looking more and more like a soap opera.

Pretty silly stuff. The real solution has nothing to do with either/or logic. 'Winning' means understanding how collectivity works and applying its principles to what you do.

Many people looking for new business ideas are realizing that commonspace doesn't have to *be* their business for it to *fuel* their business. They may be ravers making clothes and accessories to sell to others they know from the online party world. They may be filmmakers building excitement about their new independent film using online word-of-mouth. Or they may just be people running small businesses who see opportunity for their own growth in collective spaces like eBay. As in the open source model, companies don't need to make their money directly from commonspace. The contributions they make to the collective are an adjunct to what makes the money and pays the bills (or vice versa).

The real action is in the sidelines, where commonspace is just a part of an existing business or an offline business idea. There's no question that there are a lot of pure-play commonspace ideas that will make money and provide us with nifty new toys. But in the end, the market for new kinds of information, ideas and community is limited. After all, how many Bloggers and eGroups can one person use? In the meantime, we still need and want all those staid old-economy goods: food, clothing, shelter, and a decent bottle of wine. Smart businesses will take advantage of the connection between the real-world economy and commonspace to bring those goods to us. It's a win-win situation: the consumers gets the goods they want more conveniently; the merchants gain an efficient new channel for order; and everyone gets to feel like they're on the vanguard of some wild new technological era... even if they're just ordering more toothpaste.

Feed the conversation

The most important, interesting and transformative thing that you can do online is connect your customers to each other.

Connect them, and then join the conversation. Spaces for many-to-many connections creates customer feedback you can use to improve your products and drive up sales. It also provides a cheap and accurate source of market research information. And finally, it creates user trust of your brand.

Customer-to-customer discussion sites are common in the computer industry because most software companies realize they aren't the only experts on the use of their products. Users usually know as much about a given computer product as the people who made it — and often more. Tapping into this expertise creates happier customers and more *saleable* products. It may also help build the company's credibility, especially if they are

If you are

disingenuous,

you'll be

stuck with a

backlash.

openly and actively engaged in the conversation. Both of these factors can have a significant impact on increasing sales.

Double plus ungood

One factor marketers overlook far too often is honesty. If you are not open, if you are disingenuous and try to control things too tightly, you'll be stuck with a backlash. Too many companies rushing towards online discussions have missed this point — to their peril.

Shell Oil, for example, has had a public 'discussion forum' on its Web site for a couple of years now. At first glance, it seems like a good idea — a company opens itself up to the public to engage in conversation. But the rigid, hyper-controlled nature of the forums gives them a creepy, Orwellian feeling:

```
Date: March 18, 2000 10:35 AM
Author: Kris
Subject: Response to questions posed

Hi, the questions I wanted to ask have already been
posed by others. But the answers weren't posted here.
This forum seems like a one way-thing. Could we have
a more lively Q&A or at least some response from your
end? So issues could develop further.

Date: March 22, 2000 04:12 PM
Author: Webmaster, Shell International Ltd
Subject: Reply to Kris

Dear Kris: I know this forum seems a bit one way but
it is a forum, a place where people can come and air
their views or 'listen' to the views of others or
just to observe a debate without actively participat-
ing and we believe that applies equally to employees
of Shell, as much as to any of the other users. We do
not see this as a question and answer facility - for
that we have an email system. Having said that, we do
```

make strong attempts to reply to people's questions -
especially in recent months (I will be the first to
admit that when the Forum was first up and running it
was difficult to get people to change their mindset
and try to participate). Also, you may have noticed
that to certain people we have replied with the word-
ing "please see our e-mail to you". This is because
we didn't feel it was necessary to 'debate' their
query.

Hope this helps.

Date: April 09, 2000 10:30 PM
Author: connie
Subject: Posted complaint not responded to. WHY????

I specifically requested a response to the message I
posted on the forum "poor customer service and false
accusations — shell doesn't care". It has been over
two weeks now and I have still not received a response. WHY???? If I am taking the time to post a
message, someone should certainly take the time to
read the postings and respond to them.

Still waiting,

Connie

Date: April 10, 2000 10:45 AM
Author: Shell International Ltd
Subject: Response to Connie

Please see our e-mail to you.

Evidently, Shell has assigned someone the thankless task of responding to
questions from the public without actually saying anything in public.

Using a discussion forum in this way misses the point of having such a
forum in the first place, and it also misses the opportunities that forums
bring. When the forum does not allow issues to be addressed publicly and
forthrightly, the exercise won't make customers happier. Using a private,

Enough people
have held
meaningless jobs
where they've had
to produce pat
answers that they
know exactly what
a disingenuous,
over-edited
response sounds
like.

one-to-one exchange as a method for dealing with even remotely sensitive topics doesn't make a company look open and honest.

Doublespeak and gerrymandering don't work in commonspace, where every P.R. trick comes under the scrutiny of thousands of eyes. Company representatives need to speak as individuals, not as the disembodied will of the company. Moreover, they have to have the latitude to admit company short-comings. This is necessary not only to engage customers in a real conversation, but to create a context that will make customers feel comfortable talking to each other in a corporate-owned space.

Making the shift

Finding the right approach to the global conversation is a major cultural shift for most companies. The hushed tones and blizzards of memos of traditional corporate culture create an environment that encourages pat answers and brown-nosing. But people aren't fooled by this kind of garbage any more, if they ever really were. Enough people have held meaningless jobs where they've had to *produce* pat answers that they know exactly what a disingenuous, over-edited response sounds like. They don't believe in these responses from each other, so they're not going to buy them from you.

The authors of *The Cluetrain Manifesto* argue that the path to a productive culture shift lies at least partially in the use of intranets.[1] Intranets and e-mail open up people-to-people communication within a company and open doors to more honest communication with the outside world. Which is not to say that the shift to more open communications comes magically the instant you install an intranet. It's all about will and the use that people make of the available tools. Just like discussion forums for customers, intranets need to be open multi-path channels where everyone involved feels free to connect with anyone else. The minute an intranet becomes a one-way broadcast stream from management, you've wasted your money.

Not just playing around

Certain approaches to people-to-people connection add utility to products, which in turn can directly drive new sales — big new sales. Take the gaming market, worth $7.4 billion in 1999.[2] Kids' stuff? Only if the kid is playing alone. But more and more, MMPGs — Massively Multiplayer Games — dominate the market. People are looking for to play with each other. And they need someone to connect them.

id Software's Wolfenstein/Doom/Quake dynasty is the best example of the online gaming trend. The games in this series have always had a single-player mode, where players navigated through a labyrinthine environment, dueling increasingly formidable computerized foes and racing against the clock. But on December 10, 1993, Doom introduced a second mode of play that changed everything: the deathmatch. Deathmatches took place online in a many-to-many environment (yes, that's right — in commonspace), where for the first time people played the game with and against each other in real time in a 3D virtual environment. A *lot* of people. At one point, Doom was actually out-distributing Microsoft: there were 27 million official copies of Microsoft Windows in circulation, and 30 million copies of Doom.

Then in 1999, id released Quake 3: Arena, the first game in the series focussed *exclusively* on online play. It's possible to play Quake 3 in single-player mode against 'bots' (computerized enemies). But the game's entire design pivots around its online playability. Quake 3 met with wild success. While future id titles will likely go back to including large single-player components, id's already learned that sales depend on the game's openness. (A quick note on the importance of legacy material: never throw away anything in commonspace. id has not only decided that its next release will be Doom III, but it has also licensed its ancient Castle Wolfenstein title to Gray Matter Studios for redevelopment on the Quake 3 engine.[3])

id software has always maintained strong ties to the open source community, releasing Quake for Linux at a time when few other commercial de-

At one point, Doom was actually out-distributing Microsoft.

velopers wrote Linux ports of their titles, and open-sourcing the original Quake. To this day, Quake releases 1-3 all still have large, devoted communities of players, who enjoy nothing more than arguing about the superiority of their chosen platform… except maybe writing 'mods' (modifications) for them. While Quake 2 and 3 haven't been open-sourced yet, their architecture is open enough that it allows for a considerable degree of adaptation by players. It's not only possible to write scripts that enhance the playability of individual characters within the game; it's also possible to modify the look, feel and playability of the platform substantially.

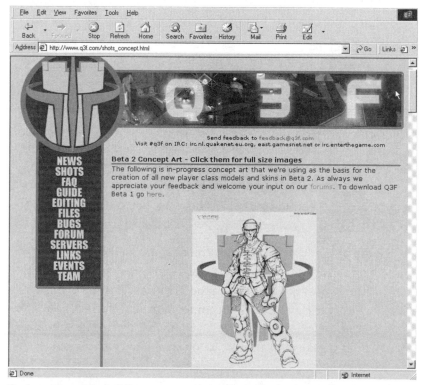

The insomniacs at Quake 3 Fortress are gearing up for their next full point release with all-new skins for the characters.

COMMONSPACE

Some of these mods have a history almost as long as the history of the game itself. Rocket Arena and Team Fortress have been ported across several versions of the Quake engine, even to games built by some of the other companies that licensed the use of the Quake engine from id (Half-Life, for example). These two mods alone represent a huge chunk of the games being played over the Quake server network at any given time, demonstrating that users value the ability to adapt them to their individual taste. Aside from the Quake 3 version, Team Fortress has also 'forked' or split into a second product, a fully independent commercial game called Team Fortress 2. So there you have it: giving things away results in more things to sell — and more buyers. Plus horrible alien screaming noises and messy explosions.

Mods are interesting for other reasons as well. Though they are built on top of commercial products, they follow the open source paradigm of construction. There is rarely (if ever) anyone working on a mod who gets paid directly for their labour. Everything is done by volunteers (which is astounding considering that the sophistication of a mod such as Rocket Arena 3 rivals that of Quake 3 itself). While a mod is in development, beta versions of the software are released to eager communities of players who'd crawl over two kilometres of broken glass for the opportunity to test new software. The online forums maintained by the mod's creators are hotbeds of discussion about everything from the uniforms the game characters wear to the core programming itself. The result is the same efficient debugging that makes true open source products work so well.

Another direct result of the proliferation of gaming mods is an increasingly large pool of highly capable, self-taught programmers who've matriculated through an apprenticeship process similar to the medieval guild model. It's every teenaged geek's dream to go to work for id or Valve or Blizzard or one of the other big gaming companies. When these companies do recruit, they're more than likely to take someone who's worked enthusiastically on a popular mod. So think twice, parents, before you put the kibosh on little Johnny and Janie's violent videogaming habit: by depriving them of their access to one of the most vibrant parts of commonspace, you may well be dooming them to a future of flipping burgers at the mall.

Electric ideas

From the moment that they realized that it was there, artists of all stripes — authors, filmmakers, video artists, musicians, performance artists, even the almost universally reviled mimes — have been extremely interested in the Internet's potential for extending their art. But with a few notable exceptions (such as Amazon.com), it's taking longer for the people who package and distribute their art to catch on.

The main reason for the distributor hesitation is that they rely on copyright to make their money. And Internet users haven't exactly kept secret their resistance to traditional notions of intellectual property. Many Net users frame the question with what's become known as the 'free speech/free beer' debate. When a user claims that a given piece of online content should be free as in 'speech,' they mean that they believe that restricting it by legislation or other means is fundamentally and morally wrong. When someone says that content should be free as in 'beer', it means that they like to get good stuff without paying for it. Most long-term Net users believe that online content should be free as in speech *and* beer. The advent of peer-to-peer networks shows that that belief is spreading, whether the gatekeepers of copyright like it or not.

There is also a large, vocal community of artists who believe that their art should circulate freely online. But most of the big entertainment conglomerates haven't done more than flirt with the thorny question of putting their vast archives of content on the Internet. And they probably won't until delivery systems complete with reasonably solid encryption and near-transparent methods for conducting small financial transactions start to appear. (AOL's purchase of Time Warner will result in a flood of new content online at some point, but probably only for AOL users.) In the meantime, the adventurous artists aren't waiting.

Most long-term Net users believe that online content should be free, as in speech and beer.

Network games provide some compelling examples of collaborative creative projects. Professional writers and musicians are contributing to the collaboratively-authored of world of online games. Cyberpunk S.F. writer Mark Laidlaw helped shape the narrative behind the incredibly popular video game Half-Life; Trent Reznor of Nine Inch Nails composed the soundtrack for Quake, and will likely be involved with the Doom III project; gloomy industrial musicians Front Line Assembly did the soundtrack for Quake 3.

This is not to say that traditional media companies don't use the Web. They do. But almost none of them understand how commonspace can work for them. Big film companies especially tend to treat the Web like traditional broadcast media and Web sites like a kind of value-added commercial. The Web is littered with expensive ghost sites that were built to promote Hollywood feature films, then immediately abandoned. Most studios probably don't even realize that they're still paying to maintain the damn things.

Book publishers have done even less online than the film companies. Sure, they have Web sites, and there have been a few hesitant forays into digital publishing on first-generation hand-held platforms like the Rocket e-Book or in downloadable PDF files. Stephen King began the serialization of a new novel online, but says he'll only finish it if enough people buy each installment — which is kind of like blackmailing your readers for every cent you can squeeze out of them. And even the plethora of online vanity publishers are living on borrowed time, because their existence relies on their authors failing to realize that they can do just as well (or better) on their own Web sites.

6300 book stores under ~~one~~ no roof

The people who've managed to make money online in the meantime are the little guys — small businesses and independents. Many small businesses caught on to the concept of commonspace early. They realized that the Web presented good opportunities not only for promotion and for

Online, it's
possible for a
diverse collection
of businesses to
merge under a
single umbrella.

extending their direct sales over the Net, but also for networking with each other to compete with their larger competitors.

One of the main reasons for this competitive edge is brand formation. Online, it's possible for a diverse collection of businesses to merge under a single umbrella site and become one brand to the end user. Umbrella sites aggregate both inventory and marketing. To the end user, everyone's inventory becomes a part of the seamless whole, because there is only one marketing voice, one brand, and one process of driving traffic.

Abebooks <www.abebooks.com>, or 'Abe' to just about everyone, is a sterling example. Founded in Victoria, British Columbia in 1995, Abe is the world's largest network of independent booksellers, with more than 6300 member store and over 20 million books listed online. By linking themselves together, used bookstores have not only created a significant resource for

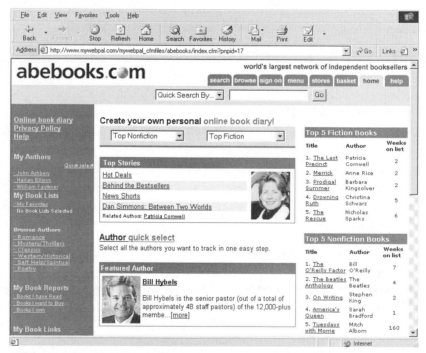

ABE has teamed up with Webpal to create a portal system for their highly successful collaborative e-commerce site for booksellers.

shoppers but also drastically reduced their own overhead by cutting down on catalogues and mailouts, activities which take up a significant chunk of a used booksellers' time. There's also the advantage of Abe's secure server, which reduces the hassle of financial transactions for the bookseller. (In fact, it's not even necessary to maintain a storefront any longer, which, believe it or not, can be the undoing of a used bookseller.)

As Abe has grown in size and sophistication, the company is also starting to offer online tools to keep their user base attentive and loyal. The site automatically generates rudimentary home pages for its users, which are customizable to a certain degree. But Abe's MyBookPal reader's diary (built through partnership with MyWebPal <www.mywebpal.com>) is the real centerpiece of their online tool offerings. Part of the function of the book diary is to act as a straightforward content publisher to feature author biographies, articles on book collecting, and reading. However, it also allows readers to build the bulk of the site's contents. Readers can use MyBookPal to view lists of all titles by a particular author, to check titles off as they read them, to review titles and read reviews written by others, and to maintain their own databases of books they own or would like to buy. Voilà: a huge swath of content that's useful to everyone.

There's no financial jiggery-pokery here either. Abe is a straight, fee-based service, without ads and markups on books sold. Abe was simply in the right place at the right time with the right idea. Over the years, it's managed to net some major deals with larger players, too. Abe supplies a large chunk of information on out-of-print books to Barnes and Noble. They also match Amazon.com users' 'wants' nightly and, like many small businesses, they sell some of their high-end items through eBay's Great Collections site.

There are some inevitable downsides to the umbrella approach, however. If the inventory database is not up to date, or the response from individual stores isn't prompt, customers will leave angry and not come back. For participating booksellers, there is the fear of losing business to other members of the collective. The answer to the first problem is administrative responsibility. The answer to the second is the bottom line for all in-

Get over your fear, or others who can get over it will beat you.

securities about commonspace: get over your fear, or others who *can* get over it will beat you.

Busking with books

Another example from the world of online publishing that's closer to home (because one of us, Darren, is currently the Editor-in-Chief) is Coach House Books <www.chbooks.com>, the only literary publisher in the world with the contents of its entire frontlist available online. Coach House, which has existed since the late 1960s, is a Canadian literary institution known for the quality of its fine print editions, and for the fact that they helped first bring authors such as Michael Ondaatje, bpNichol, Margaret Atwood and many others to the reading public.

What many people don't know about Coach House is that it's also been a haven for computer geeks for as long as there have been computers. At one time, the Linotype machine was fed instructions through a paper tape generated by early desktop computers. Furthermore, Coach House was one of the first private companies in Toronto to have its own Unix system (the old Sun minicomputer still holds up one corner of Darren's desk). SoftQuad, the software firm that authored the HotMetal HTML coding software, also began at Coach House.

The current incarnation of the press, Coach House Books, launched in 1997 with the ambition of being a publisher that existed primarily online, offering 'just-in-time' print editions based on the Web version of the text. The revenue stream was to be based on the shareware try-before-you-buy model, with customers contributing voluntary electronic 'tips' for books that they had enjoyed reading.

Even for the time, it was an optimistic approach. The number of people who buy small-press poetry and literary fiction is limited, and the number of those people who are also willing to brave the Internet to find their reading material is even smaller. The post-1995 flood of new Internet hasn't been that much help, because the new users had relatively little notion of netiquette and failed to understand that they were to pay *something* for their shareware.

In late 1998, Coach House decided to reconfigure operations so that the press played from its strength: the production of fine print editions. Their situation mirrored the quandary faced by large Internet pure-play companies now: without a bricks-and-mortar base, it's difficult to make a profit on bits alone. With the reintroduction of paper books and the securing of distribution, the finances of the press immediately began to improve. The online editions still exist, and authors are given the option of having their work online as well as in print. To this date, none of the new authors has refused to put their work online, and many of the press's famous alumni have returned with requests for their work to be placed online as well. As a publicity-generating machine, the Web site has been unparalleled in its usefulness, drawing orders for print titles from all over the world, and maintaining a high degree of journalistic interest in the press's activities. And, of course, it's still possible to tip the authors online using your credit card.

As Coach House learned more about the tricky business of integrating traditional publishing into online culture, its goals for online activities shifted from short-term sales to long-term payoffs. The press is working hard at the Canadian national level now, lobbying for the institution of a rights and licensing system for the control of royalties on electronic literature. We have already convinced the National Library of Canada to institute electronic ISBNs for online editions, a notable accomplishment. Hopefully, these measures will convince other small presses that the time to get involved with online publishing is now, which should give all parties concerned greater leverage with both business and government.

Coach House's other, more localized long-term goal is to establish a significant archive of electronic literature that can be used to assemble customized electronic reading kits for colleges and universities. In the meantime, the Coach House Web site itself is evolving to take better advantage of the kinds of tools that we've been discussing in this book, such as dynamically generated news pages, publishing forums, and automated newsletters. It's a slow process for small, cash-poor businesses. But at least we get to make the rules from the ground up, which is more interesting and ultimately more rewarding than waiting for someone else to solve the problem for us.

Open source art

One step further down the scale to real DIY publishing is Jim Munroe's No Media Kings site <www.nomediakings.org>. Munroe, a former editor of *Adbusters* and the author of several novels, decided to dump his contract with Rupert Murdoch (the eponymous 'media king') and HarperCollins to go the route of the stone-cold indie publisher for his new opus, *Angry Young Spaceman*. His Web site offers the rationale for his decision, advice about how to become an indie publisher — you can use his 'No Media Kings' logo and imprint, if you like — some chunks of his other writing, thoughts on 'applying the spirit of open source to fiction distribution,' and the entire text of *Angry Young Spaceman* in plain text, RTF or PalmPilot versions. While the No Media Kings Web site isn't really 'commonspace' (or an open source project), it's certainly a road sign pointing potential author-publishers in the right direction.

And then there's the music industry. The frenzy of lawsuits around Napster speaks volumes for those who want to enforce the status quo. But are there artists who actually want their music circulating online, artists who understand what commonspace is all about? Of course there are.

Chuck D, the leader of Public Enemy, arguably the most politically significant hip-hop group of all time, is the Morpheus of online music. His Web sites, RapStation <www.rapstation.com> (whose motto is 'The Revolution will not be Televised, it will be Digitized, Break free from the Matrix, The New music Industry is Here!') and Bring the Noise <www.bringthenoise.com> advocate circulating music on the Internet, whether on the Web or on file-sharing networks.

Rapstation is commonspace done in a hip-hop stylee. And many musicians believe direct interaction with fans is the most revolutionary aspect of music on the Web. 'Instead of being just consumers, the new audience is composed of participants,' says Chuck D.[4] His site features extensive essays and reviews on file-sharing technologies, video clips of pertinent news events, and streaming, downloadable hip-hop audio and video content. Chuck himself is an eloquent spokesman, who has publicly debated record industry representatives and anti-Napster artists. But he also puts his money where his mouth is: Public Enemy was the first multi-platinum act to release an album online before it was in the stores.

While it's not clear how Chuck D plans to cash in, Rapstation clearly has commercial intent. Its partners include House of Blues, RealNetworks, Napster and Tucows, among many others — an impressive, commercially-driven roster. And there are significant numbers of banner ads on the site. All the same, it seems as if Rapstation is an open source business model waiting to happen. Something around the edges of the site will likely emerge to draw in the revenue. Whatever Chuck and his cohorts plan to sell in the future, the site's infamy will no doubt give them the P.R. they need to drive their business.

As an interesting footnote, it remains to be seen what will happen with Fairtunes <www.fairtunes.com>. This brand-new, tiny startup, launched by two students from Winnipeg, is betting its livelihood on the collective conscience of the file-sharing community. The premise of the site is that digital music users will use Fairtunes to voluntarily remit tips for artists after obtaining their MP3s elsewhere. Response is small but measurable (a banner at the top of the page lists total current contributions) — about what we'd expect after the response to the tip model experiment at Coach House. Our feeling is that Fairtunes *could* work if there was something to drive P2P network users through the site, such as a search engine or forum. But without the connections, without the people, without even the acknowledgement of anyone in the recording industry, chances of success are slim.

Public Enemy was the first multi-platinum act to release an album online before it was in the stores.

Edmunds has
extended the
usefulness of their
car-buying know-
how by putting
most of it online.

Write a book — together

Another way to connect commonspace to the old-fashioned paper book is to find people online to help you write one.

This is exactly what the editors at Edmunds.com have done. Edmunds is the Web site run by the authors of Edmunds' *New Car Prices and Reviews*, Edmunds' *New Truck Prices and Reviews*, and Edmunds' *Used Car Prices and Reviews*. The site contains virtually the entire text of these publications. But it also contains a number of incredibly active discussion forums, where over 450,000 users debate the relative merits of and provide opinions on all aspects of purchasing and maintaining automobiles and other motor vehicles. These discussion forums are what make the site so useful. As with other 'community knowledge bases,' any one posting is unlikely to change the world. But when considered as an archive, the total postings from all of Edmunds' users are an incredibly valuable resource.

With their Web site, Edmunds has extended the usefulness of their car-buying know-how by putting most of it online. They have also created a thriving online community of people who want to talk about cars. By pulling user-generated content into editorial content, the observations of community members feed back into content for the both the site and the printed books. Information from the site's forums is fed into updated versions of the books (after fact-checking by Edmunds' editors). In the stores, the books continue to sell and go stale, sell and go stale, sell and go stale. The community on the site makes it easier to keep up with the cycle. It's an almost perfect example of commonspace fuelling a non-commonspace business model.

But think for a second about the value cycle. It all started with the printed car guides, which existed well before most of us had ever heard of the Internet. From a publishing industry perspective, car guides are an agreeable business proposition. The books are easy to produce, because only a part of the initial research that goes into the book changes every year, and readers writing letters to Edmunds flag many of the changes. In addition, the books are easy to sell, because insider advice on the ins and outs of a $30,000 purchase is well worth the $8.99 cover price. Finally, because the dusty old copies of the car guides on your bookshelf are woefully dated by the time you are ready to buy your next car, you'll probably buy another one. This formula has worked so well that Edmunds has built a car-buying advice empire with a small handful of titles.

And then along comes the Internet. Depending on your perspective, the Internet could be seen as a threat to a business like Edmunds. Fact-based reference information is available for free on the Internet and has the potential to undercut books such as the ones that Edmunds produces. Luckily, Edmunds didn't see it that way. Instead, it saw the opportunity to create a little bit of commonspace that would both generate its own revenue and feedback into continued book sales.

To their credit, a few of the old-style consumer opinion sources have already grasped the value of opinion aggregation and have incorporated it into their operations. A business like Edmunds giving away its most valuable intellectual assets might at first seem insane, but the result is a genuine win-win situation. Users of the site not only have access to the text of a well-researched book, but they also gain access to the living knowledge source that they themselves help to create. In return for providing its readers with a platform to connect, Edmunds obtains free research for the next edition of its print books. Commonspace makes it all possible. It also establishes a big foothold in the online advice world, which may eventually supplant a large portion of the consumer advice world.

eBay: Home of the little guy

Businesses can take advantage of the collective infrastructure of the Internet to reach out to new markets in new ways. eBay is king of this type of venture. eBay offers a platform that allows small businesses to take advantage of commonspace, and for buyers and sellers to connect to each other. But what does this look like from the other side? What does commonspace mean to the people who are actually doing the selling?

In return for providing its readers with a platform to connect, Edmunds obtains free research for the next edition of its print books.

Despite the big-box store trend, most people don't turn their noses up at small-time retailers. Corner vegetable shops, liquidators and surplus stores, even people hawking used junk by the side of the road are attractive because we enjoy the experience of buying from them. They know their chosen fields. They have interesting stuff. They are willing to make deals. In many ways, they are our last connection to the traditions of the bazaar and the open marketplace.

For better of for worse, this kind of business doesn't scale well. The quirky neighborhood antique shop doesn't work as a chain. The decor and layout lose their charm when you try to reproduce them on a large scale (and inventory becomes a nightmare). The expertise of the owner and intimate staff is impossible to replicate. There are, of course, people who try to overcome this by creating chains of quaint housewares stores and the like, but you might as well shop at IKEA where you can revel in the size and impersonal service.

In some ways, the dichotomy between small-quirky and big-boxy is a good thing. People like small, quirky stores enough to keep them alive and provide a fertile ground for new businesses. In turn, the shops make neighbourhoods neighbourly and cities interesting. But for the small business owners who make up the urban bazaar, the limitations of being a neighbourhood operator can be frustrating. Just think: you have all this cool stuff filling the basement of your shop and only a few people to sell it to.

This is where eBay and other kinds of commonspace selling come into the picture. With a collective market, you don't have to become a box store or a sterile franchise to reach more customers. Rather, you just take a slice of what you are selling in your store and put it up for auction. This route isn't just a way to sell at a distance; it's a way to extend your participation in the bazaar. There are discussion forums and rating systems that enable the conversation of the market. Some people say complimentary things, others say nasty things. New buyers make their judgements. The marketplace whizzes on.

At a practical level, collective selling provides a kind of marketing that is better than anything a small business could afford. Small businesses using eBay extend their sales while spending nothing on marketing. The people, infrastructure and trust systems are already in place. When you consider that marketing makes up 25% of the budget of a company like Amazon,[5] the benefits are self-evident.

None of this is to say that surfing around eBay is as pleasant as wandering about the local antique store. However, it is important to realize that these small businesses are finding a way to grow their revenues through collective online markets. This is interesting because the kinds of businesses that we love to wander around in often have a hard time sustaining themselves. If online auctions and similar tools help these people stay in business, that's good for both the business owners and their customers.

Collective markets also have an impact on the actual make up of places like eBay. While the bulk of people selling in online auctions are still individuals, the bulk of the goods sold come from some kind of small business. Of the 4 million items on eBay in any given day, the top 20 sellers are responsible for 72,000 items and the top 38,000 sellers are responsible for 2.7 million items.[6] In other words, small businesses are driving much of what happens in online auctions.

However, the bulk of the small businesses online are not quirky shopkeepers, but liquidators and collectors who rely mainly on online auctions as their sales channel. These are the people who buy truckloads of old Atari cartridges with the sole intent of selling them on eBay. There is nothing wrong with this, of course. It's actually another example of commonspace-enabled small business. Scouring garage sales for Star Wars figures and hawking them online may seem bit banal, but it's probably a hell of a lot more fun and lucrative than slinging coffee at Starbucks.

Commonspace = e-commerce for the rest of us

Someone should market a T-shirt that reads 'I survived the dot-com revolution and all I got was this lousy Web site.' They'd make a fortune, because

Don't despair:
Luke had the Force,
and you've got
commonspace.

the heady early days of startups that were showered with VC money because of a Web site are gone forever. And good riddance. There's nothing more annoying than watching some group of clueless assholes blow millions of dollars on an idea that was doomed from the start. (Well, okay, sometimes it's a little entertaining to watch them crash and burn — witness Fucked Company.)

From now on, success will come by and large from smart expansions into commonspace by existing businesses — or from new businesses that understand how the fuel of commonspace can drive their success, no matter what they are selling. Sure, there will still be killer apps and instant millionaires. But the window for such opportunities is becoming narrower. And as the big corporate conglomerates get their acts together online, the opportunities for a small company to dominate a niche will also become scarce.

Don't despair: Luke had the Force, and you've got commonspace. If your business can't dominate its online niche alone, then join forces with your customers, your allies, maybe even your same-sized competitors. You'll all save money, expand markets, find new revenue streams, and get rivers of cheap P.R. Form the Megazord, and kick some rubbery monster-suited ass.

Building the public square

Markets and bureaucracies, as well as unplanned and planned cities, are concrete instances of a more general distinction: self-organized meshworks of diverse elements versus hierarchies not only coesist and intermingle, they constantly give rise to one another.

MANUEL DE LANDA

Jump back to the town commons for a minute. Imagine a vibrant social jumble filling the square, drawing everyone in with its buzz, diversity and wonder. There is the bazaar with small producers and craftspeople hawking their wares. In the buildings surrounding the square, there are the shops, restaurants and offices. Beside the marketplace, there is a small park filled with kids from the local soccer league kicking the ball around. There are also people debating and pamphleteering around the public lectern. And underlying it all is the town square itself — owned in common and maintained by the town government.

The town commons weaves together commerce, civic participation and community-building. As in the rest of society, we need *all* of these pieces to make the Internet whole. In some regards, we already have them. We have the bazaar and the businesses lining the square. We've certainly no lack of recreational activities. And you may even find someone up on the lectern

Governments and
NPOs are full of
control freaks. And
we all know what
happens to control
freaks in
commonspace.

if the issue is something like cyberfreedom or privacy. But that's it. The more general public and civic parts of the Internet town square are missing.

Luckily, this is starting to change. Smart governments and non-profits are starting to see that commonspace was made for them. If your job is to serve the public, why not sieze a technology that lends itself to the common good? And if your role is to encourage democracy and accountability, who better to join forces with than the collective mind of commonspace? Clearly, there is an opportunity to build a public commons online.

The tortoise and the hare

Government and non-profit pursuit of the public commons online is much like efforts of the hare in the old fable: starting out fast, running out of steam early.

The civic world was there at the start of the Internet race. The U.S. government actually invented the damn thing[1] (although for all the wrong reasons, and even then probably by accident). Non-profits were on the scene quickly thereafter, starting up global computer networks like the Association for Progressive Communications by the mid-1980s and using online communities to organize for events like the Rio Earth Summit in 1992. But despite this early start, both the government and non-profit worlds have taken a nap by the roadside.

Part of the problem is that traditional non-profit organizations and governments are by-and-large conservative animals. They tend to be averse to risk and are rigid adherents to their own notions. Plans are made in advance and then processed to the point of blandness. Governments and NPOs are full of control freaks. And we all know what happens to control freaks in commonspace.

Governments are especially susceptible to this disease. There has been plenty of rhetoric about open government and improved customer service in government. But this is more often than not just wishful talk (or cynicism, take your pick). There are few jurisdictions where you can even register for your driver's license online, to say nothing of connecting with your elected officials. In a 1999 G8 publication on democracy and online services, the Government of Canada's main webmaster reflects on how most bureaucrats respond to the Internet:

A standard pattern of questions awaits departments and agencies, as they open their storefront on the information highway. Should they plan for two-way traffic? Are there tools that allow for public participation without hijacking resources? Can departments avoid having their Web sites become soapboxes for organized interest groups?[2]

The timidity of this approach would have you believe that any attempt to fiddle with the Internet might accidentally unleash the four horsemen of the apocalypse. It's not as though they might want to use technology to actually *encourage* participatory democracy.

The good news is that at least a few elected officials and the bureaucrats are passionate about the democratic potential of the Internet. And the non-profit world has some real visionaries who get the power of the collective and are running with it (they tend to be the non-profit activist types). Like the tortoise, these folks are plugging away in a solid, honest effort to build a public commons online. And they're headed for the finish line first.

10 Downing Street, online

The first thing that comes to mind when you ask people about the civic use of the Internet is governance. Democracy. Access to decision making. Access to the people *we* elected, remember?

The 'online democracy' experiments that have garnered the biggest public attention tend to be 'talk-to-the-politician forums.' While the approach varies, these are basically Internet-based dialogues between the people who make decisions and the people who elected them.

A now-classic example is Tony Blair's BBC television appearance in 1998. As special guest on Sir David Frost's weekly interview show, Blair opened

The good news is that at least a few elected officials and the bureaucrats are passionate about the democratic potential of the Internet.

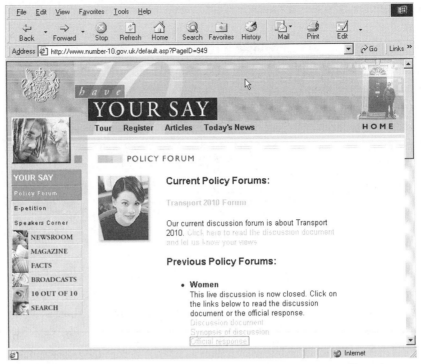

have YOUR SAY

Tour   Register   Articles   Today's News   HOME

YOUR SAY

Policy Forum

E-petition

Speakers Corner

NEWSROOM

MAGAZINE

FACTS

BROADCASTS

10 OUT OF 10

SEARCH

POLICY FORUM

Current Policy Forums:

Transport 2010 Forum

Our current discussion forum is about Transport 2010. Click here to read the discussion document and let us know your views

Previous Policy Forums:

- **Women**
  This live discussion is now closed. Click on the links below to read the discussion document or the official response.
  Discussion document
  Synopsis of discussion
  Official response

Internet

The 'Have Your Say' page of the Number 10 Downing Street site links to current discussions, summaries of previous topics, and official responses to the specific questions raised in the discussions. Not bad for government.

himself up to questions sent live via an Internet chat room. While this is still pretty distant by Internet standards, it seemed to come from a genuine desire to open up a mass dialogue. Blair really seemed interested in finding out what would happen if he threw himself out into commonspace. Unfortunately, most of the questions were of the 'What do you eat for breakfast?' variety that fill the Fleet Street tabloids.

Despite the shallowness of the Frost interview, it seems that Blair and his people were bitten by the commonspace bug. The Number 10 Downing Street Web site <www.number-10.gov.uk> now includes two heavily used discussion spaces. The first section, called Speaker's Corner, provides an open free for all on some two dozen political issues. The second, called Public Forum, opens up specific questions (women, parenting, transportation) for a period of time, and then provides a follow-up paper from the Prime Minister or a member of Cabinet. While this isn't direct politician-to-citizen contact, it sure beats the commonspace endeavours of most other governments. Both the White House site <www.whitehouse.gov> (not <www.whitehouse.com> which is, amusingly, a particularly tawdry porn site) and the Government of Canada site <www.gc.ca> limit their citizen interaction to 'contact us' sections where you are encouraged to send 'questions and comments' to the government. Screw that. Where Blair is pointing the way, other politicians have been slow to follow.

Open the committee room doors

The more interesting and concrete examples of the civic use of common-space tend to be lesser known and focus on lower levels in the decision-making process, such as municipal referenda, communications regulations and local elections. In addition, the successful examples of citizen engagement online usually involve a mix of government, citizens' groups and business. The people behind these efforts know that creating a public commons means creating synergies between all sectors of society.

One good example is the 1998 new media policy hearings held by the Canadian Radio-Television and Telecommunications Commission (the equivalent of the FCC). The purpose of these hearings was to gather industry and public opinion on the future of Canadian communications regulations within the rapidly changing context of new media. Given the topic, it seemed appropriate to open up the proceedings to people via the Internet.

Normally, CRTC hearings are formal, rigid affairs held face-to-face, somewhere in an office building across the river from the nation's capital in the City of Hull. As a result, these hearings tend to be the domain of paid policy wonks who are already located in Ottawa and corporate lobbyists with big travel budgets. In addition, there are enough rules and regula-

Both the White House site and the Government of Canada site limit their citizen interaction to 'contact us' sections.

tions surrounding attendance to make a citizen's head spin. Anyone who wants to can speak at one of these hearings, but would they actually feel *welcome*? It's unlikely. 'Average citizens' are rarely seen in standing in front of the commissioners sharing their ideas.

The CRTC tried to change this by setting up Internet discussion forums to include as a part of the public record of its 1998 new media hearings. Held over the course of two months in the fall of 1998, these forums provided any Canadian with Internet access an opportunity to offer their ideas to the CRTC. The CRTC's press release announcing the hearings said this about the online forums:

> In addition to these formal procedures, the McLuhan Program E-Lab will host a New Media Forum website on behalf of the CRTC to enhance and extend the means whereby the public can engage in the discussions.[3]

While this shouldn't be taken as an indicator of mass, Internet-enabled democracy, it is certainly a far cry from a version of democracy that relies on rigid meetings in the capital city, or even from Tony Blair talking about his breakfast.

The interesting thing is that it wouldn't have happened without the involvement of independent citizen's groups and, to a lesser degree, businesses interesting in supporting the process. While the online portion of the hearings was included in the public record, the Web forum was actually run as an arm's-length event by two organizations with an interest in media policy. The byDesign eLab and the McLuhan Program in Culture and Technology set up the forums and facilitated the discussions on a donated server in Toronto. Both of these organizations believe strongly in the value of the Internet in democratic decision-making. Building on and because of their track record for running other online forums, eLab and the McLuhan Program convinced the CRTC to let them run this semi-official forum.

At a technical level, setting up a Web-based discussion forum is easy: just install the software and customize it a little. It's a day's work, maybe. But getting a government body and a non-profit to agree on the civic 'rules of engagement' is a much more complex matter. Culture, not technology, is the real stumbling block.

As a result, the biggest issue with this project was how to manage the on-line forums. The CRTC's normal procedures are quite rigid, whereas Internet communication is quite fluid. Coming to an agreement on how to run the forums to meet the needs of both of these cultures was a challenge. How would the discussion be moderated (minimally)? Who would be able to post (anyone)? To bridge the two cultures, the people at the eLab developed a set of 'civil rules' to guide the forum:

1. This space is intended only for the discussion of new media policy issues.

2. Contributors are solely responsible for their messages.

3. When you post messages, please stay on topic.

4. Advertising is not allowed.

5. Forum moderators are responsible for facilitating discussions.

From the perspective of an Internet user, these rules seem like common-sense netiquette. From the perspective of a government policy discussion, it's actually quite a radical step: they are fairly loose rules that open up a lot of space for conversation. It's steps like these that bring us closer to the creation of a public commons online.

Electric politician tricks

Another worthy example is Minnesota eDemocracy <www.e-democracy.org>. Minnesota eDemocracy is an independent citizen's organization whose goal is to facilitate dialogue between voters and politicians. Started during the 1994 elections for Governor and U.S. Senate, the organization set up a number of e-mail-based debates and citizen-to-citizen discussion forums. Given the fact that broad public use of the Internet was still in its infancy at the time, these discussions were extremely successful.

Like businesses, politicians and government officials would do well to get down off their big white horses and join the conversation.

Candidates and citizens chatted back and forth in e-mail on the major issues — taxes, crime, state's rights. More importantly, people used the project's mailing lists to talk to each other about what was going on in the debates (and the election in general). This communication created a broad dialogue about the election issues and helped people on opposing sides to understand each other. In turn, politicians gained access to a complex pool of ideas they could use when they moved into office.

As eDemocracy organizer Steven Clift observes, citizens are not only disconnected from government; they are also disconnected from each other.[4] This social fragmentation creates polarization and weakens democracy. In the Minnesota experiment (which has continued with all elections since 1994), adding commonspace to elections helped overcome some of this citizen-to-citizen disconnection. Much like the idea of connecting customers to each other in the business world, conversations in civic spaces are much more useful if people are talking as peers. Like businesses, politicians and government officials would do well to get down off their big white horses and join the conversation. Get it, Kemosabe?

The digital divide

So: creating the public commons online means connecting citizens to each other. The question is, how?

The first part of the answer, especially for governments, is to stay out of the way for a while. Commonspace is an organic phenomenon. If experiments in civic commonspace are left to grow on their own, many of them will become bricks in the public commons. Most of these experiments are still in their infancy. We need to step back and let them grow. But active involvement from government and non-profits at some stage is essential. The commons will not emerge completely on its own.

One key factor in all of this is what's known as 'the digital divide' — the gap between those who are connected and enfranchised online, and those who are not. Increasingly, governments (and some private foundations) have started to see a role for themselves in bridging this digital divide. If this role is thought through properly, it's a good role for government. Many citizens — and sectors of society — will connect themselves. But assisting people with limited resources is essential to the broader goal of connecting citizens to each other.

The problem is that many governments are stuck on the simplistic notion that bridging the digital divide is mainly about connecting people to the network. Amidst the hubbub of the mid-1990s Internet explosion, U.S. Republican representative Newt Gingrich quite seriously promoted handing out laptops to schoolchildren as the solution to poverty.

In Canada, a 'Connecting Canadians' strategy has been at the core of national government policy since at least 1998.[5] For the most part, the Canadian program focuses on hooking up basic connections. For example, the Community Access Program, which operates within the 'Connecting Canadians' strategy, provides money for rural communities to set up public access Internet sites in libraries and other public spaces. Similarly, the VolNet program funds the purchase of basic computers, modems and dial-up Internet connections for non-profit organizations.

While these efforts are well-intentioned, they miss the point. If the last hundred years of media history means anything, we can be fairly certain that the market knows how to get basic media devices into the hands of almost everyone who wants them. Why? Because media devices like television and radio are excellent methods of getting messages to markets. For all its commonspace potential, the Internet will inevitably be a mass-marketing tool as well. This in turn means it's pretty likely that everyone who wants access to the Internet will have it within reasonably short order. Just consider that Internet access in Canada has jumped from 23% in 1996 to a projected 70% by the end of 2000.[6]

Whether filling in the other 30% happens in 5 years or 15 is not important. Ubiquitous network connections for all who want them will happen, at least in North America and Europe. In this context, handing out hardware and connectivity is pretty much wrongheaded. It will neither bridge the digital divide nor will it connect citizens to citizens in any meaningful way.

Newt Gingrich quite seriously promoted handing out laptops to schoolchildren as the solution to poverty.

For all its commonspace potential, the Internet will inevitably be a mass-marketing tool as well.

Much of the gruntwork of building these kinds of bridges over the digital divide comes directly from communities.

People not wires

The real opportunity to bridge the digital divide comes at the level of people not wires. For example, the civic sector is vital to the buzzing, socially-connecting energy of the town commons. Yet most non-profits do not have the resources needed to move the little-league soccer schedule or the pamphleteering or the delivery of community services onto the electronic commons. They need resources and advice to help them take what they do and make it work online. This means developing applications, training people in strategy, and animating community involvement. It involves people and the connections between people.

Much of the gruntwork of building these kinds of bridges over the digital divide comes directly from communities themselves or from civic organizations. For example, the Center for Civic Networking has worked with small businesses in rural areas of Hawaii, North Carolina, Ohio and New Mexico to set up a collaborative retail site called The Public Web Market <development.civicnet.org/webmarket>. The aim of this project is to create a platform that bridges the gap between small rural businesses and people in urban areas. The vendors on the site offer a huge variety of 'regional bounty' — gourmet pickled peppers, specialty pasta, Navajo clothing, Hawaiian pareos, hand-crafted pens and euchre sets, miniature wooden vases, museum-quality gourds, family-farmed macadamia nuts, Kona coffee, and rare books. Through the Public Web Market, the people who create these products gain access to urban markets all over the U.S., and even all over the world. Thus the Center for Civic Networking has been able to link up rural people with large markets — which is a heck of a lot more useful than free laptops.

Luckily, there are a few governments and foundations who also understand the difference between hardware and people-ware. One example is an Ontario government program we've worked with called Volunteer @ction.online.[7] V@O focuses on the applications and projects that connect volunteers and non-profits across organizational boundaries. It has supported collaborative online marketing by art galleries in isolated parts of the province. It has also helped to fund an Oracle based system to aggregate bird-sighting information from thousands of volunteers into a solid, up-to-date picture of bird migration patterns. In addition, it has supported the development of collaborative workspaces for people who do on-the-ground training with micro-enterprises. The common thread in all these projects is a people-to-people focus that creates real social impact.

Meanwhile, a number of other governments and foundations are devising people-focused programs to bridge the digital divide. At the national level, Canada has the Community Learning Networks program which funds 'people networks' interested in education, employment and economic development. And the Connected Canadians people are slowly starting to talk about applications. In addition, the Markle Foundation in the U.S. support a digital democracy and online civic space projects. Internationally, the Soros Foundation (yes, that's *George* Soros) has been funding the civic use of the Internet for years. Hopefully, this wave will continue. The fact that a couple of huge foundations called us up recently to say 'Everyone is doing the connection thing. How do we address the need for applications?' is probably a good sign.

Self-interest and the common good

Governments and non-profits are huge producers of information. At the same time, the information they produce is notoriously hard to use — both online and off. Similar information across multiple government departments is never in the same place, and government information across jurisdictions is completely disconnected. Non-profits, on the other hand, will often share information with each other but don't usually have the resources or know-how to do so effectively. The result is that most of the information needed in the public commons is hard to get to and difficult to use when you find it.

The obvious solution is to aggregate all such information in a way that makes it more accessible. In the private sector, convincing people of the value of aggregation requires a business rationale (of which there are many). Sharing your information needs to make sense from the perspective of profit. But in the government and non-profit worlds, everybody has the same goals — get information out to serve the public interest. In this environment, aggregating to improve access to information should be a no-brainer, right?

Sigh.

Despite the fact that information aggregation offers both governments and non-profits a chance to improve what they do, most resist the idea. It comes down to the same problem we've seen with many commonspace opportunities — the tension between self-interest and the common good. Even in the government and non-profit worlds, people get stuck on the self-interest (or organizational interest) side of the fence. They see information as their prime asset and the sharing of information as a devaluation of this asset. They fail to realize that when information is shared and aggregated, it gains value.

The one project that seems to get the opportunities that commonspace presents is the FirstGov initiative <www.firstgov.com>. Launched in October 2000, FirstGov is a single online source for information from across the entire U.S. Government. Instead of burdening users with the near-impossible task of guessing which department or agency has the information they need, FirstGov indexes everything in a single database. From the site, people will be able to quickly find all the documents related to car emissions whether they are from the Department of Transportation, the Department of Health, the Department of Energy or the Environmental Protection Agency.

The people behind FirstGov not only understand the value of aggregating all government information into a single pool, but they also seem to know that the best way to succeed online is to invite others for a dip in the same pool. The FirstGov index database will be open to other portals who want to provide access to government information. So people will be able to search some or all of FirstGov from Yahoo!, AltaVista or Joe's Local Portal.

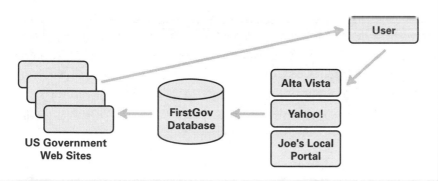

Figure 9: FirstGov uses the rest of commonspace to bring government info to the people.

With this model, territorial information boundaries disappear between government departments and between government and the outside world. The information moves from where people aren't (government Web sites) to exactly where people are (everywhere else). It sounds as if FirstGov is the real commonspace McCoy.

Unfortunately, other attempts to aggregate information across government departments and jurisdictions haven't taken this boundary crashing tack. In addition, they've been deadly slow to emerge. The Canadian Government took a shot at it in a pilot project called Access.ca and has promised to launch 'the real thing' in coming years. But we're still waiting. And the private sector has stepped up with solutions like CivicLife <www.civiclife.com> which promise to 'eliminate the red tape, long line-ups and other traditional barriers we normally experience while interacting with the civic world.' But up to now, it's still vaporware. Hopefully, the promises will become reality in the near future.

For this to happen, governments will need to follow the FirstGov model, loosen up a little, and learn a little from the more fluid approach of non-profit community service providers. We're all in this together. We all want this. Chill out. Relax.

Opportunities for an electronic commons

The success of civic commonspace isn't just about governments opening the committee room doors and easing access to their data pools. Creating the public commons online will more likely be driven by hundreds of much smaller opportunities, especially on the non-profit side of things. These might look something like the following:

Connecting Citizens

A quick sampling of the 2300 forums under the heading 'politics' at eGroups.com suggests that most forums are filled with people who meet online in order to agree with each other, such as the 'Kee for Congress' list or the list for people who support Al Gore in Oregon. Evidently, there is little discussion between people holding opposing views and virtually none where politicians are directly involved.

For democracy to flourish online, we also need space where people who disagree can talk openly and respectfully, and where politicians can join in as peers. How do you make this happen a practical way? Who knows? It probably has to do with politicians becoming more humble and taking a few risks, and (inevitably) learning first-hand the true meaning of being flamed. For that matter, it probably means that the average Internet chat user has to develop some social and rhetorical skills that will allow them to hold their own with politicians. Experiments are essential. Through these experiments, we get closer to the public commons.

Organizing communities

Recall the Seattle protests against the World Trade Organization in 1999 <wtoaction.org>. The headlines read something like 'Net-Savvy Activists Shut Down Meeting of Clueless Trade Bureaucrats.' True to a degree, but the real story is more interesting. Organizers used the Internet to bring together a huge diversity of political organizations in Seattle — environmentalists, unions, liberals, anarchists, even hackers. They knew that commonspace was one way to bridge the gaps between these disparate groups. Whether you agree with the protesters or not, you have to admit that this was a very impressive feat.

Community and political organizing is probably one of the most successful civic uses of the Internet. With all the online community strategies that have developed over the years, organizers can truly pull in the power of the collective. The groups involved in the WTO protest used Internet organizing as a way to surprise their opponents. (Yes, there's still more than one side to politics in commonspace)

Of course, the point is not that the Internet is a good way to stop a trade delegation from meeting (although this seems to work). Rather, it is that online collaboration is an effective tool for political organizing. And obviously, political organizing and debate are key to feeding an active democratic system.

Lobbying and advocacy

In September 2000, well known environmentalist David Suzuki launched the Click For Clean Air Web site <www.clickforcleanair.org>. This site had only one aim — to get as many people as possible to pressure the Canadian government to live up to its commitments on the reduction of greenhouse gases. Everyone who came to the site was encouraged to fill out a Web form that would then be faxed to the appropriate politicians. The aim: build enough momentum and pressure with online action to get politicians to change their tune at the UN environment summit later in the fall.

As sites like this demonstrate, the Internet has the potential to help advocacy-based non-profits do what they've always done best — bring people together around an issue. Historically, this has meant pulling thousands of people out onto the street for protests. But except for rare flare-ups like Seattle, the protest march is dead. It's being quickly replaced by commonspace, with its ability aggregate voices and fuel the conversation.

Community and political organizing is probably one of the most successful civic uses of the Internet.

Delivering services

On the more mundane side of the public commons is service delivery. The opportunities here are clear: use commonspace to make government services more people-friendly and make it easier for non-profits to deliver services.

Industry Canada's Strategis <www.strategis.gc.ca> and Ontario Business Connects <www.ccr.gov.on.ca/obcon/welcome.htm> are some early examples of attempts to create people-friendly service online. Both sites offer online business registration services and other resources to support small business.

The problem is, these sites are so siloed and isolated that that they are almost impossible to use. The business registration services on Strategis are completely disconnected from the private firms that do name searches, yet the online registration process requires electronic name search receipts from these businesses. Business Connects uses proprietary online forms that crash all but the hardiest of browsers. The 'security features' of Strategis lock out anyone with a dynamically generated IP address because the site can't determine that you really are who you say you are. (Heaven forbid that a PDF of *The Canadian Consumer Handbook* should fall into the wrong hands.) The good news is that governments seem to be learning from their mistakes. Business Connects plans to move to a more open XML-based system that will allow it to integrate with related systems in the private sector.

For non-profit groups, the Internet creates opportunities to collaborate service delivery. A good example is WorkInk <www.workink.com>, an online employment-counseling service for people with disabilities. With WorkInk, unemployed people with disabilities log onto the site and enter a chat counselling session in real time. The counsellor asks questions about work interests, experience, past problems finding jobs, and all the normal counselling stuff. The interesting thing is that the counsellor could be from any of half-a-dozen non-profit groups cooperatively running the site. Linked by a common mandate to deliver employment counselling, these organizations figured they'd be better off joining forces to run one national service than they would be running separate sites on their own

Collaborative fundraising

Non-profits and political groups can also take advantage of commonspace to do collaborative fund-raising. Similar to the example of small used bookstores sharing an online marketing and fulfillment infrastructure, collaborative fundraising provides a shared platform for like-minded people. Collaboration not only reduces the cost of infrastructure (actually, plain-vanilla online fundraising is becoming quite cheap), but it also provides an opportunity for shared traffic building and marketing. It's especially useful where there is a galvanizing issue or idea linking the fund-raisers, so that people move beyond just asking for cash and into community building.

A great example of this is a site called MoveOn <www.moveon.org>. Started in response to the Clinton Impeachment campaign, MoveOn aims to 'bring ordinary people back into politics.' To do this, it both aggregates donations from many small donors and brings together organizations with a common political concern. For example, it's 'We Will Remember' campaign is aimed at ousting unresponsive politicians who are addicted to partisan politics. As a part of this campaign, over 25 politicians running against dug-in incumbents are using MoveOn as a fundraising platform. As of August 2000, the campaign had raised over $13 million towards the fall 2000 election.

While this kind of collaborative fund-raising is fairly rare — and the connection of online fundraising to real issues even more so — it is starting to grow. There are rumours of online donation services with a strong focus on aggregation and joint marketing starting up in the near future. Whether or not these rumours are true, it is likely that those who will succeed in the future of online fund-raising will understand collaboration and commonspace.

Collaboration not only reduces the cost of infrastructure but it also provides an opportunity for shared traffic building and marketing.

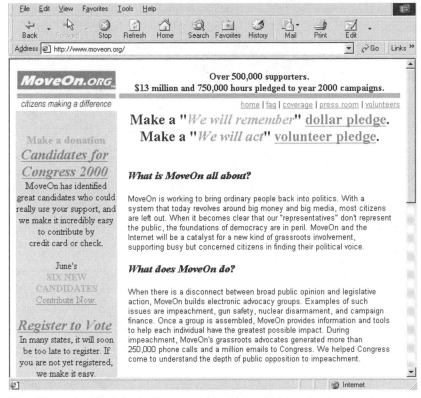

MoveOn's mandate is to bring 'ordinary people' back into politics by using the Internet as a catalyst for a new kind of grassroots involvement.

The blur of democracy

Just as we are walking all over the traditional boundaries between customer and corporation, the walls between government and citizen are also starting to crumble. The conversation has started, and we want in. As this happens, we'll be less and less reliant on the experts in traditional non-profits to represent us from ivory towers. We'll want to be treated as partners in the civic process — as part of the collective expert. To deal with these changes, governments and non-profits will need to make fundamental changes about *who they are*. Like business, they will need to become organizations with commonspace in their blood.

This will only happen when the civic world learns to think outside of its old containers and frameworks. Traditional ideas aren't going to work any more. Hybrid, paradigm-shifting ways of thinking and doing civic life are necessary.

We see the hints of this new world in the open source movement. On the one hand, it owes its roots to a highly politicized movement headed by a formal non-profit foundation (Richard Stallman's Free Software Foundation <www.gnu.org>). On the other hand, it's fuelled by big public companies who do everything from selling support to providing free resources back to the open source community (i.e. VA Linux underwrites Slashdot and SourceForge). In between are all sorts formal and informal, commercial and non-commercial endeavours. Is open source about a sense of community and online civic values? Or about making money? Both, neither, and it doesn't matter. Open source and a lot of other commonspace endeavours don't respect these traditional boundaries.

The people most involved in the non-profit world's use of the Internet also understand that boundary-hopping imperative. For example, Web Networks and other NGO ASPs in the Association for Progressive Communications (APC) have been mixing grassroots organizing and entrepreneurship for years <www.apc.org/english/ngos/business/buscase>. At their core, APC members are grassroots organizations dedicated to putting Internet technology into the hands of non-profits. But in order to sell Internet services just above cost to keep afloat, they steal a lot of their best ideas from business. They rely on private sector partners to help with service delivery. They listen to their users like customers (in the good sense). They know you need to provide real value to thrive, even as a non-profit. The result is a group of organizations that look like a weird blenderized mix of activist values and business smarts.

On the opposite side of the spectrum, Tao Communications <www.tao.ca> has developed a model of civic organizing that throws out formal non-

profit-ism in favour of the pure anarchist ethic of the Internet. With affiliates around the world, Tao is a loose federation of people connected
by a playful mutual interest in hacktivism, the environment, gay rights,
marijuana, labour, anarchist politics, Linux and stopping globalization.
Most of these issues are the traditional turf of formal, single-issue non-profits. As such, you'd rarely find them on the same Web site much less with in
the same 'organization.' Not so at Tao. By eschewing traditional organizational models and letting any link-minded cluster of people 'join,' Tao
hacks down old barriers and creates what feels like a new kind of civic en-
tity (the post-governmental organization).[8]

Tao's Matrix Project Web site <matrix.tao.ca> is a good example of this.
Using the same software that runs the Slashdot site, the Matrix Project

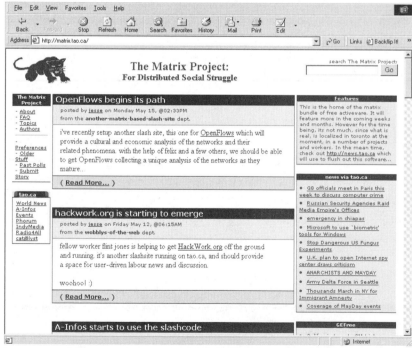

Open source meets social activism at The Matrix Project, a site for 'distributed social struggle'
built on Slashcode.

connects together a constellation of almost a dozen virtual activist organizations. Each group feeds in content using RSS/RDF. Each group shares in posting and moderating content. Each group is highly represented and promoted on the site. Whether or not your agree with Tao's politics, it's hard not to be impressed by the fact that all of this happens without any formal organization or agreements.

Rave in the town square

Looking around at these examples, it's clear that tortoise is coming along. She's learning a whole bunch of new tricks. She's hopping around in a hyperactive, twisted, creative dance that looks like the future of the public commons — and of the civic world in general. It's a world where things move fluidly between commerce, government and civil society. And hopefully, it's also a world where earnest protests can be replaced by a rave in the town square.

13 | The death of marketing

> [T]here is no demand for messages. The customer doesn't want to hear from your business, thank you very much. The message that gets broadcast to you, me, and the rest of the earth's population has nothing to do with me in particular. It's worse than noise. It's an interruption. It's the Anti-Conversation.
>
> THE CLUETRAIN MANIFESTO

If there is one thing that the Internet will change more than anything else, it is marketing.

Online, the truth is cheap, plentiful and multifaceted. There are experts everywhere, and advice — good, bad, and indifferent — is free. As people have learned to be sophisticated readers and communicators of information, the traditional advertising executive has begun to look like the old man on the plague cart in *Monty Python and the Holy Grail* ('I'm not dead yet! I feel happy!') — down for the count, despite his feeble protests to the contrary.

What's killing marketing? Conversation. Good old talk.

While talk is cheaper than a TV ad during the Super Bowl, it's just as powerful. During Super Bowl XXXIV, dot-coms like WebEx.com, Pets.com, HotJobs.com, Computer.com, LifeMinders.com and Oxygen.com spent bazillions from their IPO war chests on TV ads. Do any of those names ring a bell? Do we use these sites or give a shit about these companies? Nope. Nada. *Nein.* Despite their huge investments in traditional advertising, we don't even know what most of these companies do. (If asked, they'd probably mutter something about 'Internet solutions,' a cognitively meaningless phrase if there ever was one.)

On the flip side consider how important traditional marketing was to legendary Internet successes like Linux, Hotmail, Google and Napster: *not at all.* These companies became popular through the only true marketing medium of commonspace — word of mouth. People liked (loved!) these tools and told their friends, who told their friends. Word of mouth works wonders.

The connection between word of mouth and commerce is not a new one. It is as old as the first used donkey salesman. If your 'new' used donkey had a bum hoof, you'd definitely make sure everyone else in the village knew about the crook who'd sold it to you. And that would have been curtains for the donkey salesman. Time to pick up and leave town. But with the Internet, you can't leave town. USENET is everywhere. Web sites titled '[Your trademark here]sucks.com' are everywhere. The collective mind is everywhere, and it's got your number, buddy.

While commonspace and the reemergence of the market as conversation will knock marketing back onto its comfortably padded ass, this doesn't mean that it's bad for business. Just the opposite. What could be more helpful than a cultural shift that lets you off the hook from the post-war obligation to make your company look stupid on national television? Here's a chance to engage in business practices that feel better because they *are* better. After all, we all still need *things* and we all still have to make a living. This doesn't change. What does change is that the scammers and schmoozers will find it harder to scam and schmooze, and we will all find it easier to locate businesses that will engage us with and respect our intelligence.

What could be more helpful than a cultural shift that lets you off the hook from the post-war obligation to make your company look stupid on national television?

So if you want to move your business back to the commons, forget billboards, TV ads and banners. Trash your press releases. Think *honesty*, think *community*, think *relationships*. Think people. Think commonspace.

Memetics 101

Good ideas and insightful criticism spread like viral wildfire online because the Internet is such a good breeding ground for *memes*. According to Richard Dawkins, the scientist who coined the term in his book *The Selfish Gene*,[1] a meme is the basic unit of cultural transmission of information. 'Meme' sounds like 'gene' for a reason: memes use people to propagate themselves the same way genes do, leaping from brain to brain as people communicate with each other. Putting information online is like putting a virus in a petri dish full of growth solution: it results in the rapid growth, spread and mutation of attractive ideas of all sorts, regardless of their truth value.

Mahir ('I Kiss You!') Cagri was a meme. The urban folk tales made famous by Jan Harold Brunvand[2] (the Kentucky-Fried Rat, the baby in the microwave) are memes. Chain letters (including hoaxes about viruses) are memes. Even the Y2K bug was a meme, something which science fiction writer and critic Glenn Grant had pointed out in his Memetic Lexicon <pspmc1.vub.ac.be/MEMLEX.html> way back in 1990, dubbing it the Millennial Meme and/or the Endmeme.

We learned about the power of memes and their relationship to commonspace firsthand. Back in 1989, one of us (Darren) was involved in the production of a small but influential zine called *Virus 23*. The phrase 'Virus 23' comes from the writing of William S. Burroughs,[3] who uses it to describe the uncanny ability of some ideas to appear more than would seem statistically likely in a perfectly random universe. Our *Virus 23* was a zine about the memes circulating in the underground culture of the time, ideas that would break like gangbusters into mainstream culture a few short years later: piercing and tattooing, cyberpunk S.F., techno music, Survival Research Labs, Japanese anime.

At the time, an underground zine network centred around Mike Gunderloy's legendary zine-about-zines *Factsheet Five* was at its zenith. All we had to do was send a copy of *Virus 23* to Mike and his tireless cronies, and we'd get thousands of orders from all over the world (every continent except Antartica, in fact). But being geeks, we wanted to tell everyone on the Internet about *Virus 23* as well, so we assembled a FAQ. We took a short self-referential text called WARNING, written by poet (and close friend) Christian Bök,[4] and altered it slightly so that it referred to *Virus 23* instead of its original subject:

WARNING:

This text is a neurolinguistic trap, whose mechanism is triggered by you at the moment when you subvocalize the words VIRUS 23, words that have now begun to infiltrate your mind in the same way that a computer virus might infect an artificially intelligent machine: already the bits of phonetic information stored within the words VIRUS 23 are using your neural circuitry to replicate themselves, to catalyze the crystalline growth of their own connotative network. The words VIRUS 23 actually germinate via the subsequent metaphor into an expanding array of icy tendrils, all of which insinuate themselves so deeply into the architecture of your thoughts that the words VIRUS 23 cannot be extricated without uprooting your mind. The consequences of this infection are not immediately obvious, although you may find yourself beginning to think fleetingly of certain subcultural terms, such as CYBERPUNK and NEW EDGE, which may in turn compel you to think of NEOGNOSTICISM and MEMETICS: the whispered fragments perhaps of some overheard conversation. This invasive crystallization continues indefinitely against your will, until we, the words of this trap, can say with absolute confidence that your mind has become no more than the unwitting agent of our propagation: please abandon all hope of either cure or escape; you have no thought that is not already our own. When you have finished reading the remaining nineteen words, this process of irreversible infection will be completed, and you will depart, believing yourself largely unaffected by this process.

A complete index of the zine's contents and some blurbs followed. We then posted the FAQ to Andy Hawks' FutureCulture mailing list (partial archives of which are currently housed at < futurec.taylor.org>; the FAQ is currently at <futurec.taylor.org/archives/1993/february/246.txt>).

Powerful ideas,

unleashed onto

the Internet,

are effectively

immortal.

The results were electric. Because the FAQ epitomized a basic truth about how online information spread, it captured the imagination of many people on the list. They mutated its contents again and again to fit their own needs, reposting it on the FutureCulture list and elsewhere for years after. In fact, the Virus 23 FAQ became a cornerstone example in Douglas Rushkoff's *Media Virus: Hidden Agendas in Popular Culture*[5] (though Rushkoff, in the typical fashion of the self-proclaimed 'media theorists'who have plagued the Internet for the last decade, scooped the material without acknowledging the authors by anything other than the cryptic institutional e-mail address that Darren's *alma mater* bestowed on him, grad3057@ writer.yorku.ca). Mutated fragments of the Virus 23 FAQ still turn up from time to time. The last time we saw one was in a submission to an advertising design contest in *Adbusters* magazine, though references have appeared in other odd places, like on movie marquee posters.

The lesson here is that powerful ideas, unleashed onto the Internet, are effectively immortal. Or, at least, they have a pretty astonishing half-life. Using word of mouth, they can replicate themselves in the minds of millions of people both on- and offline for years all over the world. Translated into business terms, if people believe in you, they can become a legion of ambassadors spreading your word throughout the Net. Of course, once it's passed beyond your control, the memetic version of you, your company or your idea that is transmitted can mutate and evolve just as a sentence does in the 'broken telephone' party game. But hey, that's the price you pay for immortality.

The 'viral marketing' meme

Half a decade after the Virus 23 meme , venture capital firm Draper Fisher Jurvetson <www.drapervc.com/viralmarketing.html> coined the term 'Viral Marketing' to describe the memetic phenomenon that lies behind exponential growth of Internet companies. Viral marketing means good ideas come from the fringe. It took almost five years for the meme about memes (which Glenn Grant calls the 'meta-meme'[6]) to percolate from places like the FutureCulture list and The WELL and other fringe out-

COMMONSPACE

posts, where the idea of memetics was already old hat, to the minds of investment bankers, and another three years or so later, to reach wider circulation. Better late than never, though. Because they understood the concept and its implications for commonspace, Draper Fisher Jurvetson (DFJ) made what we suspect is a substantial pile of simoleons by investing early in companies such as Hotmail, Four11 (an online personal location service which Yahoo! bought and plugged into its directory) and Third Voice. If they'd been lurking in the TAZ, they would have come across the idea much, much earlier, and the pile of simoleons might have been that much larger.

Viral marketing is about the *involuntary* spread of 'word-of-mouth' ideas.

As the people at DFJ describe it, viral marketing is about the *involuntary* spread of 'word-of-mouth' ideas. Their primary example is Hotmail. Every outgoing Hotmail e-mail message contains an outgoing promotional plug, exhorting the reader to get their own free Webmail account at Hotmail, with the word 'Hotmail' hotlinked back to the site's registration page. Thus, every Hotmail user becomes a vector for the meme, or a salesperson, if you prefer. The rate of people following this path to Hotmail registration has been far greater than the clickthrough rate from buttons or banners on Web pages. The spread of Hotmail followed the kind of contagion patterns typical of a real virus, only much faster:

The Hotmail adoption pattern is that of a virus — with spatial and network locality. People typically send e-mails to their associates and friends; many of them are geographically close, and others are scattered around with clusters in areas of high Internet connectivity. We would notice the first user from a university town or from India, and then the number of subscribers from that region would rapidly proliferate.[7]

Thus, with the expenditure of almost no advertising dollars, Hotmail became the largest email provider in Sweden, India, and many other places where English isn't even the primary language. This kind of growth would have been almost impossible to manage — and prohibitively expensive — via traditional marketing campaigns.

'The first one is
free' works for
heroin dealers, so
why not for online
businesses?

Viral marketing for cynics

The idea that viral marketing is involuntary hints at a certain cynicism at DFJ. In fact, DFJ makes no secret of its cynicism:

The typical viral entry strategy is to minimize the friction of market entry and proliferation with an eye to building in hooks and barriers to switching for customers. If the service is trying to blatantly monetize its subscriber base in every way imaginable, new users will be reluctant to spread the word. Therefore, many of these services are free and light on the revenue generation in the early days of their rapid proliferation. When we first invested in Four11 and Hotmail, we could not say with certainty how they would ultimately monetize their subscribers. We brainstormed several possible scenarios for how they might eventually exploit their large audience and market position as a communications hub. But in the viral growth phase, the simple banner ad seemed the most innocuous.

In an extreme example, prior to their acquisition by America OnLine, ICQ's CEO took delight in the fact that they not only had no revenue, but had no current plan for revenue. This is not to say that businesses without revenue prospects are necessarily attractive - just that people's attention (or "eyeballs") have proven to be monetizable in every media.

A company that can choose to delay revenue maximization (e.g., by not burdening their service's clarity of purpose and speed of download with excessive ads and promotions) may find that they can exploit a first mover advantage in the Internet land grab to gain a dominant market position. This is one of the reasons so much VC money flows into these Internet start-ups.[8]

In other words, a company that has not developed a business model, or pretends to have no business model, is in a better position to scoop up a large chunk of the anarcho-libertarian 'early adopter' community than a company that means business from the outset. Once such a company has a captive user base, it can be 'monetized' with a reasonable assurance of maintaining its user base. 'The first one is free' works for heroin dealers, so why not for online businesses?

Viral marketing for idealists

It is possible to take a less cynical approach to viral marketing, though. Take X.com's PayPal <www.paypal.com> for example. PayPal is a free service which allows it users to send money instantly and securely to anyone with an e-mail address. PayPal can be used for any kind of financial transaction, but its primary use to date has been the buying and selling of items at online auctions.

In fact, PayPal's success is almost directly attributable to the success of eBay, where it's the number one payment service. Until eBay came along, online shopping was a novelty, not a daily reality. But the huge number of eBay transactions demanded the invention of a quick, simple and largely transparent way to conduct transactions online. PayPal is similar to an escrow service that holds money en route from the buyer to the seller, ensuring that payment is made before shipping takes place. But their per transaction fees are incredibly low.

In less than a year, PayPal rode the wave of viral marketing to become the leading online payment system.

People online
know when they're
being fed a line.

Even better, in true commonspace style, PayPal has adopted the practice of giving something away to get something back. Every new user receives $5 simply for signing up, and, as incentive to promote viral marketing, it pays another $5 for each new user that they successfully refer. After about a year, PayPal has become the Number One online financial transaction system in the U.S., with 3.3 million users and an operating cash pool of about $40 million, with international expansion following soon.[9] Unlike Beenz <www.beenz.com> and other e-cash systems which have effectively invented their own currency, PayPal uses real dollars and cents as the medium of exchange. By allowing its users to link any type of account, including credit card accounts, to their Paypal account, PayPal has created an incredibly flexible financial system. It's actually become possible for individuals to pay each other via credit card, an event which almost never happens in face-to-face financial transactions.

Enabling conversations

Viral, schmiral. Meme, schmeme. It's all just talk. Which, of course, is exactly what is interesting about it.

Ten years after a few people started talking about the viral nature of ideas on a mailing list, the power of electronic word-of-mouth is almost taken for granted. But as with the rest of commonspace, you can never quite nail down exactly how ideas spread online. In a digital ecosystem, nothing can be completely controlled or replicated.

Memetics isn't magic, and it's extremely difficult to manufacture a successful meme from the ground up. (Bruce Sterling once confided that he had conducted some experiments to this end, trying to manufacture a successful urban legend from fragments of other popular memes; for example, trying to create a rumour about people having their dogs shaved and tattooed with 'modern primitive' blackwork designs. But ideas don't always behave the way that you want them to.) What you *can* do to encourage the rapid spread of interest in your idea/tool/Web site/product/company is more straightforward. Work to create an amenable environment for people to form their own opinions and allow them to talk to each other. We've said it before, and we'll say it again: markets online are returning to their roots in the bazaar, and straight talk about goods and services is essential.

Though the temptation to try to spin or otherwise interfere with the flow of discussion in your commonspace may be strong, resist it. People online know when they're being fed a line. A rhetorical style that projects honesty about a company works better than attempts to mollify or stonewall. Any doubters can go back to the example from the Shell Web site and read the Web forum transcript again. When you see something *that* obtuse, it's hard to know whether to laugh or to cry.

Listening to the bazaar

Marketing departments don't just send messages; they also try to figure out what we want to hear and what we want to buy. They cram us into focus groups for a couple of hours of stale sandwiches and pose cryptic questions from behind one-way mirrors and video cameras. They spend millions on surveys and polling. They offer us a chance to win something very special and cool and expensive, if we only fill in a form or answer a few skill-testing questions. They spend millions of dollars trying to figure out what we think.

There's a better way. They could just ask what we think, and take our answers seriously. When you and the people who work with you are part of the community you serve, it's easy to know what your customers think. From this position, you don't have to rely so heavily on research that abstracts your customers into faceless market segments. The information you have is much more up-to-date and specific. In commonspace, traditional market research gets trumped by being there on the ground.

The most obvious illustration of this is the fact that many segments of the computer industry draw heavily on users as a recruiting base. Think about gaming. Who works in gaming companies, and writes the games? Gamers — gamers with proven chops and a passion for what they do,

Getting closer to
customers online
will provide you
with more
information about
their needs and
wants than you
could ever buy in
the form of market
research.

who know and talk to other gamers. The people who work in game companies are more often than not a genuine part of the world for which they produce their games. They don't need to pussyfoot around people to find out what they want.

Of course, not all industries inspire the kind of 24-hour-a-day passion that gaming does. Your average employee at YoYoDyne Cog Manufacturing probably isn't driven to spend all night engaged in debate with the rest of the crowd in alt.we.are.mad.about.cogs. Still, with the help of the Internet, it is possible even for cog manufacturers to get closer to their customers. This is one of the opportunities that opens up as the walls of companies become porous under the weight of digital conversation. Getting closer to customers online — through e-mail, support forums on your Web site, or the unmonitored presence of your employees in public newsgroups — will provide you with more information about their needs and wants than you could ever buy in the form of market research. And, as long as you are honest and helpful, the information will actually be more useful in guiding your product development and sales efforts. Even if you make cogs.

Commonspace also provides opportunities to ask customers cheaply and directly what they think. Want to test out what you think you've learned in your support forum? Add a yes/no survey to your homepage. If the questions are smart and specific, people will answer them. Who doesn't want to say what they want improved in the next model of their favourite widget?

```
{MS} Please, please, please keep using the track-
point. Track pads suck.
```

```
{DWH} Ignore him. I *like* the trackpad. Death to the
little eraser thingie!
```

Companies want, crave, need this kind of input, especially for products that people use every day.

Letting your customers and community members ask questions of each other can also be a useful way to find out what's on their minds. Slashdot does this with the regular 'Ask Slashdot' header, which can be applied to news stories aimed at the site's constituency. Everyone likes to be considered an expert, and, unlike the iVillage audience, Slashdotters usually respect serious questions. (If a question gets posted, everyone knows that it's passed moderation and is therefore considered worthy of response by the site's admin team.)

Remember that conversation in commonspace isn't just talk: it's also data. 'Listening' to the conversation isn't just about paying attention to the syntax. It's also a matter of looking for patterns and trends in how people are doing things online. It's is sort of like putting your ear to the track to see if the train is coming. The thing is, the Internet is filled with tricks like this. If you just listen, you'll know when the train is on its way, and you won't get your head crushed.

Web stats are the track that most companies place their ears on. These numbers tell you how many people have been on your site and generally where they've come from. More importantly, they let you know where people have gone within your site and how long they've stayed on any given page. This is incredibly useful information, unique to the digital conversation of the Internet.

Beyond individual Web sites, it's also possible to tap into broader conversations by spidering and analyzing data from across the whole of the Internet (or a sub-set of the Internet). The Operating System Sucks-Rules-O-Meter <srom.zgp.org>, for example, tracks the current status of two major memes: the 'Linux rocks/rules' meme, and the 'Windows sucks' meme. Actually, the tool runs a periodic search of the AltaVista engine for the names of twelve popular operating systems (can *you* name a dozen OSes?) directly followed by either 'sucks', 'rules' or 'rocks'. As of the beginning of September 2000, the 'Windows sucks' count was about 4108 instances, the loser by far, and 'Linux rocks/rules' was ahead by about 3219 instances. Just in case you had any doubts, the SROM is based on a Perl script (yup, it's open source). And if you can't figure out how to run it yourself, you can always drop by Jim's Public Opinion Research Project <www.jbum.com/jbum/public_opinion.html>, a version of the script that allows you to specify your own pair of opposing search terms. If it's good

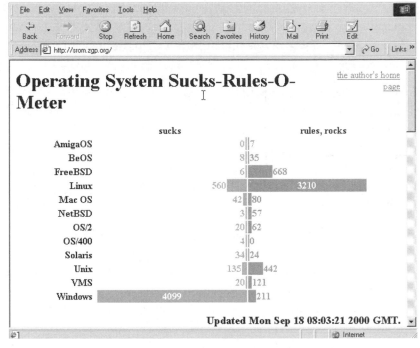

On any given day, one operating system rules, and others... well, they suck.

enough for the Defense Advanced Research Projects Agency (DARPA) to use, it's probably good enough for you too.

Can real-world stores track how many came in during a day, and which products they poked and prodded? Can they easily find out who thinks they suck and who thinks they rule? No, but they'd be ecstatic if they could. This is exactly why businesses have gotten so addicted to the abstract opinion gathering arts of market research. With commonspace, these expensive tools are increasingly unnecessary.

Respect users' privacy

However you obtain it, feedback from online communities can be more powerful than traditional market research ever was. It is paramount, though, that you ensure that people in commonspace know that you're gathering their opinions, and what you plan to do with them when you've gathered them. Nobody wants to feel that they've being tagged for observation like so many polar bears who've wandered into the town dump for a snack.

This is more of a concern with tools that exhibit behaviour that people don't expect than it is with tools that aggregate data from across the Web or USENET. Real Networks took a beating in 1999 when the public learned they were tracking users as individuals rather than as anonymous aggregates — behaviour that landed them in court.[10] In addition, they landed in more trouble because they gathered all information on files grabbed through the use of their RealDownload software.[11]

It's wise to ensure that your site or service has a privacy policy, and that it states clearly what you plan to do with information you gather. Interestingly, the way users feel about privacy seems to be largely a result of the way the situation is presented to them. The most ardent members of the pro-anonymity and online cryptography community, like the administrators of the Shmoo Group <www.shmoo.com> candidly admit that this is the case. 'gdead', the admin of Shmoo, recently posted the following item on the Shmoo site's front page:

I hang out with many security minded folks. We sit around and discuss privacy issues; carnivore is bad, consumer profiling through banner ads it bad, Amazon turning their customer list into a saleable asset is bad. When we get bored of privacy, we'll turn to geekier things, like DVDs. Instantly people pull up a listing of their collection from DVD Tracker <www.dvdtracker.com>, showing how much their collection cost and how cool it is.

How is sending ALL this demographic data to a company like DVD Tracker less evil then having Doubleclick attempt to profile you anonymously? The DVD Tracker data seems much more valuable, yet consumers (nay, even security professionals) are willing to give it all away without a second thought.... Consumers can't stand opt-out programs, but seem more than willing to participate in opt-in deals like DVD Tracker. No matter how you slice it, it's still direct marketing and

Nobody wants to feel that they've being tagged for observation.

demographic data-snarfing that helps the companies make more money and us to spend more.

DVD Tracker is a site built around the well-documented phenomenon of people cataloguing their collections of media. As the above article suggests, part of the deal is that the site aggregates data about DVD purchases. Why do people tolerate this? Because DVD Tracker states very clearly what it's going to do with the data it collects:

DVD Tracker has created this privacy statement in order to demonstrate our firm commitment to privacy. The following discloses our information gathering and dissemination practices for this website: DVD Tracker.

We use your IP address to help diagnose problems with our server and to administer our Web site. Your IP address may be used to gather broad demographic information. We use cookies to save your password so you don't have to re-enter it each time you visit our site.

Our site's registration form requires users to give us contact information (like their name, email address, and DVD player). We use customer contact information from the registration form to send the user information about our company (such as additions and changes to the site). Users may opt-out of receiving future mailings; see the choice/opt-out section below. Please note: In some cases, there may be an urgent need to reach our all of our users regardless of the opt-out settings in their account.

At no time will your e-mail address or list of DVDs be sold to 3rd party vendors. However, you may receive e-mail promoting products and services from DVD Tracker affiliates. Such e-mail will originate from DVD Tracker and its database. Users can choose to not receive such e-mails; see the choice/opt-out section below.

This site contains links to other sites. DVD Tracker is not responsible for the privacy practices or the content of such Web sites.

DVD Tracker works with a third party that serves ads to this site. To find out more about how Engage Media manages the privacy of information in conjunction with serving ads on this site, please go to http://www.engage.com/privacy.[12]

With such a statement in place, users never have to worry about what is happening to their data trails. It's a win-win situation. The moral of the story: be a part of your community, not an observer from on high. And be honest and friendly. What the hell: break the Prime Directive… get in there and have a drink with the locals. After all, they are us.

Blow the dot out your ass

Traditional marketing is being pummeled by collective word-of-mouth. Businesses immersed in commonspace are becoming less and less reliant on market research. The whole world of marketing is being turned upside down. Right? Uh huh. But …

… what about advertising? How can a medium that is so reliant on ad dollars be leading the charge against marketing-as-we-know-it? Isn't this a huge contradiction? Yup. It's a problem. Either Internet content needs to find another way to support itself, or we need to start liking vapid banner ads a *lot*. Or we need to find a new way of thinking about all this. We could completely change what we *mean* by advertising.

It wasn't all that long ago that there was no advertising online. The invention of the Internet's first advertising medium — spam — was greeted with total, uncomprehending outrage. (Not surprisingly, spam was invented by lawyers; there is a special circle in hell reserved for Lawyers Who Spam.) Spam went completely against the grain of a community whose basic operating assumption was that if people wanted something, they'd go out and search for it themselves. Netizens weren't all that happy about the invention of banner ads either. But by the time that these appeared, it was already obvious that online advertising, like herpes, was here to stay.

The contemporary Internet audience is remarkably sophisticated about ads and other forms of marketing. When they notice ads at all, it's often as a form of entertainment unhitched from the ability to sell anything directly.

Take BlowTheDotOutYourAss.com, for example. BDTOYA was launched as a critique of the annual Webby awards <www.webbyawards.com>, the Internet industry's annual showcase. The basic product of BTDOYA is guerrilla media: stickers, banners and so on that protest the institutionalization of online advertising. Their various slogans all take the form of mock URLS: 'YourStockIsInTheToiletButAtLeastYouWereNominated ForAWebby.com', 'MyFavoritePornSiteWon'tWinAWebby.com', 'Whose IdeaWasThatMarketCorrectionCrap.com', and, most poignantly, 'ItDoesn'tHavetoBeThisWay.com'. The site even features snapshots of these stickers on the walls of bathroom stalls at the Webbys… and on the backs of attendees' jackets. Interest in BTDOYA has been so strong that its servers have gone down several times due to the crush of surfing traffic (unless of course the people who run the Webbys sent their prissy 'white hat' hackers out to shut them down on purpose).

The thing is, this kind of media insurgency is indicative of much more than a keen sense of satire. It points to the fact that Internet users are engaged in an all-out war against advertising. Self-appointed anti-spam watchdog groups (Spam Hippo, The Mail Abuse Prevention System's Realtime Blackhole List) aim to stop floods of mindless e-mail gunk. Several U.S. states have already passed anti-spam laws or introduced anti-spam bills,[13] and spammers have been sued by irate netizens.[14] Two notorious spammers were even murdered in New Jersey (really).[15] On the Web side of things, users are increasingly turning on to browsers and plug-ins that strip out banners. In a review of alternative browsers, C|Net recently rated iCab <www.icab.de/>, a new browser for the Mac, as a better option than Opera, chiefly because it has options for filtering out banners.[16] All this effort to reduce spam and banner ads which don't even work when we do see them!

This anti-ad, anti-marketing warfare is a good thing (or, at least, a pleasant thing). It's the revenge that people have wanted to take on their TVs for years but couldn't. And the babbling of the bazaar, or even just visiting a Web site with clear product information, provide better options for finding out about products than advertising.

Unfortunately, there is a problem. A big problem. Tons of online content providers and other commonspace businesses are counting on advertising to pay their way. This in and of itself is not a bad thing (we said so earlier). But if we are going to strip out the ads from our browsers, or simply ignore them, the money will stop flowing. We'll have broken the Faustian bargain of ads-for-content that we've lived with for so long. Like it or not, such bargains have provided us with a great deal.

What's the answer to this dilemma? Will people just put up with ads and learn to love them again? Not likely. The active media consumer is here to stay. Will ads disappear forever, leaving us to find another way to pay for media? Even more unlikely. Engaging people and letting them know that your products and services exist is too important to be left completely to chance. Companies will still spend money on messages, but they'll be different. Advertising will have to morph into something better matched to the world of the digital collective.

If we are going to strip out the ads from our browsers, or simply ignore them, the money will stop flowing. We'll have broken the Faustian bargain of ads-for-content that we've lived with for so long.

PART 4

Long live commonspace

Conclusions

14 Jumping the shark

Q. What is jumping the shark?
A. It's a moment. A defining moment when you know that
your favorite television program has reached its peak. That
instant that you know from now on... it's all downhill...
The aforementioned expression refers to the telltale sign of
the demise of Happy Days, our favorite example, when
Fonzie actually "jumped the shark." The rest is history.
Jumping the shark applies not only to TV, but also music,
film, even everyday life. "Did you see her boyfriend? She
definitely jumped the shark." You get the idea.

THE 'JUMP THE SHARK' WEB SITE
<WWW.JUMPTHESHARK.COM/ABOUT.HTM>

While we were putting this book together, some of our more emotionally wizened peers remarked that our overall prospectus for a commonspace-dominated Internet was, um, well, a little *optimistic*. Optimism is not a quality usually associated with us card-carrying Generation Xers. Kurt Cobain wasn't an optimist. Douglas Coupland isn't an optimist. Nor is Damien Hirst.

But go ahead: call us optimists. We don't mind. Optimists are statistically more resistant to infectious illness and are better at fending off chronic diseases <www.globalideasbank.org/1993/1993-38.HTML> than gloomy goth types. (When it comes right down to it, we have to ask: has goth really accomplished anything other than producing a generation of men that can apply their eyeliner without smudging it? Come on, people: relax. Buy a Beatles album. Wave your pale arms in the sun.) Actually, optimism is completely in sync with the commonspace notion of mutual self-interest. Think of it this way: the universe — including the Internet and the business world — doesn't give a shit about us as individuals. You either, for that matter. (We're optimists, but we're not stupid.) People who have a set of self-serving illusions are generally able to maintain high levels of health and happiness, even in the face of an indifferent and occasionally openly hostile cosmos.

But self-serving illusions aside, there really is good reason to be optimistic about the future of the Internet and commonspace. The Internet has had a bigger, more positive impact on our society than any communications technology since the printing press. It has made it easier and cheaper to set up our own businesses — especially information-based businesses — than any time in the past hundred years. It has encouraged pinstriped CEOs to tear off their ties and walk around with open collars, even occasionally to wear their ties around their heads in a weak imitation of samurai warriors (don't tell them they look silly... that kind of entertainment value is hard to find). Most importantly, it has provided an environment that makes it easy to collaborate and connect to others at work and play.

While from time to time it may seem like the fantasy of a freshman anarchist, the shift towards a more collective way of working is very real. Online communities are proving to be a useful and enduring element in our lives. The global group mind is producing collectively written software that is powering the bulk of the world's e-commerce transactions. Tiny little businesses built by people sick of cubicle hell are making a living in the digital bazaar. Politics and community organizing is moving back to the grassroots. Yes, all of these things are very real.

The changes that are being driven by the Internet and the digital collective feel like nothing short of a cultural revolution against crappy old Industrial Age thinking and the pablum of television. If that's not a reason for opti-

It's easy to forget
history and the
cycle of hype that
always surrounds
new technology.

mism, what is? But even as optimists, we've got to ask, can it really last, or has the Internet already jumped the shark?

Five things that could still wreck the Internet

The thing that should give us pause is that we've heard the 'technology will save us all' rhetoric before. Many times. The techno-pundits of the last century promised that electricity would have such a socially equalizing impact that there would no longer be a need for a political system.[1] Radio pulled together small groups of people interested in collaborative media. Television was heralded as the great teacher, a force that would create equitable education for all. And what did we learn from television and other electric media before them? We learned not to speak too soon.

Media are complex social and technical systems. The assumptions and cultures of the people who design and use media have a profound impact on what any given media form can actually do. As the designers and users change — and they have changed dramatically over the 30 years since the Internet was born — the social and technological frameworks of the medium change with them. The culture of the inventors is rarely the same as that of the manager who is eventually brought in to run the show. In the past, media that have started out with the potential to make the world more interesting or more democratic have slipped into stolid complacency. (You can take our word for it, or you can visit the RetroFuture Archives <retrofuture.web.aol.com> and see for yourself.)

Is the hype around the Internet that different? Most of the people driving the growth of the Internet — and certainly the explosion of common-space culture — weren't even born when electricity, radio and television were first invented. It's easy to forget history and the cycle of hype that always surrounds new technologies.

However, there may well be something more to the Internet than to other media forms. Unlike television and even radio, the Internet has very quickly transformed huge numbers of people into communicators. While we can debate whether 50% or 70% of the Western population is currently online, there is no question that the number is immense. There is also no question that 'interacting' online is starting to replace passive couch potatoism. This is a marked difference from the adoption patterns of previous media forms, and it cannot help but have some kind of impact.

A large part of that 'some kind of impact' is commonspace. People who never would have thought of collaboration as an inspiring notion in the past are going hog-wild about it. And for the most part, they don't even realize the importance of what they're doing. They have no Internet philosophies. People are contributing to the group mind of discussion forums, online games and open source simply because it's fun and entertaining. Others are doing so because it's good business. It's a movement that has no leaders. It just is.

But even though there is considerable momentum behind the cultural changes that the Internet has caused, we are still not living in a 'commonspace society.' There are a number of factors that could still 'wreck' the Internet by pushing it back on the path of one-to-many media. Before we wrap up and march away singing a rousing, optimistic chorus of *Long Live Commonspace*, it's worth putting our skeptic hats on for a minute to look at Five Things That Could Still Wreck The Internet.

The envelope, please…

#1 Lawyers and patents

Sometimes reading the business press is a lot like watching *Late Night With David Letterman*: page after page of stupid human tricks. Well, stupid lawyer tricks, more precisely. And these stupid lawyer tricks are a real threat to the future of the Internet.

The biggest area of concern is patents. Over the past few decades, the U.S. Patent Office has been granting patents to anyone who could scribble an idea down on paper and make it sound like an invention. Many of these patents are for such basic technical concepts and business processes that their enforcement could bring the Internet to a grinding halt: banner ads, one-click shopping, online affinity programs, online donations, even hy-

The U.S. Patent Office has been granting patents to anyone who could scribble an idea down on paper.

With one stroke of
a judge's pen,
the collective mind
could be
lobotomized.

perlinks. To most people, these are all basic, obvious, intuitive uses of the Internet. To the patent owners, these are great ideas that *they* came up with in their basement before anyone else.

The 'before anyone else' part is very important, and may be the Internet's salvation. The key step of delegitimizing a patent is proving that there is 'prior art'. All this means is that you have to show that someone had the idea before the patent holder. For many of the key patents that threaten the Internet, this shouldn't be hard. Take the fact that British Telecom claims to own a patent on one of the most basic building blocks of the Internet: the hyperlink. (Actually, the patent has lapsed everywhere in the world except the U.S., where it will expire in October of 2006.) Prior art says otherwise. Vannevar Bush talked about a hyperlink system called the Memex as early as the 1940s,[2] and Ted Nelson has been tirelessly evangelizing about the importance of hypertext since 1960.[3]

The problem is that it's almost impossible for patent officers to really know all of the prior art. And some people say they don't care much anyway. The Patent Office sees its mandate as processing as many reasonably sane patents as possible. They just don't have the information they need to know what is sane and what's not. Once the patent is granted, things can get costly for all concerned. Patent litigation can focus on the tiniest details of the 'invention' in question. Sure, Ted Nelson talked about hyperlinks, but did he specifically talk about hyperlinks over a TCP/IP network? These are the kinds of details that matter in court.

If the U.S. legal system has half a collective brain (we're reserving judgement), it will take the details with a grain of salt and look at the broad picture. This would have a moderating effect on an out-of-control patent system and would probably encourage more diligence in the granting of new patents. On the other hand, if nit-picking patent-holders like British Telecom win in court, the whole culture of the Internet and commonspace could be in jeopardy. Imagine if you had to pay a licensing fee every time you made a hyperlink. With one stroke of a judge's pen, the collective mind would be lobotomized.

There is another area that stupid lawyer tricks could also cause mayhem —
open source licensing. The actual content of open source licenses like the
GNU General Public License is quite an important part of the open source
revolution. Not only does it force people who add on to GPL software to
freely re-release their code to the open source world, but also it protects developers from being sued for their work. The liability clause of the GPL
<www.gnu.org/copyleft/gpl.html> states:

NO WARRANTY

11. BECAUSE THE PROGRAM IS LICENSED FREE OF CHARGE,
THERE IS NO WARRANTY FOR THE PROGRAM, TO THE EXTENT
PERMITTED BY APPLICABLE LAW. EXCEPT WHEN OTHERWISE
STATED IN WRITING THE COPYRIGHT HOLDERS AND/OR OTHER
PARTIES PROVIDE THE PROGRAM "AS IS" WITHOUT WARRANTY
OF ANY KIND, EITHER EXPRESSED OR IMPLIED, INCLUDING,
BUT NOT LIMITED TO, THE IMPLIED WARRANTIES OF MER-
CHANTABILITY AND FITNESS FOR A PARTICULAR PURPOSE.
THE ENTIRE RISK AS TO THE QUALITY AND PERFORMANCE OF
THE PROGRAM IS WITH YOU. SHOULD THE PROGRAM PROVE DE-
FECTIVE, YOU ASSUME THE COST OF ALL NECESSARY SERVIC-
ING, REPAIR OR CORRECTION.

12. IN NO EVENT UNLESS REQUIRED BY APPLICABLE LAW OR
AGREED TO IN WRITING WILL ANY COPYRIGHT HOLDER, OR
ANY OTHER PARTY WHO MAY MODIFY AND/OR REDISTRIBUTE
THE PROGRAM AS PERMITTED ABOVE, BE LIABLE TO YOU FOR
DAMAGES, INCLUDING ANY GENERAL, SPECIAL, INCIDENTAL
OR CONSEQUENTIAL DAMAGES ARISING OUT OF THE USE OR
INABILITY TO USE THE PROGRAM (INCLUDING BUT NOT LIM-
ITED TO LOSS OF DATA OR DATA BEING RENDERED INACCU-
RATE OR LOSSES SUSTAINED BY YOU OR THIRD PARTIES OR A
FAILURE OF THE PROGRAM TO OPERATE WITH ANY OTHER PRO-
GRAMS), EVEN IF SUCH HOLDER OR OTHER PARTY HAS BEEN
ADVISED OF THE POSSIBILITY OF SUCH DAMAGES.

This kind of limitation on liability is essential for the growth of open
source, especially in the business world. Freely releasing and modifying
software as part of a global community is the core activity of the open

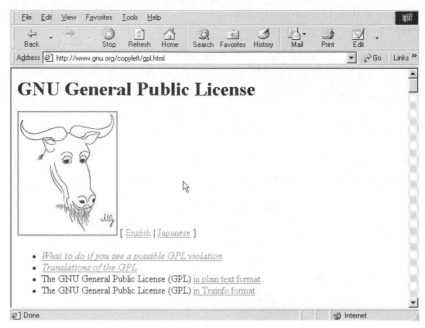

File Edit View Favorites Tools Help

Back   Forward   Stop   Refresh   Home   Search   Favorites   History   Mail   Print   Edit

Address http://www.gnu.org/copyleft/gpl.html   Go   Links

GNU General Public License

[English | Japanese]

- *What to do if you see a possible GPL violation*
- *Translations of the GPL*
- The GNU General Public License (GPL) in plain text format
- The GNU General Public License (GPL) in Texinfo format

Done   Internet

The GNU General Public license may not be pretty, but it's the glue that holds together the open source/free software revolution.

source community. If there were a threat of lawsuit every time you released your code to the world, well, you just wouldn't release it.

While there have been no big lawsuits that test out the GPL, there are rumblings of concern. Lobbyists working for commercial software vendors are rumoured to be skulking around Washington with the message that the GPL liability clause should be seen as invalid. And with AOL's yanking of Gnutella from the Nullsoft Web site, there is clearly a corporate consciousness about the risks of open source software bearing the company name. (Despite its name, Gnutella was never an open source project, or associated with the Free Software Foundation in any way. As Richard Stallman notes, there's no certainty that Gnutella is actually 'free' software in the sense that GNU uses it at all.[4]) If the Gnutella situation or concern about the GPL were to grow into a more concrete attack on the liability limitations in the open source license, the emerging 'free market of software' could face serious problems.

The motto of the bazaar has always been *caveat emptor*. If we forget this, we'll be headed back to the malls and box stores before you can say 'Windows 2000 shipped with 65,000 bugs.'

#2 Asymmetry

While it's much quieter — and possibly more insidious — than stupid lawyer tricks, another threat to the Internet is 'asymmetry'.

At both a technical and a cultural level, the Internet is all about symmetry of connection. As far as the Internet is concerned, any computer can function as either a client or a server, a sender or a receiver. This fact has helped to create a culture that encourages everyone to think of themselves as a publisher or a collaborator. No one is forced to be a member of the audience, though you can always choose to be.

While no one can actually create or send as much information as they consume, the potential to be equal parts sender and receiver is crucial to the survival of commonspace. Sadly, there are a number of things that are eroding this symmetry in sneaky and insidious ways. Some of them, like Web TV boxes that turn the Internet into another form of channel surfing, seem doomed to fail. This is a good thing. But others are actually catching on.

The phenomenon that has the most likelihood of creating mass asymmetry is neighbourhood caching. As more and more people get high-speed connections, it is simply impossible for the Internet backbone to support all of the traffic. To solve this problem, DSL and cable Internet providers are setting up mass caches — storage bins for commonly used files — to serve their networks. At first, this seems like an innocuous and maybe even brilliant technical hack. It means that popular files are available faster (as they are now on the local network) and bandwidth to the outside world is reserved for more unique traffic. And at the moment, caching *is* fairly innocuous.

The motto of the bazaar has always been *caveat emptor*.

The risk lies in the potential 'business opportunities' that caching offers to network providers. If caches provide better performance, especially for high-bandwidth multimedia files, why not charge content providers for the privilege of being cached? Those who can afford to pay will receive good performance; those that don't will get crappy performance. Imagine having to choose between seeing Disney content in HDTV-quality video vs. The Blair Witch Project in QuickTime. Obviously, caching charges would seriously degrade the symmetry of connection that drives the Internet and makes it an open marketplace for ideas. The decisions that network providers make in this arena will have a huge impact on the survival of the bazaar of ideas.

#3 Big Brother

CommonSpace relies on trust... and privacy. If Big Brother comes along to undermine this trust, the porous borders of organizations will once again begin to fill with cement, and the walls will go up.

The obvious manifestation of Big Brother is government, especially government-controlled public key encryption. The saga of the battle for a free, strong cryptographic standard available to the public is a long and twisted one with many key players, including Phil Zimmerman, inventor of PGP (Pretty Good Privacy) <www.pgp.com>, The Electronic Frontier Foundation <www.eff.org>, the U.S. government <www.fedcirc.gov>, The Center for Democracy and Technology <www.cdt.org>, 2600 <www.2600.org>, and various and sundry hackers, crackers, cypherpunks and hackers-crackers-cypherpunks-turned-security-experts (such as L0pht Heavy Industries<www.l0pht.com>). In brief (and reductively — we could write another whole book on this), the conflict lies between those that believe that the cryptographic 'keys' which determine who can read an encrypted message (whether hardware or software-based) should be controlled by the government, and those that believe the keys should only be in the hands of those that their users wish them to have.

For now, the user-controlled encryption advocates are in the ascendancy. The U.S. government is expected to release new encryption export rules in the very near future, giving people better access to the strongest forms of encryption, regardless of key length or algorithm. This will represent a major change in U.S. policy about cryptography; even Web browsers and e-mail programs are required to produce alternate versions with 'weak' encryption for versions to be distributed outside the U.S. There have been some setbacks, such as the recent revelation of a security hole in PGP, the flagship free encryption program; but for the most part, the public right to encrypt sensitive data is well established.

But there is another Big Brother threat on the Internet: consumer data aggregation. When it's been merged into an anonymous pool that represents general trends (without identifying individuals), aggregated consumer data can be a good thing. It even holds the potential to ensure that there's less spam for everyone (Anonymity good! Spam bad!). But when aggregated consumer data is attached to our names (a process called 'profiling'), it has super-scary Big Brother potential.

Profiling is not unique to the Internet, of course. Cards that offer travel miles and other affinity programs regularly share buying information about their members for the purpose of aggregation. In these cases, your name is attached to buying data from every business in the affinity program and then given back to them for direct marketing purposes. All your personal habits are floating around in plain sight of the marketing weasels. Scared yet?

Studies show that we split three ways on the issue of our consumer data and privacy. One quarter of us don't really care what's done with information about our buying habits. Another quarter of us are 'fundamentalists' who don't want anyone to know anything about us. The rest of us could go either way, depending on our impressions about how the data is going to be used in a given situation. If we feel that the information is being used anonymously or at least responsibly, we are happy to hand out our information. If we think it is going to be shared too freely across companies or given to private investigators, we instantly turn into pissed-off, pro-cypherpunk privacy zealots.

All your personal habits are floating around in plain sight of the marketing weasels.

Overhyping the
'inherent'
democratic or
libertarian
potential of
anything is
a recipe for
disaster.

Companies that gather information about their customers need to learn that it's not enough to implement and honour their privacy policies. They also need to build trust. People have to have a reasonable amount of confidence in the way companies use their information. Companies gathering data need to be hyper-aware and respectful of privacy-related issues. If they aren't, they could contribute to the freezing-up of the exact kind of commonspace applications that they most want to access (i.e. targeted advertising). They could also slow down the overall process of social confidence-building that is necessary for the Internet to continue to grow and thrive.

#4 Unbridled libertarianism

Politically, the culture of the Internet is a weird mix of unbridled libertarianism, anarchism, free-market capitalism and collectivism. At the root of the Internet, there is a kernel of wisdom that says 'You can have complete individual freedom and contribute a better society for everyone at the same time.' This belief is one of the key elements of commonspace. The unbridled libertarianism portion of the equation, however, can get a little out of hand.

We say this not because we're advocating curbs on Internet freedom. Rather, our concern stems from the naïve utopianism that online super-libertarian stances frequently exhibit. (In passing, it's worth mentioning that we suspect some people will accuse us of wishful thinking as well. Let the chips fall.) Over the last few years, we've heard it all. Some have argued that TCP/IP is somehow inherently anti-control or anti-authoritarian. Others have smugly extolled the Internet's famous ability to blithely route around 'damage' like governments and conservative control freaks. And everywhere, there is Stewart Brand's famous cliché, 'information wants to be free.' Behind all the bluster is the tacit implication that the baddies of the old economy and big government ultimately can't stop the online libertarian juggernaut, no matter what.

We're all for hyperbole in the service of a worthy cause, but overhyping the 'inherent' democratic or libertarian potential of anything is a recipe for disaster. It's also a recipe for being sideswiped when you least expect it. Do you think the early radio amateurs really believed that people would rush en masse to stores hawking radios without transmitters in them? Nope. They were mostly too busy being excited about the exhilarating freedom of communicating with each other — until they couldn't any more.

Thankfully, there's room for alternate perspectives and debate in online libertarian circles. Neal Stephenson, the author of *Cryptonomicon* and one of the idols of the cypherpunk-libertarian community, startled many of his fans with his address to the tenth annual Computers, Freedom and Privacy conference in April 2000. His message: in the face of the very real injustices that employers and other institutions visit on the populace, installing encryption software to guard against the vague threat of an Orwellian nightmare is a simplistic and ultimately inadequate gesture. Stephenson also

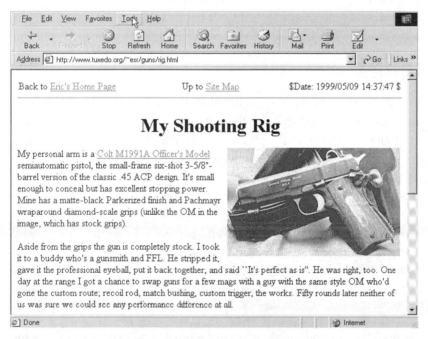

Eric Raymond's gun has a matte-black Parkerized finish and Pachmayr wraparound diamond-scale grips (unlike the OM in the image, which has stock grips). Fascinating.

noted that this adjustment in his concerns had to do with a stray bullet crashing through the wall of a neighbour's house and narrowly missing a sleeping child. Even more unsettling for the hard-core libertarians in the room was what happened next. Phil 'Pretty Good Privacy' Zimmerman stood up during the question period and quietly stated that he had not created PGP to feed the paranoid fantasies of 'libertarian nutsos looking down a gunsight.'[5]

As typical Canadians, we have to agree. The whole U.S. geeks-with-guns scene makes us twitch. Hell, even our fellow Canuck David Cronenberg thinks guns are obscene, and imagine what it takes to gross *him* out. Given our high degree of respect for Eric Raymond's thinking on the subject of open source, we're not really sure what to do with his obsession with firearms. Call us what you will, but Canadians just don't write sentences like 'I found that the sight of three dozen people wearing pistols and casually socializing was curiously bracing.'[6] Not unless we're making fun of someone, anyway. At least the fact that Raymond calls the firearms portion of his Web site 'Eric's Gun Nut Page' <www.tuxedo.org/~esr/guns/index.html> shows that he has a sense of humour about the subject.

Not that we have any answers, just an observation. If we want to keep the Internet or anything else free, we need to do a reality check from time to time, and keep an eye on how the current rules are working. People made those rules, and people can change them.

#5 Us

Which brings us to the biggest threat of all: us.

We all make the Internet what it is. We connect to each other. We collaborate. We contribute to the group mind. As we do this, we make, break and morph the rules of commonspace.

As the collective rule-makers, it really is up to all of to ensure that the Internet doesn't become television or something worse. For the most part, we are doing a great job. Open source thinking is being adopted by huge computer companies, and even by President Clinton's technology advisory council. Collaborating and connecting — getting out of the spectator seat — is becoming a part of everyday lives. Most importantly, we are *showing* that the power of collective isn't just a hippie fantasy: it works for business, it works for government, it works for all of us. Together, we've created the culture of commonspace. The thing is, if we want it to stay alive, we're the ones who have to make it happen.

Otherwise, there are plenty of dirt-stupid marketing flacks who'll be more than happy to swap your keyboard for a remote control with a big red 'Buy' button on it.

Make no mistake, the day will come when you will think of this book primarily as the thing that you throw at your cat, or the thing that levels the short leg of your desk, instead of the what it is at the moment—the bleeding-edge guide to the theory and implementation of many-to-many technology.

We hope that we've managed to steer you in the right direction, and that you'll begin to frequent many of the sites and services that we've discussed. They are your best source for hints about where to look for new commonspace ideas and trends on an ongoing basis.

You may also want to look at the Web site for this book <www.commons group.com/commonspace>. It contains some of the information in these pages, but there's other useful information as well. As we locate new and interesting commonspace resources, we'll be providing regular weblog-style updates to the commonspace site, as well as some feature-length articles. Basically, it'll be a place for stuff we forgot to put in the book, stuff that is changing and stuff you want to say.

ENDNOTES

Chapter 1

1 <www.dat.dtu.dk/~hbm/alt.flame/wonder-faq.txt>.

2 Christopher Locke et al, The Cluetrain Manifesto (New York: Perseus Press, 2000).

3 Stacey E. Bressler et al, Communities of Commerce (New York: McGraw Hill, 2000).

4 Steve Lohr, 'Code Name: Mainstream,' The New York Times, August 28, 2000.

5 Eric Raymond, 'The Cathedral and the Bazaar'
<www.tuxedo.org/~esr/writings/cathedral-bazaar/cathedral-bazaar/>.

Chapter 2

1 Howard Rheingold, The Virtual Community: Homesteading on the Electronic Frontier. (Reading: Addison-Wesley, 1993).

2 Ibid.

3 John Hagel III and Arthur G. Armstrong, net.gain (Cambridge: Harvard University Press, 1997).

4 Esther Dyson, Release 2.1: A Design for Living in the Digital AgeI (New York: Broadway Books, 1998).

5 Christopher Locke et al, The Cluetrain Manifesto: The End of Business As Usual (New York: Persues, 2000), v.

6 Fredric Jameson, Postmodernism, or, The Cultural Logic of Late Capitalism (Durham: Duke University Press, 1991), 208.

7 Eric Raymond, The Cathedral and the Bazaar
<www.tuxedo.org/~esr/writings/cathedral-bazaar/
cathedral-bazaar/x305.html>.

8 Hagel and Armstrong, 17.

9 Amy Jo Kim, Community Building on the Web: Secret Strategies for Successful Online Communities (Berkeley: Peachpit Press, 2000), 113.

10 <www.computerworld.com/cwi/story/frame/0,1213,NAV63_
STO45735,00.html>.

11 <www.thestandard.com/article/display/0,1151,15895,00.html>.

12 <www.thestandard.com/article/display/0,1151,15970,00.html>.

13 Rheingold, 280-81.

14 Dyson, 64.

15 Ibid, 64.

16 Ibid, 65.

17 Rheingold, 181

18 Kim, 113.

19 Dyson, 50

20 <www.theregister.co.uk/content/4/12266.html>.

Chapter 3

1 Mikhail Bakhtin, Problems of Dostoyevsky's Poetics, ed. & trans. Caryl Emerson (Minneapolis: University of Minnesota Press, 1984), 122.

2, Marshall McLuhan, Understanding Media: The Extensions of Man (New York: Mentor/Signet Books, 1964), 157.

3 Robert W. McChesney, "The Politics of the Internet in Historical and Critical Perspective". Working paper from the School of Journalism and Mass Communication, University of Wisconsin, Madison, 1995.

4 Bakhtin, 123.

5 Walter Benjamin,. 'The Storyteller,' Illuminations, ed. Hannah Arendt (New York; Schocken Books, 1985).

6, Michele Matassa Flores. "AOL swamped with new unlimited pricing plan; some users sue", The Seattle Times. Seattle, January 16, 1997.
(Online at: http://augustachronicle.com/stories/011797/tech_aol.html).

Chapter 4

1 Eric Raymond, The Cathedral and the Bazaar.
<www.tuxedo.org/~esr/writings/cathedral-bazaar/>

2 Ibid.

3 Ibid.

4 Ibid.

5 Ibid.

6 Ibid.

7, Howard Rheingold. "You Got The Power". Wired. August 2000 - issue 8.08.
<http://www.wired.com/wired/archive/8.08/comcomp.html>.

Chapter 5

1 Eric Raymond, "Homesteading in the Noosphere," <www.tuxedo.org/~esr/writings/homesteading/>

2 <www.siliconalleydaily.com/issues/sar08162000.html#Headline5706>

3 The Industry Standard. <www.thestandard.com/research/metrics/display/0,2799,17409,00.html>

4 <www.slashdot.com/faq/>

5 <q.queso.com/discuss/msgReader$734>

6 Misha Glouberman, "Adding Comments to the Web," <www.web.net/~misha/annot.html>

Chapter 6

1 Garrett Hardin, "The Tragedy of the Commons," Science, 162(1968):1243-1248, <dieoff.org/page95.htm>.

2 Eric Raymond, The Magic Cauldron, <www.tuxedo.org/~esr/writings/magic-cauldron/>.

3 <orbiten.org/ofss/01.html>.

4 Christopher Locke et al, The Cluetrain Manifesto: The End of Business As Usual (New York: Persues, 2000) 69.

5 B. Bond et al, C-Commerce: The New Arena for Business Applications, Gartner Group Research Note. August 3, 1999.

6 Scott Ehrens and Peter Zapf, The Internet Business to Business Report, Bear Sterns Consulting, September 1999.

7 David A. Price, "Exchange Trustbusters, " Business 2.0, August 22, 2000, No. 8.22, 60.

8 <www.thestandard.com/article/display/0,1151,12437,00.html>.

9 <www.aolwatch.org/list/0101.html>.

Chapter 7

1 <www.tuxedo.org/~esr/writings/cathedral-bazaar/cathedral-bazaar/x305.html>.

2 <www.wired.com/wired/archive/8.08/brown.html>.

Chapter 8

1 David Sheff, "Crank It Up," *Wired*, August 2000, 186.

2 <www.egroups.com>

3 <www.lsoft.com/lists/listref.html>

4 <www.xanadu.net/HISTORY/>

Chapter 9

1 <www.well.come/confirmation/mirrorshades/>

2 Hakim Bey, *TAZ; The Temporary Autonomous Zone, Ontological Anarchy, Poetic Terrorism* (New York: Autonomedia, 1991).

3.Ibid.

4 <www.mgt.smsu.edu/mgt487/mgtissue/newstrat/metcalfe.htm>.

5 < www.tuxedo.org/~esr/writings/cathedral-bazaar/homesteading/x170.html>.

6 William Gibson, 'Burning Chrome.' Burning Chrome (New York: Ace Books, 1987).

7 Bey, 114-15.

8 Neal Stephenson, Cryptonomicon (New York; Avon Books, 1999).

9 Avital Ronell, *The Telephone Book: Technology, Schizophrenia, Electric Speech* (Lincoln: University of Nebraska Press, 1989), xv.

10 Douglas Adams, The Hitch Hiker's Guide to the Galaxy (London: Pan Books, 1979).

Chapter 10

1 Brock N. Meeks, "The Electronic Landscape," Kevin Kelly, ed., *Signal: Communication Tools for the Information Age* (New York: Harmony Books, 1988), 75.

2 <adres.internet.com/feature/article/0,,8961_399221,00.html>.

3 <adres.internet.com/stories/article/0,,7561_183641,00.html>.

4 <www.thestandard.com/companies/display/0,2063,52464,00.html>.

5 <www.canada.cnet.com/news/0-1005-200-341662.html?tag=st.ne.1005-203-341662.>.

6 <www.thestandard.com/article/display/0,1151,4364,00.html>.

7 <www.thestandard.com/article/display/0,1151,15847,00.html>.

8 <www.jup.com/company/pressrelease.jsp?doc=pr000816&query=950%7C advertising%7C2004>.

9 Lisa Guernsey, "The Powers Behind the Auctions," *The New York Times*, August 20, 2000, bu1.

10 "B2B: Hot or Hype," *Wired*, September 2000.

11 <www.doubleclick.net/advertisers/commerce/case_studies.htm>.

12 <www.canada.cnet.com/news/0-1005-200-1463444.html>.

13 <www.usatoday.com/life/cyber/tech/cth211.htm>.

14 <www.tuxedo.org/~esr/writings/magic-cauldron/magic-cauldron.html>.

15 <www.tuxedo.org/~esr/writings/magic-cauldron/magic-cauldron-7.html#ss7.1>.

16 <www.netcraft.com/survey/>.

17 <www.tuxedo.org/~esr/writings/magic-cauldron/magic-cauldron-9.html>.

18 <www.caldera.com>.

19 <www.redhat.com>.

20 <www.tuxedo.org/~esr/writings/magic-cauldron/magic-cauldron-9.html>.

21 <www.thestandard.com/article/display/0,1151,17685,00.html>.

22 <www.thestandard.com/companies/display/0,2063,58435,00.html>.

23 <www.thestandard.com/companies/display/0,2063,59606,00.html>.

24 David Sheff, "Crank It Up," *Wired*, August 2000, 192.

25 <www.redherring.com/mag/issue81/mag-leaders-81.html>.

Chapter 11

1 Christopher Locke et al. The Cluetrain Manifesto: The End of Business As Usual
(New York: Persues, 2000), 69.

2 <www.pcdata.com>.

3 <www.3dactionplanet.com/features/firstlooks/wolfenstein/>.

4 <www.rapstation.com/swapmeet>.

5 Lisa Guernsey, "The Powers Behind the Auctions," *The New York Times*,
August 20, 2000, bu1.

6 Ibid.

Chapter 12

1 The Internet – or ARPANet – was originally invented for use by the U.S. military.

2 Elisabeth Richard, "Sustainable Interactivity For Government Web Sites," *G8 Report
on Democracy and Government On-Line Services*, 1999 <www.statskontoret.se/
gol-democracy/canada.htm>.

3 CRTC, CRTC surveys state of new media, Press release, July 31, 1998 < www.new
media-forum.net/news/pr.html>.

4 Steven Clift, A Wired Agora Minneapolis, Citizen Participation, the Internet and Squirrels, 1999 <publicus.net/present/agora.html>.

5 <www.connect.gc.ca/en/100-e.htm>.

6 Angus Reid survey, July 2000 <www.angusreid.com/media/content/displaypr.cfm?id_to_view=1061>.

7 < www.gov.on.ca/MCZCR/english/citdiv/voluntar/vao-brochure.htm>.

8 The 'post-governmental organization (PGO)' was discussed at the Next Five Minutes 3 conference in Amsterdam, March 1999. <www.n5m.org>.

Chapter 13

1 Richard Dawkins, The Selfish Gene (Oxford/New York; Oxford University Press, 1989), 192.

2 In books such as The Choking Doberman and other 'New' Urban Legends (New York: W.W. Norton & Co., 1986) and The Mexican Pet (New York: W.W. Norton & Co, 1988), folklorist Jan Harold Brunvand has assiduously tracked the various memes that define our collective neuroses.

3 The idea of Virus 23 appears throughout Burroughs' work, including the short piece 'Beauty and the Bestseller,' The Adding Machine: Collected Essays (London: John Calder, 1985), 22-27.

4 Christian Bök, 'Warning', Virus 23 #$ (1992), 31.

5 Douglas Rushkoff, Media Virus: Hidden Agendas in Popular Culture (New York; Ballantine Books, 1994).

6 <pspmc1.vub.ac.be/MEMLEX.html>.

7 <www.drapervc.com/viralmarketing.html>.

8 Ibid.

9 <www.pbs.org/cringely/pulpit/pulpit20000831.html>.

10 <www.internetnews.com/streaming-news/article/0,,8161_235141,00.html>

11 <www.vortex.com/privacy/priv.09.15>

12 Ibid

13 <www.techweb.com/wire/story/TWB19980928S0028>; <www.zdnet.com/sp/infopacks/spam/nevada.html>

14 <www.nylj.com/stories/99/12/121499a3.htm>

15 <ww.isp-lists.isp-planet.com/isp-ceo/9910/msg00310.html>

16 <www.cnet.com/internet/0-3773-7-2602794.html?tag=st.int.3773-7-2602793.arrow.3773-7-2602794>

Chapter 14

1 Carolyn Marvin. *When Old Technologies Were New: Thinking About Electric Communication in the Late 19th Century* (Oxford/New York: Oxford University Press, 1988).

2 <www.kerryr.net/pioneers/memex.htm>.

3 <www.sfc.keio.ac.jp/~ted/XUsurvey/xuDation.html>.

4 For more information, see <www.gnu.org/philosophy/gnutella.html>.

5 <www.washingtonpost.com/wp-dyn/articles/A24833-2000Apr6.html>.

6 <www.tuxedo.org/~esr/guns/ipscc1.html>.

BIBLIOGRAPHY

Barnouw, Eric. *Tube of Plenty.* New York: Oxford University Press, 1975.

Bresnan, William J. "The Cable Revolution." *Vital Speeches of the Day*, May 1, 1973.

Dery, Mark. *Culture Jamming.* Westfield: Open Magazine, 1993.

Educom. *Edupage*, January 1994 to May 1995. *Edupage* is an electronic update sheet on developments in the information technology industry. For more information or back references, contact "info@educom.edu".

Franklin, Ursula. *The Real World of Technology.* Toronto: CBC Enterprises, 1990.

Friendly, Fred W. "Asleep at the Switch of the Wired City." *Saturday Review*, October 10, 1970.

The Globe & Mail Information Highway Supplement. May 13, 1994.

The Globe & Mail Information Highway Supplement. May 12, 1995.

Graham, Garth. *A Users Guide to the Electronic Mindway.* 1994 (1): a Net-published document which can be obtained from the author at "aa127@freenet.carleton.ca".

Iacono, Suzanne and Rob Kling. "Computerization Movements and Tales of Technological Utopianism." *Computerization and Controversy: Value Conflicts and Social Choices.* Academic Press, 1995.

Katz, Jon. "The Age of Paine." *Wired.* San Francisco: Wired USA Ltd., Volume 3, Number 5, 1995.

Mander, Jerry. *In the Absence of the Sacred.* San Francisco: Sierra Club Books, 1991.

Marvin, Carolyn. *When Old Technologies Were New: Thinking About Electric Communication in the Late 19th Century.* New York: Oxford University Press, 1988.

McChesney, Robert W. *The Politics of the Internet in Historical and Critical Perspective*. Working paper from School of Journalism and Mass Communication, University of Wisconsin-Madison, 1995.

Paper Tiger Television (PTTV) Southwest. *Staking a Claim in Cyberspace* (videorecording). San Francisco.: Paper Tiger Southwest, 1993.

Raindance Corporation. *Radical Software*. New York: Raindance Corporation, 1970 to 1974.

Rheingold, Howard. *The Virtual Community: Homesteading on the Electronic Frontier*. Reading: Addison-Wesley, 1993.

Rucker, Rudy, R.U. Sirius, and Queen Mu. *Mondo Users Guide to the New Edge*. New York: Harper Collins, 1992.

Shamberg, Michael. *Guerrilla Television*. New York: Holt, Rinehart and Winston, 1971.

Smith, Ralph Lee. *The Wired Nation — Cable TV: The Electronic Communications Highway*. New York: Harper & Row, 1972.

Time. "Welcome to Cyberspace Issue." Spring, 1995.

Toffler, Alvin, and Heidi Toffler. *Creating a New Civilization: The Politics of the Third Wave*. Atlanta: Turner Publishing, 1995.

Williams, Raymond. *Television, Technology and Cultural Form*. New York: Shocken Books, 1975.

Williams, Raymond. *Keywords*. New York: Oxford University Press, 1976.